VERSIONS OF ANTIHUMANISM

Stanley Fish, one of the foremost critics of literature
has spent much of his career writing and thinking
This book brings together his finest published work
material on Milton and on other authors and topics
literature. In his analyses of Renaissance text:
interpretive problems that confront readers,
critique of historicist methods of interpre
argues, is key to understanding which piece:
relevant to literary criticism. Lucid, provocat
able, this new book from Stanley Fish is requi
teaching or studying Milton and early modern ....

STANLEY FISH is the Davidson-Kahn Distinguished University
Professor and a professor of law at Florida International University.
He has previously taught at the University of California at Berkeley,
Johns Hopkins University, Duke University and the University of
Illinois at Chicago, where he was Dean of the College of Liberal Arts
and Sciences. He has received many honors and awards, including
being named the Chicagoan of the Year for Culture. He is the author
of fourteen books and is an on-line columnist for the *New York
Times*.

VERSIONS OF ANTIHUMANISM

Milton and Others

STANLEY FISH

CAMBRIDGE
UNIVERSITY PRESS

CAMBRIDGE UNIVERSITY PRESS
Cambridge, New York, Melbourne, Madrid, Cape Town,
Singapore, São Paulo, Delhi, Mexico City

Cambridge University Press
The Edinburgh Building, Cambridge CB2 8RU, UK

Published in the United States of America by Cambridge University Press, New York

www.cambridge.org
Information on this title: www.cambridge.org/9780521176248

First published 2012

Printed in the United Kingdom at the University Press, Cambridge

A catalog record for this publication is available from the British Library

Library of Congress Cataloging in Publication Data
Fish, Stanley Eugene
Versions of antihumanism : Milton and others / Stanley Fish.
p.   cm.
ISBN 978-1-107-00305-7 (Hardback) – ISBN 978-0-521-17624-8 (Paperback)
1. Milton, John, 1608–1674–Criticism and interpretation.
2. English literature–17th century–History and criticism.   I. Title.
PR3588.F577 2012
821′.4–dc23
2011046102

ISBN 978-1-107-00305-7 Hardback
ISBN 978-0-521-17624-8 Paperback

To the Memory of Michael O'Loughlin,
Who Now Enjoys the Garlands of Repose

Contents

vii

Acknowledgments

The following chapters have been previously published.

Chapter 2 appeared in *Cardozo Studies in Law and Literature*, 21.1 (2009) and appears by permission of University of California Press.

Chapter 3 appeared in *Milton in the Age of Fish: Essays on Authorship, Text and Terrorism*, ed. Michael Lieb and Albert C. Labriola (2006) and is reprinted by permission of Duquesne University Press.

Chapter 4 appeared in *Milton Studies*, 44 (2004), and is reprinted by permission of University of Pittsburgh Press.

Chapter 5 was published as the afterword to *Milton in Popular Culture*, ed. Laura Lunger Knoppers and G. Semenza (2006) and is reprinted by permission of Palgrave.

Chapter 8 was published in *Writing and Political Engagement in Seventeenth Century England*, ed. Derek Hirst and Richard Streier and is reprinted by permission of Cambridge University Press.

Chapter 9 first appeared in *Representations*, vol. 7 (1984) and is reprinted by permission of University of California Press.

Chapter 10 appeared in *Revenge of the Aesthetic*, ed. Michael Clark (2000), and is reprinted by permission of University of California Press.

Chapter 11 appeared in *Soliciting Interpretation: Literary Theory and Seventeenth Century English Poetry*, ed. Elizabeth D. Harvey and Catharine Eisamen Maus (1990), and is reprinted by permission of University of Chicago Press.

Chapter 12 appeared in *Visionary Milton: Essays on Prophecy and Violence*, ed. Peter E. Medine, John T. Shawcross and David V. Urban (2010) and is reprinted by permission of Duquesne University Press.

Introduction: intention, historicism and interpretation

A NOTE ON METHOD

Although it is not fully argued in the essays collected here, underlying the readings I offer of Milton and others is a position on the relationship between intention and interpretation. Indeed, my argument is that it is not a relationship, but an identity. Interpretation just is the act of determining what someone meant by these words (or this picture or that film or that gesture). So the answer to the very old question, "What is the meaning of a text?" is: "A text means what its author or authors intend," period.

Simply to propose this thesis is, I know, to provoke a host of objections. Why focus on intention which is subjective and elusive when you have the text which is material and immediately available? How does one determine intention anyway? How do you get inside people's heads? What evidence, apart from the text, is relevant? What about the intentions of authors long dead? What about authors who have conflicting intentions? What about committees and legislative bodies? Can they be said to have intentions?

There are answers to these questions, but before I offer a few of them I want to point out that while the intentional thesis is radically historical, it is not historicist as that word is usually understood. Let me explain. The intentional thesis is historical because it identifies meaning with a purposive act performed by an author at a particular moment. The question is not: "What would Milton have meant by *Samson Agonistes* had he written it in the wake of 9/11?" but: "What did Milton mean by *Samson Agonistes* in 1670 or 1648 or 1659 or 1661?" (all dates proposed by various critics). To answer the second, and genuinely interpretive, question you have to do the historical work of figuring out what Milton had in mind when he wrote (or dictated) the play's words, and that involves reading those words in the light of an intention Milton could have had at the time of composition.

That is why the dispute about the date of *Samson Agonistes* is interpretively relevant. Archie Burnet observes in his introduction to the new

Variorum Commentary (Duquesne University Press, 2009) that none of the proponents of various dates "can avoid the autobiographical approach." That is, they all read the words as composed by a man who was situated in this or that historical context, and the success they have, or think they have, is then cited as evidence that the preferred date is the right one. The procedure, Burnet complains, is circular: "*SA* is interpreted as evidence of Milton's thoughts and feelings after the Restoration, and such thoughts and feelings are, in turn, interpreted as evidence of the poem's post-Restoration date." But this circularity, far from being vicious, is the shape interpretation always takes: it tacks back and forth between the hypothe-sizing of an intention and the details that are at once its product and its support. If and when those details fill the poem's landscape and seem answerable to the intention the critic has posited, the interpretation has achieved plausibility and, sometimes, persuasiveness.

This does not always happen. Interpretation can fail, and when it does, it is because a text or a piece of a text has not been linked up to an intention in a way that seems inevitable. (Yes that must be what he meant!) It's not a lack of historical evidence; it's a failure to bring a piece of historical evidence together with an argument for an author's intentional use of it. In the past 350 years, any number of quotations and citations from a variety of sources have been put forward as the key to Milton's enigmatic phrase "two-handed engine" (*Lycidas*, 130), but so far none of the candidates has won general acceptance from the critical community. It has not proved difficult to find references to a two-handed something-or-other in poems, sermons, proclamations and tracts; what has proved difficult is tracing any of the references back to Milton's door or, more properly, to the intentional context within which he was writing.

Not that it hasn't been tried. Just as those who propose various dates for the composition of *Samson Agonistes* cannot "avoid the autobiograph-ical approach," so can no would-be solver of the riddle of the two-handed engine avoid making biographical/intentional arguments. As Richard Streier has observed, a catalog of mentionings (here's a two-handed engine and there's another and another) won't do the job. Piling up historical evidence is not an interpretive strategy; all the evidence in the world will be irrelevant if it has not been shown to be (a) within Milton's ken and (b) related strongly to what he was trying to do.

That is why intentionalism is historical but not historicist. An historicist analysis, at least of a certain kind, would go directly from the noting of some set of historical facts (political, agricultural, economic, military) to an interpretive conclusion. In 1638 there was widespread concern about X;

Lycidas was published in 1638; therefore *Lycidas* is about X. This is of course a caricature of the historicist method which typically is marked by deep learning and sophisticated cultural analysis. But in the end what the method amounts to is *surrounding* the literary text with historical materials (perhaps in obedience to Louis Montrose's celebrated formula: the textuality of history and the historicity of texts) and assuming that by doing so you will have said something about the text's meaning. No, what you would have done is place the text next to an elaborate and elaborated account of the moment of its composition and declared, but not proven, a vital connection between them. Proof, or at least something that could be offered as proof, would require that you begin with a hypothesis about the author's intention – to justify the ways of God to man, to write a pastoral poem with a glance at the state of the clergy, to explore the relationship between faith and positive law by focusing on the example of Samson – and then see if that hypothesis can be fleshed out and thereby confirmed by materials the author can plausibly be said to have known. (What did he know and when did he know it?) It is not a question of whether to be historical or not (a choice never available to us), but a question of which history is to be the primary lens. It should go without saying that when you're dealing with the product of a purposive design, as a poem or epic or play surely is, the primary lens must be the lens of a historically formulated purpose; once in place, that lens – the lens of intention, of the inquiry into what the author was up to – will pick out from the vast and inexhaustible riches of history and histories the items that are, or at least might arguably be, relevant. Naïve historicism (and there's more than a little of it around) has no principle of selection; it is impossibly democratic and accords relevance to anything and everything, and is therefore not a method of interpretation at all but the mere collecting of data.

If collecting data is not interpreting, neither is intellectual history. You can of course ask an intellectual-history question about a text and your question might very well contain the word "mean," but the meaning you are in search of would be more properly called "significance." Questions about significance (in the sense I am using it) regard a literary text as an instance of something or as a piece of information about something rather than as a message from an author to his readers. What does Marvell's "Upon Appleton House" tell us about agrarian conditions in the middle of the seventeenth century? What is the significance of Donne's sermons for the history of prose style? What does Milton's work for Cromwell's government tell us about the intersection of poetic and political careers

in the period? These are historians' questions, and while answers to them
might be useful in prosecuting the interpretive task – the interpreter can
perhaps do something with the information they elicit – they are not
asked in the spirit of that task. To be sure, you might say that these are
larger questions because they expand the focus of investigation from
the narrow act of intentional composition to the broader context of the
culture in which that act occurred, but the panoramas that have been
opened up by historical inquiry cannot be directly imported back into
the interpretive task and serve as an answer to *its* question. That would be,
as I say in "Why Milton matters; or, against historicism," picking up the
stick from the wrong end.

The case is even clearer with that branch of intellectual history called
reception history. Here the questions are: "What did Blake think Milton
meant in *Paradise Lost*?" or: "To what uses was *Paradise Lost* put by politicians
and generals in the nineteenth century?" or: "What do eighteenth-century
editions of Milton tell us about his reputation?" Again legitimate and interesting questions, but, again, answers to them are not answers to the question,
"What does *Paradise Lost* mean?" because they have not emerged in the
course of an inquiry into Milton's intention.

One consequence of the fact that a work means what its author or
authors intend is that the meaning of a work cannot change, although our
understanding of what that meaning is can and does change. (That's the
history of literary criticism.) So it cannot be true, as John Carey claims
(*TLS*, 2002) that "September 11 has changed *Samson Agonistes* because
it has changed the readings we may derive from it while still celebrating it
as an achievement of the human imagination."

There are several judgments all mixed up in Carey's statement: (1) the
judgment that religiously inspired violence is abhorrent; (2) the judgment
that because he was a great poet, Milton could not have lauded or excused
religiously inspired violence; (3) the judgment that if Milton did in fact
laud or excuse religiously inspired violence he is not a great poet; he is a
"monstrous bigot" (Carey's phrase); and (4) the judgment that however
plausible a reading of *Samson Agonistes* that failed to condemn Samson's act
may have been on September 10, it is entirely unacceptable one day later.

The first judgment is debatable. The second and third judgments rest
on a dubious theory of literary value. The fourth judgment makes
interpretive validity depend on events that occurred long after the author
wrote. Milton may or may not have condoned religiously inspired violence;
it's the business of interpretation to settle the point if it can, but 9/11 or
anything else that happened after 1671 cannot legitimately be brought into

the process. After 9/11 those who had always read *Samson Agonistes* as a glorification of its title figure may recoil from the play; they may find their view of Milton changed, but they won't find their reading changed, that is, if it is really a reading and not an instance of what has been called "presentism," the practice of importing present significances into past literary productions. Presentism is a form of intellectual history and it has its place. It is perfectly OK to ask about the new conversations a work may enter into by virtue of current events, but it's not OK – it's a category mistake – if the answer is turned into an interpretation of the work. *Samson Agonistes* can't change even if the things you think about when reading *Samson Agonistes* change.

Presentism as a mode of interpretation is an alternative answer to the question: "What is the meaning of a text?" Presentism says that the meaning of a text is the meaning it has for contemporary readers. (The legal analogue is the idea of the "living constitution," the constitution that changes as society's circumstances and needs change.) But this can hardly be a method of interpretation because the only constraints in play are the interpreter's current interests and desires. Presentism substitutes for the question "What does it mean?" the question "What do we want it to mean?" Asking that question is not interpreting; it's just making it up.

The second alternative to the intentional thesis (a text means what its author or authors intend) is textualism, the idea that the meaning of a text is determined by the meanings its words would have had at the time of the text's production; just get yourself a good historical dictionary and you'll be able to figure it out. The problem with this so-called method is that (a) a dictionary did not write the text and (b) an author is not bound by the standard meanings he might find in his dictionary, should he choose to consult it. The meaning a word has is a matter for the author to decide. True, if he decides to employ non-standard meanings (as poets often do) he will pay a price in the difficulty of communication. Standard dictionary meanings are useful because readers will assume their use as a default matter, and if an author wants to assure the highest level of easy communication with his readers, standard dictionary meanings will be the vehicle of choice. But the text alone (a phrase without a referent; there is no text apart from the specification or assumption of intention; there are just marks) won't tell you whether its author made that choice or made another. It is again a question of intention, and rather than declaring its intention and thus being self-sufficient, a text only emerges into readability when an intention has been posited for it, and the dictionary won't tell you what that intention is. To be sure, standard dictionary meanings can be part of the evidence for an intention, but they can't be fully determinative unless it has been established by independent means that the author resolved – intended – to be bound by them. Textualism is a non-starter. You can't have an interpretive method that is impossible to perform.

In a way intentionalism is a non-starter too because it is not a method. That is, the intentional thesis – a text means what its author or authors intend – doesn't tell you how to go about interpreting; it just tells you that if you are interpreting – rather than doing something else, like data collecting or intellectual history – you are trying to figure out what someone meant by these words; it also tells you that if you're not doing that, you're not interpreting. To put it another way, the intentional thesis does no work; it just stipulates what kind of work there is to do and then withdraws, leaving you to do it.

And how do you do it? The short answer is "empirically." Because the intentional thesis is silent on matters of procedure (it doesn't even tell you who or what the intending agent is), it leaves all interpretive questions unsettled, including the question of what is to count for evidence of an author's intention. No piece of evidence is ruled either in or out in advance; any piece of evidence might prove to be relevant – might prove to be evidence – if a line can be drawn from it to the specification of the author's intention. You never know what's going to turn up or whether you will be able to do something interpretively with what does turn up. There is no theory guiding you – interpretation is not a theoretical activity – just the search for pieces of a puzzle, the puzzle of what someone meant by these words, by words like "two-handed engine."

So in the readings that follow I am not being directed by the intentional thesis as I would be if it were a theory or an "approach" (it's not an approach to interpretation; it *is* interpretation). I'm just proceeding in the understanding that it is interpreting I'm doing and not something else.

THE READINGS

Because intentionalism is not a theory of interpretation but a specification of what it is (and isn't), the theory of interpretation an author may have is irrelevant to interpretations of his work, except as a piece of biographical data. Knowing that your author believed this or that about interpretation will not tell you how to interpret him. You interpret him by trying to figure out what he meant, and you do that even if he himself had a different (and wrong) idea of what interpretation involves, if he were, for example, a textualist or a presentist. (Theorists of legal interpretation often spend a lot of time worrying about the theory of interpretation the founders had; but interpreting their words can only take one course – the intentional course – no matter what they might have had to say on the matter.)

It is then a matter of coincidence and serendipity that Milton was himself an intentionalist. His intentionalism – his conviction, expressed in *The Doctrine and Discipline of Divorce*, that you must look behind Christ's words to the spirit informing them – is part and parcel of his antiformalism, his refusal to rely on rules, texts, kings, prelates, surfaces, images or any outward conveyance for guidance and illumination. When Mammon offers to install interior lighting in Hell and asks: "And what can heaven show more?" (*PL* I, 273b), he gives voice to a form of thinking, a cast of mind, against which Milton does continual battle – the settling of questions of meaning and value by the way things appear, by configurations in the empirical world, by the evidence of things seen.

Here, a master text is Michael's rebuke of Adam for having concluded from some apparently pleasant interplay between the descendants of Seth and a bevy of attractive women that nature's ends are being fulfilled. "Judge not what is best / By pleasure, though to Nature seeming meet"(*PL* XI, 603–604), Michael admonishes, which means: "Don't reach moral or interpretive conclusions by attending to how things seem" (advice Adam has already failed to heed when he falls by submitting to what "seemed remediless"); look deeper for the significance of anything said or done; look to the relationship between actions, words and even thoughts, and the imperative, always in force, first to discern, and then to do, God's will. Keeping the Sabbath because Scripture says so is to risk committing a sin unless your resolution flows from faith and not the "mere" text; breaking the Sabbath is a pious act if it is done at the prompting of the Spirit (*Christian Doctrine*, book 2, chapter 1).

It is clear, then, that Milton's intentionalism is also a morality. He is not interested, as a theorist of intention might be, in intention in general; he is interested in whether agents (including himself) have the right intentions, and, as it turns out, there is only one. This does not mean that there is only one act you can properly intend, but that whatever act you perform – keeping the Sabbath, breaking the Sabbath; staying married, getting divorced; using scatological language, avoiding scatological language; tearing down the temple, not tearing down the temple – must be an expression of the intention to obey God and glorify him. If it is that, then no matter how mean or great in worldly eyes ("though worlds judge thee perverse") it will have been a righteous and praiseworthy act. As Herbert says in "The Elixir," "Who sweeps a room, as for thy laws, / Makes that and th' action fine." And Milton echoes him (I am not suggesting direct influence): "were it the meanest underservice, if God by his Secretary conscience enjoin it, it were sad for me if I should draw back" (*The Reason of Church Government*).

In this severe ethic, the danger to be avoided is the assertion or promotion of the self as an entity with powers, motives and achievements of its own. The positive project is the stilling of the self, which, again, does not mean refraining from doing or saying anything, but refraining from saying or doing anything for which one could take credit. It's called "giving God the glory" and Milton does it when he attributes his writing to the inspiration of his muse (the Holy Spirit) and when he declares (in *The Reason of Church Government*) that if God makes a poet a vessel of his word, "it lies not in man's will what he shall say, or what he shall conceal." (Herbert's view, as we shall see, is even more stringent; his constant theme is that the stilling of the self is an impossible project and that the very effort to prosecute it assures its failure because it itself involves a claim of human agency.)

If the self's chief error is to believe in its own independence and efficacy, the primary instrument of that error is language, which can be responsibly or irresponsibly deployed in ways that mirror the pious or impious actions men can perform. Just as fallen creatures must give the glory to God and refrain from claiming independent agency, so must language subordinate itself to the task of praising God and describing his handiwork and refrain from substituting its representations for the real thing. Hobbes, among many others, finds in the ability to speak the main difference between men and animals, but he also finds in the ability to speak the vehicle of man's departure from the straight and narrow. For "With words men can represent to others that which is Good in the likeness of Evill, and Evill in the likeness of Good" (*Leviathan*).

Words can be either the vehicle of our aspirations if we use them rightly, as aids and prods to something more significant than they, or the instrument of our self-worship, if we do not look through them but accept the significances they present (and we have conceived) as the horizon of understanding and truth. It is no accident that when Satan detaches himself, or claims to detach himself, from God, the first thing he does, involuntarily, is to give birth to Sin – a prideful deviation from God – who is received by his associates as a "sign" (*PL* ii, 760), that is as a representation, something secondary, derivative. But in time the devilish host forgets the secondary, unreal status of sin and signs, grows "familiar" with them and finally learns to love them ("Becam'st enamoured"). At that point the rebellious self – the self detached from deity – and the new empire of signs – signs detached from a tethering ground – go their own way, unconstrained by a higher reality, creating meanings and values ad libitum. (It is a diabolic perversion of the godly command: "be fruitful and multiply.")

Although Satan meets God's loyalists with newly invented artillery and gunpowder, his first weapon is the pun. He opens the war in heaven by "scoffing in ambiguous words" (*PL* VI, 568), that is, by using language in a way that, rather than pointing to a prior and stable referent, turns back on itself, plays with itself, and keeps on going, impelled only by the narcissism of self-reproduction. Satan's puns are the linguistic equivalent of the boast he makes earlier when Abdiel tells him that he and his followers are but creatures: "We know no time when we were not as now; / Know none before us, self-begot, self-raised / By our own quick'ning power" (*PL* V, 859–861). The puffing up of language as a source of infinite semantic fecundity and the puffing up of the creature as a self-generating entity are one and the same. If the self is to be stilled lest it fall into the sin of claiming sufficiency, language must be stilled too.

That's a hard lesson for a poet; it veers toward antihumanism and indeed antihumanism is the logical extension of the requirement that man renounce all his powers and acknowledge a total dependence. The authors whose works I discuss in the following pages respond to this requirement differently. Milton tries to have it both ways, but in the end he is more a humanist than an antihumanist. If the desire for fame is, as he says, the last infirmity of the noble mind (*Lycidas*), it is an infirmity he never leaves behind, wishing as he does to leave behind something the world will not willingly let die (*An Apology Against a Pamphlet*). Rather than renouncing the claim to virtue and virtuous deeds, he portrays himself in his prose tracts as being in training for virtue. Aware that at best he could only "arrive at the second rank among the Latins," he resolves instead "to fix all the industry and art I could unite to the adorning of my native tongue." Knowing that this sounds boastful (as indeed it is), he adds "not to make verbal curiosities the end, that were a toilsome vanity, but to be an interpreter and relater of the best and sagest things among mine own citizens throughout this island in the mother dialect" (*The Reason of Church Government*). In other words, I'm not going to traffic in vanity; I'm just going to get famous. Every time Milton disavows an impure motive, he reveals another one. Every effort at humility turns into a gesture of pride. Even when he tries to give the glory to God, he spoils it. The "abilities" he pledges to use in the service of virtue, are, he says "the inspired gift of God rarely bestowed." It is more than implied that he is one of the lucky gifted ones, and he passes quickly to the glorious deeds he will perform: "to inbreed and cherish in a great people the seeds of virtue and public civility, to allay the perturbations of the mind, and set the affections in right tune, to celebrate in glorious lofty hymns the thrones and equipage of God's almightiness." It is clear that the celebrator will also be celebrated, and is being celebrated now.

The posture Milton assumes in these passages – complete with hopes, ambitions and dreams of literary glory – is the one Herbert tries, vainly, to escape in his poetry. What Herbert wants to do – and "do" is the verb that must be left behind – is to somehow exist without making the slightest impression, to act without agency, to write without asserting himself, to be in the world and disappear at the same time. In the poems the first person voice is always thinking to have finally found the way, to have advanced in the art of self-renunciation and abnegation. He's always announcing, "Now I've got it, now I've figured out how to be responsive to Christ's self-sacrifice in a manner that is not self-aggrandizing" only to realize (see "The Pearl," "Thanksgiving," "Misery" and "The Holdfast") that he's right back where he started from, adding to the good deeds he had tried to disclaim the good deed of disclaiming them.

In a series of poems this game that can't be won is played out in the context of poetry. In "Jordan II" the speaker recalls his efforts to deploy the resources of his art in the service of praising God, but at the beginning of the final stanza he acknowledges that the interest he was serving in the effort was self-interest, the interest of making a good poetic showing: "So did I weave myself into the sense." The question is how can you *not* weave yourself into the sense the moment you open your mouth? What can you do? The answer comes at the poem's end: shut up. "But while I bustled / I might hear a friend / Whisper, *How wide is all this long pretence! / There is in love a sweetnesse readie penn'd: / Copie out onely that, and save expense.*" That is, stop trying, stop weaving, stop writing, stop speaking, there's no need, it's already done, it's already said.

In "The Forerunners," an early Alzheimer's poem, what the speaker can't do voluntarily (because that would be an assertion of the will) is done for him, at least in prospect, by senility. He looks in the mirror and sees white hairs which he reads as forerunners and harbingers of what is to come. He can accept aging, but he finds it difficult to accept the diminishing of his mental and verbal powers: "But must they have my brain? Must they dispark / Those sparkling notions which therein were bred?" The pun on "spark" and "dispark" (dislodge from the cranial territory) is a minor illustration of the ability he is loath to lose. More powerful illustrations follow as he trots out every argument and tradition he can think of to justify his continued engagement with "sweet phrases, lovely metaphors," but in the end he seems to resign himself to the inevitable in lines that bear the imprint of his inner struggle: "Go, birds of spring: let winter have his fee; / Let a bleak paleness chalk the door, / So all within be livelier than before." The imperatives "go" and "let" suggest agency on the speaker's part, but spring goes independently of any man's bidding, and the angel of death comes whether you invite him or not. So the "let" is a gesture in the direction of what will surely follow without his permission, the bleakness (whiteness, barrenness) of an inner landscape that will be empty of the speaker's sparkling notions. His interior will be lively because nothing of him will live there. By having become, through no choice of his own, a "clod" (l.5), a heap of dust, he will have been brought by time and decay to the state Herbert celebrates in "Aaron": "Christ is my only head . . . / My only music, striking me even dead / That to the old man I may rest / And be in him new dressed." I die only to live more truly in him.

Becoming dead to the old man by either saying nothing or waiting for nature to deprive you of the ability to say anything may be a theoretical solution to the problem of stilling the self without adding to its claims of autonomy, but it will not do for someone whose religious duty it is to work actively in the world. How does the priest or pastor who must both speak and act every day perform in a way that avoids even the tincture of self-assertion? The surprising answer given in *The Country Parson*, Herbert's manual for pastors, is to be insincere.

For Milton sincerity is a prime virtue; the integrity of the self must be maintained so that one might receive the praise bestowed on Abdiel: "Servant of God, well done" (*PL* VI, 29). Milton regularly inveighs against "set forms" in worship and in writing and prefers to any codified or pre-packaged formulation "those free and unimposed expressions which from a sincere heart unbidden come into the outward gesture" (*An Apology*). But Herbert, following in the tradition of Augustine's *On Christian Doctrine*, counsels instead of sincerity the *performance* of sincerity. The parson is described as having "composed himself to all possible reverence," which means not that he meditates until reverence wholly occupies his inner landscape, but that he puts on the trappings of reverence – pious sayings, biblical verses, theatrical gestures – preliminary to displaying them to his parishioners. What is at issue is not the presence in the pastor's heart of holiness (who could know that?), but the signs of holiness. Whereas for Milton signs are a poor and dangerous substitute for the inner essence, for Herbert the danger, indeed the impiety, is claiming to have an inner essence signs can obscure. It is in order to avoid that danger – the danger of self-assertion – that he attaches himself to the machinery of insincerity, to the rhetorical arsenal of feignings. Rather than disdaining affectation, he embraces it. He finds salvation, or at least one precondition of it, in hypocrisy.

Ben Jonson is on Milton's side, in a way. Like Milton and unlike Herbert he is a humanist, more than respectful of political and artistic accomplishments, but he is not interested in "inbreeding . . . the seeds of virtue in a great people." His aims are more local. He wants to celebrate a virtue already achieved and alive in the breasts of its bearers. The "tribe of Ben," the name he gives to these worthies, is not an army or a project; it is a club, membership of which is a matter of like recognizing like. In "An Epistle Answering to One That Asked to Be Sealed of the Tribe of Ben," Jonson declines to say very much about those who are already in: "I could say more of such, but that I fly / To speak myself out too ambitiously, / And showing so weak an act to vulgar eyes" (5–7). Not that vulgar eyes – eyes that measure worth by wealth or reputation or heraldry – could understand what he won't show them. Showing is itself the weak act; being, an entirely internal state, is the true action, recognized only by those whose inner landscapes are similarly constituted. Rather than sallying out into a world that will not appreciate it, this virtue stays at home and protects itself from "the coarser sort" (54). The person who petitions him for entry to the tribe is either already in by virtue of his virtue or will never, could never, enter. If the former, then Jonson need do nor say nothing. "So short you read my character" (73), by which he means that I don't have to present myself at length in characters (letters) because my character (the spirit) is shining through for all that have eyes, and souls, to see. That is why membership is both easy and impossibly hard. Those who gain it "not many stairs are asked to climb" (74–75); all they need do is match Jonson's faith with an answering one: "First give me faith, who know / Myself a little. I will take you so, / As you have writ yourself" (75–76). "Writ" is a joke, because no writing is necessary, nor would any writing be sufficient. Once faith recognizes faith, the work (of the spirit) is done: "Now stand, and then, / Sir, you are sealed of the tribe of Ben" (76–77).

This poem, like many others of Jonson's, is a rejection of representation and therefore a rejection of poetry itself as a medium that can do nothing except provide a meeting place in its lines for those who do not need its validation. That is why so many of Jonson's poems have a lot of trouble getting going; there isn't anywhere for them to go. The virtue they would celebrate is already fully recognized in the circle of those who share it. Embellishing their state is at once unnecessary and impossible; covering perfection with words or titles or images would be a presumption. In the absence of a subject that would be enhanced or even revealed by its art, the poetry's only subject is its own superfluity.

"On Lucy, Countess of Bedford" is a nice example. Jonson recalls his morning desire to form a creature his verse could "honour serve and Love" (4). What follows is a list of the qualities she should have, a list that is abstract and without specificity of detail, a list that will be filled out, we assume, as the poem proceeds. But in the next to last line he turns on his project because it would at best yield a fictional version of the reality he can't hope to capture. "Such when I mean to feign and wished to see" (17). If you want to see her, look right at her; don't pile words on her. That is the final advice given by his muse. "My muse bad *Bedford* write, and that was she" (18). Of course, given that he has already written Bedford in the title, the poem ends with an announcement that it need never have begun.

If the tribe of Ben is a closed shop, the poetry that issues from its members is also closed in the sense that it resolutely refuses to deliver its object in plain terms. (This despite Jonson's reputation as a poet of the plain style.) The poems circle around their subject, but, in ever more ingenious ways, avoid presenting it. The reason is given in *Underwood*, no. 84, part IV where the poet rejects the usual images that one might employ to portray the mind of Lady Venetia Digby because "these are like a mind, not it." And as for an alternative, there is none: "No, to express a mind to sense / Would ask a heaven's intelligence; / Since nothing can report that flame / But what's of kin to whence it came" (12–16). No one can know Digby who is not already himself Digby, that is, informed by the same virtue and therefore kin to – of the same kind as – the spirit she breathes. The only possible injunction is then given: "Sweet mind, then speak yourself" (17), which doesn't mean "speak for yourself" or "use your own words"; it means speak without speech, reveal yourself (to the exalted few) without discursive or painterly means, just be, do no more, add no more, and by that determined reticence refuse the twin corruptions of representation and visibility.

That is also Marvell's project, with a twist. Where Jonson wants to protect himself and his friends from the corruption of the "coarser set" and the coarse world, Marvell wants to protect the world from the corruption we inevitably bring to it. When, in the first line of "The Mower Against Gardens," he writes "Luxurious man to bring his vice in use," the vice he refers to is the vice of consciousness, or, more precisely, the vice (impossible to avoid) of allowing one's consciousness to impinge on and thereby alter innocent nature. By placing nature within the perceptual frames that define him as a limited, temporally located being, man overlays what is "plain and pure" (4) with the impurity of his categories, desires and ambitions. By merely looking at natural objects he changes their "kind" (10) and causes "A wild and fragrant innocence" (33) to be obscured by various regimes of human order. He cannot simply be *of* the world; he must have a relationship to it and that relationship always has the effect of spoiling it. The wildness of innocence is replaced by the patterns of his "tilling," a strenuous activity quite different from the tilling – indeed a non-tilling – performed unselfconsciously by the fauns and fairies: "And fauns and faeries do the meadows till / More by their presence than their skill" (34–35). That is, the fauns and faeries don't *do* anything; they are entirely without positive agency; they have no skill. The verb "to skill" means to divide and distinguish. That is the work of consciousness, the work of thought, and an activity of which the fauns and faeries are innocently free.

But what's the alternative for human beings? How can you think yourself into a state of non-thinking? This is Marvell's version of Herbert's dilemma: how can you act in a way that successfully renounces action? Marvell's answer is a form of meditation in which the workings of the mind are stilled until no sense of it as distinct from the natural world remains. Often, as in "The Garden" and "Upon Appleton House," the extinguishing of the mind's separateness from existence in general is accompanied by a slowing down of the body. The speaker of "The Garden" stumbles on melons and falls on grass; his relationship to his surroundings is narcotic, and as the drug takes effect his mind, the location of difference, merges with the boughs, sings with the birds, and ends as "a green thought in a green shade" (48); that is, as something indistinguishable from anything else in the world, or at least in the world into which the mind has withdrawn. "Meanwhile the mind from pleasure less / Withdraws into its happiness" (41–42). The lesser happiness from which the mind withdraws is the happiness of conferring identity and meaning on other things by, for example, naming them. The greater happiness is the happiness of having lost the separation from things – the distance, the perspective – that makes naming at once possible and necessary. In the state of being "a green thought in a green shade" the preposition "in," which, like all prepositions, purportedly connects items in relationships, doesn't do any work for there are no discrete items to be connected; everything is inside everything else and is therefore invulnerable to the indignity of being picked out, pointed to, named. In this line the speaker's mind achieves the condition he could only speculate (a word intended precisely) about in line 24: "No name shall but your own be found."

The condition of not being available for naming is the condition of not being available for seeing and it is toward that receding from visibility that many of Marvell's speakers move. Again, the movement must be only apparent, must not be purposeful, must be playful ("play" is one of Marvell's favorite words), must be unselfconscious. The rowers in "Bermudas" start well because they are in the middle of nowhere, "Unespied" (2). They sing, but only the winds listen, and they imagine the land they will eventually (but really not ever) reach in images that recall "The Garden": "He makes the figs our mouths to meet, / And throws the melons at our feet" (21–22). That is, no action on our part is required, no reaching after things or meanings. Of course they are engaged in the action of singing, but the song is one of praise to God, and so by definition (see Herbert's "Providence") it can add nothing to the sum of knowledge. Although, as music, the song is linear in its unfolding, its true form is ritual rather than discursive. And that is why the song is perfectly matched by the physical exercise of rowing; both are rhythmic and non-purposeful: "And all the way, to guide their chime, / With falling oars they kept the time" (39–40). In this marvelous final couplet, the oars, rather than having the job of propelling the boat forward, have the job of marking, like a metronome, the time; not time as a disposable medium rushing toward an end, but time as a spatial unit in which the same non-thing keeps happening over and over. So a scene that might in another poem be full of agency and urgency – urgency of both destination and thought – is finally absolutely still.

Nothing is ever still in the poetry of Donne, especially the mind of the poet/speaker. The workings of that mind are strenuous and its specialty is finding in situations of momentary stability the seeds of change, reversal and betrayal. Sometimes, as in "Woman's Constancy," the instability is embraced even before it is encountered. The speaker of the poem finds himself (I note but am not persuaded by the argument that the speaker is a woman) in the desired position: he is loved. But he cannot rest in the moment because he knows what will happen in the next. "Now thou hast lov'd me one whole day, / Tomorrow when thou leav'st, what will thou say?" (1–2). The mutability of his beloved is assumed; what he is interested in is how she will explain it. What will she *say*? The assumption is not only that inconstancy will occur, but that it will be justified by words, which is also the assumption that words are its engine. If the state of things is at bottom a matter of stating, then you can state – say – anything and no independent referent will stop you.

The speaker imagines the lady as a virtuoso in the art: "Wilt thou then antedate some new made vow?" (3). That is, will you invoke a prior speech-act you did not in fact perform yesterday and cite it as the reason for going back on the speech-act (saying "I love you") you did perform today? The picture is of words succeeding words and undoing whatever prior utterances have themselves brought into being. This is not a matter simply of her devising a lie. A lie depends for its status as an action on a truth it betrays; in a world where truths are endlessly made (and unmade) by words, "lie" ceases to be a useful category of opprobrium. In the same way, the self ceases to be a useful category of reference: "Or say that now / We are not just those persons which we were?" (4–5). Saying we are now not what we were goes without saying. Since what we are will always be equivalent to whatever we say and what we say "now" will always be different from what we said before, we are of course not those persons we were, and we were never those persons either except for the instant of a saying.

For a false and theatrical moment, the speaker toys with the possibility of refuting his lover's extenuations (which, remember, *he* has created in the course of creating her), but declines to do so because the inconstancy he would thus rebuke is the core of his character too: "Which I abstain to do, / For by tomorrow, I may think so too" (16–17). The "I" that may think so tomorrow is already the "I" who writes today; in the process of constructing ingenious self-defenses his lover has not offered (indeed, she has not, we tend to forget, left him; this is all anticipation), he becomes the lover, and creation, of his constructions.

This is a nasty little poem, suffused with misogyny and self-loathing. It leaves a bitter aftertaste except in the mouths of those who like it. Donne both likes it and hates it. He likes it because it gives him a chance to display his acrobatic intelligence and his ability to play endlessly on and with words; and he hates it, because at some point in the performance (I know that I am hedging between Donne as the performer and his speaker as the performer) he recoils from its self-replenishing excess. A surfeit of words is what he seeks and a surfeit of words is what makes him sick almost to the point of gagging.

In "The Triple Fool," Donne's speaker recalls the foolish moment when he thought to stop, or at least slow down, the endless proliferation of words and the emotional merry-go-round they engender with, of all things, words. He remembers resolving to "allay" and cabin the pains of love by drawing them "through rhyme's vexation" (9). "Grief brought to numbers cannot be so fierce; / For he tames it, that fetters it in verse" (10–11). The thought is that in a vertiginous world at least a relative fixity might be found in and through the forms of poetry; but that thought is immediately succeeded by another, horrifying, one: if I write my passion down and seek to stabilize and mute it, another poet can riff on what I have written and release into the atmosphere what I had hoped to contain. (The same fear is expressed with respect to a language-domesticated woman in "Elegy 7.") "Some man, his art and voice to show, / Doth set and sing my pain, / And by delighting many, frees again / Grief, which verse did restrain" (12–16). Ben Saunders perfectly captures the terrible irony the speaker recognizes: ". . . a poem about the desire to write a poem to restrain desire that results in a poem that reproduces the initial desire to write a poem to restrain desire, which in turn produces a poem about the desire to write a poem to restrain desire that reproduces the initial desire, and so on, *ad infinitum*" (*Desiring Donne*, 2006, p. 12). You can't restrain words with words; and when you try or think to try, everything you had hoped to lessen is "increased" (18). The speaker knows this all the while, for in the beginning he refers to his efforts in this mode as "whining poetry" (4), poetry that rather than sublimating the whine of a pitiful lover, extends it. Now he extends it again by writing *this* poem, another piece of whining that doubles and triples his pathetic self-pity. And if he were to write another poem entitled, perhaps, "The Quadruple Fool," he would be doing it again and once more be unable to position himself to the side of the medium (language, representation) he thinks to control and deploy; it deploys and overwhelms him.

Whereas Milton wants to put the self and representation to good Christian Humanist uses, and Herbert wants to defeat the (sincere) self by embracing representation precisely because it is secondary, and Jonson wants to protect and encase the (virtuous) self by disclaiming the power to represent it, and Marvell wants both the self and representation to disappear into the green shade of undefiled nature, Donne is trapped in the ever renewing force of representation and can't find a place or a self not already occupied by verbal forms, by "words, words, which would tear / The tender labyrinth of a soft maid's ear" (*Satire* 2, 57–58).

Hobbes agrees; it's all words, but he contrives to make this apparently unhappy fact into a technology of control and progress. He does this by dismissing the profound questions raised by the authors we have surveyed and substituting for them a question more pragmatic: how can we achieve some measure of stability in a world where nothing is stable and meanings proliferate to the point of vertigo if we let them? The answer? Don't let them. Instead, by an act of the will establish precise definitions and then permit no deviations. Accept that ours is a universe of words (" *True* and *False* are attributes of Speech not of Things") and resolve to keep that universe as tidy as possible so that the "reckonings" (calculations) that go on within it will be regular and publicly shared.

And what of everything that is not contained in our definitions? What of grand abstractions like conscience, truth, justice, liberty, equality and honor? They are to be given strict conventional definitions, definitions the virtue of which is not that they capture some essence, but that they can be worked with and relied on: "The light of humane minds is Perspicuous Words, but by exact definitions . . . purged from ambiguity; *Reason* is the *pace*; Encrease of Science, the way; and the Benefit of man-kind, the end" (*Leviathan*, ed. C.B. Macpherson, p. 116). If this care to keep the verbal foundations of society in place and in check is not taken, disaster will follow: "And on the contrary, Metaphors, and senseless and ambiguous words, are like *ignes fatui*; and reasoning upon them a wandering amongst innumerable absurdities; and the end, contention, and sedition" (116–117) and, finally, civil war.

This is not the project of Bishop Spratt's Royal Society or the logical positivists of the early twentieth century who want to pare language down so that it will be congruent with and not supplant a material reality. For Hobbes, reality is whatever the "settled significations" of a conventional vocabulary permit us to say in the context of the communal tasks that must be negotiated in everyday life. If we are furnished with a precise vocabulary that allows us to pass meanings back and forth and engage in commercial transactions with some measure of confidence, that's good enough and much better than what we would have if our ambitions – linguistic and moral – were more ambitious.

It is not that more ambitious visions are beyond men; far from it. It is, rather, that there are too many of them, and there exists no rule, except for a rule instituted by force, that can put a bound either to their desires or their conflicts. That is why Hobbes's favorite word is "artificial." An artificial language – language the lexicon of which is fixed by convention rather than by nature – is better than one that claims a correspondence with truth because the fact of the correspondence can become a matter of dispute, whereas conventions, if they are firmly in place, hold dispute at bay. An artificial system of justice, one that begins not in the hope of attaining an ideal, but in the resolution to honor contracts, is better than a system of justice with substantive aspirations because its requirement and effects can be plainly set down and measured, whereas substantive aspirations know neither limits nor humility. An artificial state, one that rests on a pedigree of positive norms laid down by the sovereign who has the power to do so, is better than a state resting on the (claimed) virtue of either its leaders or its citizens. If the people flourish in a state, it is not, says Hobbes, "because the man has the right to rule them, but because they obey him" (380); don't worry about the right of rule, just assure the obedience. And an artificial self, a self identified with a role and its obligations, is better than a self with some mysterious and non-accountable interiority. A self that acquires its shape in the context of public performances and claims no private (secret, reserved) privileges is a self you can do business with; its (conventional) word is its bond and you can count on it. The true and comforting understanding of idea of "person" is taken, says Hobbes, from the "latine": "the disguise, or *outward appearance* of a man, counterfeited on the Stage . . . So that a Person is the same that an *Actor* is, both on the stage and in common conversation; and to *Personate*, is to *Act*, or *Represent* himself" (216). In private the "secret thoughts of a man run over all things," but in public the thoughts a man should have are the thoughts of an actor whose lines are written for him. He is not a self, but a representation.

The question of course is what keeps these conventional structures – of language, justice, the state, the self – in place? What anchors the entire edifice? What prevents men from employing language to deceive and oppress? What prevents jurists from perverting justice by invoking a "higher law" which always turns out to command what they desire? What prevents the "natural person" from consulting his desires and opinions and breaking free of the artificial constraints that keep men from tearing each other apart? The answer is nothing at all aside from an act of the will that can always be forsworn. The bonds of consent to a conventionally constituted authority (of language, law, and politics) are, Hobbes admits, by their own nature "weak"; there is nothing underneath them or inside them or above them. They hold only because we fear the consequences – chaos and the war of all against all – "of breaking them." This is the ultimate and terrifying face of humanism and of the liberal state which Hobbes helps to usher in. Once you give up or stigmatize interiority, once you forsake abstraction and the guidance of ideals, once language becomes primary, and not merely instrumental to something it serves, once truth becomes a matter of correspondence between propositions, once justice is a conventional calculation, we have entered a world where everything depends upon us and we are at the same time the potential source of everything's dissolution. Sound familiar?

PART I

Milton

CHAPTER I

The Brenzel lectures

INTRODUCTION

Why read *Paradise Lost*? For that matter, why read poetry at all? What pleasure and/or instruction does it give? Is what it offers unique, or can it be derived more easily and succinctly from other sources? These are all questions too large to be answered in a short series such as this one, but I hope to gesture toward an answer by introducing you to the demands and rewards of one piece of poetry generally acknowledged to be among the most impressive productions of the human mind. My thesis is that engagement of a particularly attentive kind with that poem will tell you more about it and about poetry in general than any abstract formulations I could provide.

Let's plunge right in with a single line taken from the first book of the poem at the moment when its hero or antihero (the choice will always be yours) summons up the host of rebel angels whom he has led to disastrous defeat. As their roll is called, Milton's epic voice observes that it is these shadowy figures who will later be worshipped by superstitious men and women under names like Belial and Moloch. He wonders at the perverseness and stupidity of such worship and expresses that wonder in a single contemptuous line: "And Devils to adore for Deities" (I, 373). The message is clear; for reasons the epic voice can barely fathom, multitudes of men and women will be unable to tell the difference between devils and deities, and will bow down to the former in despite of the latter. "How could they be so stupid?" the line implicitly asks, but at the same time, the formal features of the line provide the answers to its own implied question. For if the wonder is that people would mistake devils for deities, both the rhythms and the alliterative pattern of the line imitate and

---

These lectures were written for a great teacher video produced by Jeff Brenzel. It was my original plan to read the essays on camera, but at the last moment I decided that it would be better to work from a set of quotations that I would talk about and weave into an interpretive narrative on the spot. The lectures were neither given nor ever published and so appear here for the first time.

participate in that same mistake. Not only are devils and deities equivalent in syllables; they are equivalent also in the position of vowel sounds and in the joint possession of the initial consonant "D," and moreover they are linked in the line by a mirroring structure of sound – "adore for" – which repeats and deepens the similarities that fill a line whose sense insists on difference. Here is one thing that poetry does: it says two opposing things in the same line. It says "The difference between devils and deities is enormous, and how could they miss it?" It says "The difference between devils and deities is awfully hard to discern because on the surface – in the aspects of their form – the two seem so much alike." In short, the difference is obvious *and* the difference is easy to miss.

This small line can stand in both for the experience of reading Milton's poem and for the relationship of that experience to the poem's concerns. Reading Milton's poem means being attentive to tensions and disjunctions like the ones I have described. And reading Milton's poem also involves self-conscious reflection on that to which you attend. Milton wants us to be aware of the doubleness of the line's message and he also wants us to be provoked by that doubleness to a question: "Well, which is it? Is the difference obvious and large or subtle and minute?" The answer will finally be "It depends." It depends on whether or not you or I or the characters in the poem are able to see through the surface similarities to the underlying difference that makes the surface similarities irrelevant and indeed makes them disappear. Milton's poetry not only exercises one's intelligence and perception, but *tests* it. The question here and everywhere is: "Can you tell the difference?" The answer is given in the way you read the poem, which means that your reading of the poem is a large part of its subject.

And of course it should be, since the official subject is the Fall of Man and its consequences, and you and I and everyone else *are* its consequences; so that in reading the poem, we are not only apprehending its truth, but giving evidence of its truth *in* our responses. This poetry at least is characterized by the strenuousness of its demands and also by what is at stake in the degree of success or failure with which the reader meets those demands. The poem is relentless, and it is so from its opening lines.

WHAT IT'S LIKE TO READ MILTON

The first five and a half lines identify the poem as an epic. The syntactic structure of "Of Man's first disobedience" signals a comparison with Virgil's opening in the *Aeneid* "Of arms and the man I sing." Milton places four lines between his "Of" and "sing," and the material in between begins to mark out ways in which the epic will be different. Like other epics, it will be concerned with large-scale actions, heroic – even godly – figures, nationalistic histories and ambitions and the great questions of character, moral choice and fate. The difference is that Milton's epic is Christian not only in an incidental or cosmetic sense, but to the core.

It is this fact about the epic that generates the large differences between it and its predecessors. Epics can be either tragic or comic, as in *Don Quixote* and Rabelais. A Christian epic, however, is both because it tells two stories simultaneously: a story of disaster – in this case the disastrous eating of an apple by a couple told not to do so by no less than God – and a story of redemption – of the self-sacrifice of that same God, who by taking human form and dying on the cross reverses and redeems the failure of his creatures.

What this means is that at any point in *Paradise Lost* the action taking place can be viewed under either of these two perspectives and a great deal of the reader's experience of the poem is generated by the tension between them. If one reads these first five and a half lines aloud the phrase "With loss of Eden" is de-emphasized and receives lesser stress. Line 4, "With loss of Eden, till one greater Man" in itself contains and balances the two visions – one plot-driven and inexorable, the other mercy-driven and full of surprise – that vie for our attention throughout the poem.

If we keep the focus on the "linear plot," the large question continually posed is the question of the classic detective story "Who dunnit?" – "Who brought death into the world and all our woe?" The answer seems obvious and is given in the first half line. Man did it; but in the silent space between the ending of line 1 and the beginning of line 2 that answer is complicated. We expect "and the Fruit" to be followed by something like "that act"; but it turns out to be the fruit of the forbidden tree, which for a moment raises the odd possibility that the tree did it, which in turn raises the not-so-odd possibility that the responsible party is the agent who planted the tree in the first place, that is, God.

It is by means of half-suggested interpretive possibilities like this one that the poem begins to complicate its own moral structure and to raise questions that will engage the reader in a particularly interested way. The reader is interested because this is his or her story: the story of how he or she now is, that is, fallen, mortal, full of sin. How did it happen? Who dunnit? The first answer is that man did it, which is in effect an answer that places the responsibility on the reader, makes the reader, as the son or daughter of Adam, guilty of the original crime and of the crimes he or she now commits in the father's image. No wonder readers resist the poem's official story and look for ways to extenuate the fault of Adam and Eve, that is, to exonerate themselves.

The true drama of this poem, then, is to be found not in the events of its "plot," but in the events occurring in the reader's mind, and these are above all interpretive events where a reader must choose between various ways of interpreting scenes, and the choices given amount to a test of his spiritual understanding. Each choice is to some extent the same one; will the scene be viewed from the perspective of a linear, empirical plot where cause and effect are strictly entailed and events as they unfold foreclose other possibilities, or will the scene be viewed from the perspective of Christ's redemptive act ("till one greater Man / Restore us"), an act which interrupts the logic of linear time and reflects the extravagance of mercy and grace?

One such interpretive choice is presented almost schematically in the first epic simile, an extended comparison of Satan to Leviathan. Satan, the great archangel, is described in ways that emphasize both his vast bulk and the threat he poses. He is as large as an island, and therefore presents the deceptive surface of security and stability. The story of the pilot in a frail vessel who mistakes the huge leviathan for a place of safe mooring ends disastrously even though that end is not given in the verse: when the "wished Morn" comes the leviathan, the huge whale, will awaken and submerge and drag those who have bound themselves to him down to the depths and to destruction. At this moment in the reader's experience, the threat of Satan is inflated and the danger he represents seems inescapable, so small is the pilot, so large the enemy, so small Adam and Eve, so large their foe; how could they escape; they didn't have a chance. But then with a single word the entire perspective of the scene is reversed. Line 209, "So stretcht out huge in length the Arch-fiend lay," is followed powerfully by the first word of line 210 "Chain'd" "on the burning Lake". Not only is the vast bulk suddenly emptied of its threat, but we are given an explanation:

> nor ever thence
> Had ris'n or heav'd his head, but that the will
> And high permission of all-ruling Heaven
> Left him at large to his own dark designs, (1, 210b–213)

But even as we are reassured that from a godly perspective there is nothing to be afraid of, we are provoked to wonder why God is allowing this to happen; and as soon as we begin to wonder that, we are once again questioning the logic of the Fall and resisting the assignment of blame to Adam and Eve, who are either, under one story, the helpless victims of a monstrous villain or, under an alternate story, the indirect victims of a callous God.

We must be careful not to confuse Milton's perspectivism – his insistence that we see the scenes of his story from various viewpoints – with some form of relativism. Although Milton offers us the choice between perspectives, he does not authorize them indifferently. He is not a relativist. Satan is the relativist and announces himself as one very early on in three famous lines:

> The mind is its own place, and in itself
> Can make a Heav'n of Hell, a Hell of Heav'n.
> What matter where, if I be still the same, (1, 254–256)

There are two ways to understand this assertion. Either the mind contains a firm standard which remains unchanged no matter what the circumstances; it is its own place and remains so through thick and thin; or, rather, the mind is infinitely plastic and can alter itself and its surroundings at will, making a heaven of hell or a hell of heaven. It is the second meaning that Satan intends and the claim for the creative power of the mind is imitated by the alliterative pattern of the verse and by the chiastic structure of the phrase.

What Satan doesn't see is that a plasticity so unbound leaves nothing standing, including the agent who employs it. If thought can alter reality then thought is itself as unstable, without an anchor, as the material it works on. Satan cannot at once announce the unconstrained power of his imagination and assume that he remains unchanged as that power is exercised. He cannot claim to be "still the same" if everything is changeable, and there is nothing in reference to which sameness, self-identity, can be measured or validated. The truth is that by cutting himself off from the source of all value, by rebelling from God (and here we must remember that God is not merely the name of a character), Satan turns himself into a being incapable of a stability of purpose and of meaningful action in general. One cannot fall away from the center of meaning and still pretend to be meaningful.

The epic voice comments on just this unhappy situation when it characterizes Satan's rousing call to his troops:

> with high words, that bore
> Semblance of worth, not substance, gently rais'd
> Their fainting courage, and dispell'd their fears. (1, 528b–530)

We never hear exactly what Satan's "high words" are, but Milton alerts us to what is wrong with them when he describes their intended effect in the phrase "gently rais'd." "Rais'd" is a homonym, a verbal unit that contains more than one meaning, and in this case the alternative meanings are opposites. "Rais'd" can mean either elevated, uplifted, or destroyed – in our spelling "razed" – and there is even a third suggestion, more than possible, given seventeenth-century orthography, of ras'd or erased. The pun is pointed; for what Satan is here doing is encouraging his followers to a further act of rebellion against God; that is, he is encouraging them to an act of self-destruction in the course of which they will be razed. Once one sees this possible account of the moment, the word "gently" becomes obviously anomalous. Can one gently destroy? Can "gently" have any meaning in relation to the action Satan here performs? The phrase "gently rais'd" belongs to Satan's imagined self-dramatization of the scene; this is how he sees himself, as the compassionate and caring leader; but if we are sensitive to the ambiguity we cannot join in his construction of the scene, which we will see quite differently.

It would be impossible to illustrate this moment in the poem because no single picture would be adequate to the doubleness of what is *not* presented here. Milton's verse, although it seems at first to encourage visualization, almost always frustrates visualization by disallowing any single perspective and forcing us to reason away from the images initially thrown up by its surfaces. The great critic F.R. Leavis once complained that Milton's poetry does not refer its readers to something outside its confines, but forces them to reflect on its own internal workings. This complaint is absolutely on target, although I would not see it as a fault but as an indication of what the verse demands of us – cognitive acts of discrimination that simultaneously test and refine our adequacy to the poem's great issues. If we accept Satan's own version of what is happening here by rushing past the ambiguity of "rais'd," we will leave this passage captive to the vision of the poem's arch-villain; but if we are sensitive to the workings of Milton's language, we leave the passage further instructed in the kind of thinking that will enable us to negotiate the poem's labyrinths. We will leave the passage understanding that gentleness, and all other virtues, are now impossible to a figure who has rejected the normative standard in relation to which any virtue could be defined.

Such a figure has condemned himself to meaninglessness, to incoherence, to saying, as Satan says in a late address to his troops, we are "surer to prosper than prosperity / Could have assur'd us" (II, 39–40a). This is nonsense in which prosperity is redefined as its opposite; the entire force of these words depends on the surface connections provided by the alliteration and by the cadences of the chiasmus. It sounds good, but it falls apart at the slightest analytic touch, just as it sounds good to say "I can make a Heav'n of Hell, or a Hell of Heav'n" until you realize (which you will not unless you make the strenuous effort of reflection this verse demands) that if heaven and hell can be turned into one another at will, neither of them has any meaning. Everything in the Satanic vocabulary is like these examples – surface intelligibility and coherence overstriding a moral abyss. The rebel angels do not and cannot understand *anything*, because they have rejected the frame of reference that makes understanding possible. They don't know what anything means, and their ignorance is perfectly illustrated when Mammon wonders why they just can't produce heaven in hell with a little interior decorating, some elaborate track lighting: "cannot we his Light / Imitate when we please?" (ii, 269b–270a). Cannot we use art and skill to erect tall buildings? "And what can Heav'n show more?" (ii, 273b) He really doesn't know. To him, the show of things is literally all there is and he cannot imagine a deeper content, a significance that is more than superficial. In this question – "And what can Heav'n show more?" – we see illustrated the willed poverty of the Satanic world-view, the glass ceiling of its perceptual abilities, the spiritual deadness of merely empirical vision, that is vision which cannot raise its eyes, but is captive to what the senses deliver.

Empiricism – the refusal to look beyond surfaces – is finally a form of solipsism or self-worship; for it accepts the horizons of the partial limited vision as the entire story. The birth of empiricism, of self-worship, is presented in the allegorical account of the birth of Sin, a female figure which spontaneously sprung out of the head of Satan, in a grotesque moment of self-copulation, "Likest to thee in shape and count'nance bright / . . . a Goddess arm'd / Out of thy head I sprung" (ii, 756–758a). The allegory could not be more literal. Satan produces an image of himself with which he then falls in love: "Thyself in me thy perfect image viewing / Becam'st enamoured, and such joy thou took'st / With me in secret, that my womb conceiv'd / A growing burden" (ii, 764–767a). That is, he woos himself, impregnates himself and produces a third generation of himself. With each successive self-reproduction he moves further and further away from the recognition that he is himself a creature and therefore sustained by someone greater than himself and prior to himself. He settles for images, and forgets what is real and that is why the goddess who springs from his head is called Sin and held to be "a sign." A sign is usually understood to refer to something outside of itself; a sign's meaning is elsewhere; the sign becomes a sin when it is accepted as a fully realized horizon and is substituted for the reality to which it refers. Accepting the world of signification, of signs, as complete in and of itself, independently of what it is a sign of, is sin; and it is more than accidental that sign and sin first appear in female form.

Milton is in many things a child of his times and especially so in his attitude toward women, who represent for him, as for many of his predecessors, an afterthought in the mind of God, who first made man in his image and then out of man produced a doubly derivative being, woman. As Raphael will explain later to Adam in Book VIII, the man who surrenders to passion subjects himself to a third-rate image of what is truly valuable, subjects himself as Mammon does, to mere show, to a surface, to a sign, and forgets the true meaning to which surfaces, rightly considered, point. Sin, sign, woman – all interchangeable names for the impulse Milton both feels and resists, the impulse to substitute for the true worship of God the worship of one or more of his incidental effects. "How could one be so foolish as to prefer something or someone God has created to God himself?" one might ask, a question that is in part answered when God appears in Book III of *Paradise Lost* and takes center stage.

MILTON'S GOD AND THE LOGIC OF THE FALL: "SUFFICIENT TO HAVE STOOD, THOUGH FREE TO FALL"

One of Milton's most daring decisions is the decision to place God in the foreground as a character. The critic William Empson said, with reference to Milton's God, "in a civilized narrative all the characters are on trial," and as far as he is concerned the trial of Milton's God by any reader will end in a verdict of guilty. It is not hard to see why. When we first encounter him in Book III lines 80 and following, God and his Son sit at the top of the universe and view with apparent dispassion what we might call an imminent train wreck. God reports that he sees and invites us to see Satan as an immensely powerful figure whom no bars or chains can hold. He breaks through all restraint and is seen heading directly toward Eden and the two frail creatures who are obviously no match for him. Already a host of questions, none of them favorable to this God, is provoked. Why doesn't he stop it? Why didn't he place Satan in stronger chains? Why are Adam and Eve left defenseless? Why doesn't he lift a finger? It is not that he is in doubt of what is going to happen, for from a prospect so high that "past, present, future He beholds," he sees that Satan will indeed succeed in perverting men.

And there is more. An ambiguity at line 90 suggests that this may be the outcome God has designed: "And man there plac't with purpose to assay / If him by force he can destroy" (III, 90–91a). In the syntax of the passage "purpose" can belong either to Satan or to God: it is Satan's purpose in his journey to destroy; it is God's purpose in his placement of men to set up a laboratory situation to see whether or not destruction and perversion will occur. But again he already knows that they will, and what emerges here is the picture not of a benevolent caring God, but an arrogant surveyor of the cosmic scene who operates much like a large-scale Nero watching the Christians about to be eaten by the lions, and it doesn't get any better.

When God says man will "*easily* transgress the sole Command," the adverb "easily" poses the question "Why?" (III, 94). And the most available answer is that they were without adequate defense and didn't have a chance. Then comes the most irritating and off-putting aspect of God's performance: *He knows what you've been thinking and he has an answer ready for you*: "whose fault? Whose but his own? ingrate" (III, 96b–97a). Just as the reader is, with Empson, in the act of indicting God, God turns around and indicts the reader in the person of his first parents. It was their fault, and as their heirs, it is your fault, and, in resisting me and questioning my justice you repeat the action – of disobedience – that brought death into the world and all our woe.

Nor does God merely declare this with the word "ingrate" – a word that is hurled like a spear into the heart of every reader – but he explains Adam and Eve's situation in a way that, retroactively at least, cleans up all the puzzles and problems that had bubbled up in the preceding lines. "I made him just and right / Sufficient to have stood, though free to fall" (III, 98–99). A variant of this line occurs no less than nine times in the rest of the poem. It is the key to the poem's moral logic, and in typical Miltonic fashion, it offers its own test and its own temptation. The temptation is to take this explanation as further evidence of God's guilt, to say as many readers have, if they could fall, are they not already fallen? Isn't there a propensity in them to fall, and where would it come from except from the Creator?

The proper response to this question, which raises itself, is the realization that if they could not have fallen, they could not have stood. That is, if they were so constructed as to be incapable of making a mistake, they could not receive any credit for not having made one since they would have been programmed for virtue. In order for their obedience to be theirs – something they are responsible for and can take credit for – the possibility of disobedience must be real. Readers who wish that they were failure-proof wish that they were not free agents, but to so wish is to deny them their dignity, just as their dignity would be denied if, after having made them sufficient to stand, God had stepped in and stopped the train when he saw that it was going to hit them. They were not perfect in the sense of being automatons, rather, and this will only seem paradoxical for an instant, their perfection as free agents requires their imperfection as agents who can err. Free to fall means free to stand, means free.

The doctrine of free will is at the very heart of the poem and returns us to a point made last time, that the true events of this poem occur not in its succession of events, but in the interior events of the character's and the reader's interpretive will. Adam and Eve's strength depends not on Satan being kept away from them, on God's binding him with stronger chains. Adam and Eve's strength depends on their internal capacity to maintain loyalty by obeying God's command. The poem's message to them and to us is the Nancy Reagan message: "Just say no." What this means is that the succession of plot events that fill up the poem's narrative is irrelevant. Properly speaking, the poem can have no plot because the moment a reader indulges in plot-thinking – asking questions like, "Why doesn't God stop Satan?" or: "Why does God allow Adam and Eve to separate on the fatal morning?" – the freedom of the unfallen will have been compromised because responsibility for maintaining loyalty will have been shifted from the interior field of the will to the external set of circumstances that supposedly overwhelms that will. In order to read the poem correctly, you are required to continually set aside and discount its apparent plot and cling fast to the doctrine of free will. It's very hard to do in part because one legacy of the Fall is that our wills are by no means so strongly free, and we can barely imagine a creature capable of maintaining inner strength against all outward circumstance, and it is hard in part because Milton makes it hard by providing so many opportunities for plot-thinking and for fudging the moral serenity of his vision.

In the same way Milton asks us to resist the antipathy toward God which he himself produces by presenting him as he does in these lines – as arrogant, as a know-it-all, legalistic, hard. Our relationship to God as readers exactly mirrors Adam and Eve's relationship to the command not to eat the apple. The command, as many have said, is unreasonable; it doesn't come with an explanation attached; but if it did and it were seen to be reasonable not to eat the apple, the command would not be a test of faith; it would just be a reasonable action, like stepping around a hole rather than falling into it. In order to be a test of faith the command must be arbitrary; in order for the reader's acceptance of God to be meaningful, it must not be an acceptance that flows from the fact that he's a nice guy. In one of his prose tracts, written in an effort to change the divorce laws of England, Milton defines what he calls a good temptation: "A good temptation is that whereby God tempts even the righteous for the purpose of proving them ... for the purpose of exercising or manifesting their faith or patience ... or of lessening their self-confidence and proving their weakness, that they may become wiser by experience." That is exactly Milton's strategy in this poem, where he plays God to us readers and invites us down the paths of error in the hope that by resisting them we may become wiser by the experience he has provided. In *Paradise Lost* the good temptation is always an interpretive one as we are given the choice of seeing things one way or the other, and the cumulative effect of our choices will be registered in Book IX when we witness and are asked to understand the Fall.

Most of the choices we are asked to make involve assessments of Adam and Eve's condition and the relation of that condition to what they and others say and do. The question often is: "What do we see when they are on the poem's stage?" Do we see two strong and noble creatures capable of the task assigned them? Or do we see inherently flawed creatures placed in a situation beyond their abilities? Often this is pointed out for us by the fact that Satan is our companion in seeing. We are invited quite literally to see things through his eyes and it is an invitation that we are always in danger of accepting.

The first time we "see them" it is from Satan's perspective: "the Fiend / Saw undelighted all delight, all kind / Of living Creatures new to sight and strange: / Two of far nobler shape erect and tall" (IV, 285b–288). To see "undelighted all delight" is of course not to see. Satan looks at Adam and Eve but his capacity for truly seeing them is limited by the kind of person he is. Milton believes – and I agree with him – that the shapes we see are projections of our own inner state. Satan will neither see nor understand the true delight of Adam and Eve's life together; for him the words which now fill these lines – "honor," "majesty," "worthy," "truth," "wisdom," "sanctitude" – can have no more meaning than the meaning "gently" doesn't have when applied to his action in Book I. If he could understand what truth, wisdom and honor were, he would not be himself, but another. It is a cardinal tenet of modern rationalism that you can comprehend virtues you do not yourself exemplify. Milton in contrast would say that you can only understand what you have yourself internalized. That is why he declares in another prose tract that a man who would write a true poem must himself *be* a true poem and can only praise or even recognize worthy things if he is himself worthy. In the matter of moral perception, Milton's motto is "it takes one to know one."

What do readers know – see, understand, comprehend – when they meet Adam and Eve in this poem? An early test occurs in the lines which describe

Eve's hair: "Shee as a veil down to the slender waist / Her unadorned golden tresses wore / Dishevell'd, but in wanton ringlets wav'd / As the Vine curls her tendrils, which impli'd / Subjection" (IV, 304–308a). Is subjection a surprise for the reader? Are there readers who read another message in long golden hair carelessly flowing and described as wanton? Are there readers for whom this entire pose spells not subjection but seduction and speaks a sexuality that rings alarm bells in relation to the possibility of the Fall? Are there readers who consume these lines and understand them as proof of Eve's imperfect nature and therefore as an indication once again that she is destined to be tempted since she is herself so obviously a temptress? Of course there are such readers and Milton knows it; but he wants these readers to know that in so interpreting Eve, they are betraying the limitations of their own vision. They are like Satan seeing undelighted all delight, and as if to point such readers' own interpretive failing, Milton comments on this description of Eve in the voice of his narrator: "Then was not guilty shame" (IV, 313). Not then, but now. Not in their relationship to one another, but in a fallen reader's relationship to them. The final two lines are masterful: "So pass'd they naked on, nor shunn'd the sight / Of God or Angel, for they thought no ill" (IV, 319–320). That is, *they* thought no ill, but we may if we are a certain kind of reader, if we are the kind of reader Satan is for example when a little later on in the same scene, he responds to Eve, who "half-embracing lean'd / On our first Father, half her swelling Breast / Naked met his under the flowing Gold / Of her loose tresses hid" (IV, 494b–497a). Who can resist smiling pruriently at the word "naked" and at the image of the half-swelling breast; who can resist reading much into the word "loose" and constructing from it a story of tragic propensity? Certainly not Satan. "(A)side the devil turn'd / For envy, yet with jealous leer malign" (IV, 502b–503). Do we receive this account of Satan's response with a shock of recognition? Do we measure our response against a standard we have ourselves not met? Do we push away the cynicism and sleazy sensuality that we may have involuntarily displayed? Will we be able to become wiser by experience because of the temptation Milton here presents?

Asking these questions of course raises another question which may have already occurred to many of you. What if "we" are women? The question of Milton's attitude toward women is one of the oldest in Milton criticism. It antedates the rise of feminism and found a novelistic expression in Robert Graves's novel *Wife to Mr. Milton*, a scathing account of what a young English girl had to put up with when she married a pompous, self-important intellectual bully who thought he was God's poet. The primary source of the problem is of course those famous lines from the passage we have already examined: "For contemplation hee and valour form'd, / For softness shee and sweet attractive Grace, / Hee for God only, shee for God in him" (IV, 297–299). We now know to label this last line the essence of patriarchy and there can be no doubt that a patriarchal vision is operating here, a vision in which an almighty Father generates without any participation from any mother a male heir from whose essence is further generated all of the created world and its populations. In the context of this vision, women are at best an afterthought and at worst, as we have already seen, a distraction, a source of temptation, the chief location of the possibility of turning away from internal male purity and essence to the fair but substanceless surfaces of the sensory and sensual world.

The official morality of the poem asks its characters and its readers again and again to reject the appeal of surfaces and softness and apparent physical beauty for depth, stern rigor and the true beauty of a rectified spirit. The lesson is read by Eve herself against herself in the famous scene when, upon awakening into life, she looks into a pool of water and, Narcissus-like, falls in love with her own image. "Pleas'd it return'd as soon with answering looks / Of sympathy and love" (IV, 463–464a). This moment of self-infatuation threatens to be just like the moment when Sin, likest to Satan in shape, bursts out of his own head and becomes his paramour. But Eve is saved, she tells us, by a Heavenly voice that leads her against her will to Adam who, at first sight, seems to her "Less winning soft, less amiably mild, / Than that smooth wat'ry image" (IV, 480–481a). She turns away in favor of her own self-reflection, but is called back by Adam who claims her as his other half. She yields and now in the present reads the official moral of her experiences. I now see, she says, "How beauty is excell'd by manly grace / And wisdom, which alone is truly fair" (IV, 490–491). You'll not be surprised to hear that centuries of male critics have accepted Eve's conclusion, and praised her for having achieved an obvious maturity. And you will also not be surprised to hear that in recent years feminist critics have voiced quite another response to this scene, which they read, with the help of psychoanalysis, as a story of a subject robbed of her own dignity and forced to submit to the authority of an order that defines her as ephemeral, secondary, and implicitly dangerous. Some commentators have also wondered whether in passages like this Milton may be pushing away a part of himself, performing on some of his best instincts the surgical operation his poem performs on the body and spirit of Eve.

These are questions we shall return to, for they bear directly and indirectly on the Fall. A reading of this scene that refuses its moral and grants a legitimacy to Eve's desires and impulses will find those same desires and impulses – the desire to be independent, to not be subordinate, to be in-tune with one's inner feelings – embodied in the act of eating the apple. After all, obedience means the forsaking of the self and the suppression of its instincts. It requires that one choose against everything that seems attractive and mild and that one do so on the basis of no visible evidence whatsoever. It requires faith.

Satan knows this, and that is why when he first runs through the arguments he will use in the temptation scene, the emphasis falls on the presumed susceptibility of Adam and Eve's appeals to selfhood and self-worth. He asks – and it is hard to know whether he poses these questions because they are his or because he thinks they are the right ones to ask when the opportunity for seduction presents itself – why should they be forbidden knowledge? "Suspicious, reasonless" (iv, 516a). Of course, from the perspective of the poem's official morality, the fact that the prohibition against the eating of the tree of knowledge is reasonless is what makes it a test of faith. Were it a reasonable prohibition, adhering to it would be a matter of course and not a matter of faith-bearing choice. That is also the answer to the next question Satan posits: "Why should their Lord / Envy them that? Can it be sin to know?" (iv, 516b–517). Their Lord does not envy them knowledge; he wishes them to understand that knowledge is not their God, but that he is. Knowledge, like any other good, ceases to be good when it becomes the possible object of worship, of idolatry. "Thou shalt have no other gods before Me." It cannot be sin to know, but it can be sin to deify knowledge or information. To choose knowledge over God's command would be to raise knowledge to the position of Godhood, and to do that would be to break faith with God, and in a universe where he is the source of all meaning and value, such a breaking of union would in fact be death.

Satan's entire strategy, one he probably believes in, is to drive a wedge between the goods of God's created universe and the Creator, posing a choice between them as if the goods could be good – or anything for that matter – independent of the Creator. It is independence, of both the world and of its creator, with which Adam and Eve will be tempted. Independence is a form of idolatry, of self-worship, of staying in love with the image in the pool. Satan knows because he has himself succumbed to the temptation of Godhood. He will offer them the opportunity to be "Equal with Gods" and "aspiring to be such, / They taste and die:

what likelier can ensue?" (IV, 526–527). At this moment of supreme strategical advance planning, Satan reveals the limitation of his own vision. Not surprisingly, he is himself a prisoner of plot-thinking, who sees the events unfolding in the iron-grip of empirical cause and effect: "They've been told not to eat the apple or they die. I'm going to get them to eat the apple and they'll die. What else could happen?" What could happen is quite literally inconceivable to him. What could happen is grace, mercy, the unthinkable act of a God who will himself pay the price exacted by his own law. Trapped within the mean confines of his own empirical imagination, Satan cannot reach to any such conception of Godhood. As readers of this passage, it is our obligation to so reach, although typically Milton gives us every opportunity to fail to do so. If faith is what is required, one must always remember the classic definition of faith in Hebrews 11:1: "Faith is the substance of things hoped for, the evidence of things not seen." In this poem both the characters and readers are continually asked to affirm against the evidence of things seen – against softness, physical beauty, the press of circumstance – and to choose instead a reality whose only validation is in the faithful will of the chooser.

THE DYNAMICS OF FAITH: "ON OTHER SURETY NONE"

I ended last time by remarking on the demands of faith as Milton sees them, demands that Adam and Eve failed to fulfill at the crucial moment with disastrous results, of which we are the living emblems. Let me remind you again that faith in order to be faith must be *without external supports*. Faith is not truly exercised when empirical evidence directs us to it, or when our desires coincide with it, or when the signs pointing to it are unmistakable. Performing faithfully is at once the easiest and hardest of tasks. It is easy because all that is required is a gesture of the will. It is hard because if one looks away even for an instant from the interior field in which will is exercised to the field of the external world, the path of faith will be obscured.

In Book V Adam indicates how far he is from understanding this point when he wonders what Raphael could possibly mean when he says to the unfallen couple: "If ye be found obedient" (V, 501a). Adam asks, "How could we possibly lack obedience to the God who formed us from dust and gave us this happy paradise?" Adam thinks, in other words, as some of Milton's readers have, that obedience is programmed into him, but of course if that were the case it would have no value. Remember, "Sufficient to have stood, though free to fall" (III, 99). In response to Adam, Raphael gives his own version of God's statement: "God made thee perfect, not immutable" (v, 524). This formulation is very precise because it defines Adam and Eve's perfection in terms of their capacity for falling away from it. They are perfect as free agents because they might freely become imperfect, and that freedom, whose career is placed entirely in their will, defines their possibilities and enjoins them to eternal vigilance. Raphael points out that he and his fellow angels are free in exactly the same way, capable at any moment of freely making the wrong choice and therefore capable too of making the right one. We angels, says Raphael, "our happy state / Hold, as you yours, while our obedience holds; / On other surety none" (v, 536b–538a). That is to say, nothing but our own wills maintains our present condition. There is no safety net except the one we must weave and re-weave in every moment of self-defining choice.

In illustration of what this could possibly mean for Adam and Eve, Raphael tells the story of the birth of Satan, the first event, in a sense, of the poem's plot, the moment when the harmony and corporate unity of heaven is disturbed by an agent who separates himself from corporate structures and values and becomes a self in the modern sense – free-standing, independent, his own man, in short the heroic figure of Western narrative from Prometheus to John Wayne. This first moment in the poem's plot is also the moment when its most insistent questions will be answered in a fashion: Where does evil come from? If God is God and everywhere informs the world, how does rebellion get started? How is disobedience possible?

Typically, Milton answers this question by heightening its mystery. We are told by Raphael that on a given day God declares the Son (later to be known on earth as Jesus Christ) his only begotten, and appoints him the head of all the angels. Hearing this everyone appears to react with joy, but not so Satan. Why not? The verse answers by piling up reasons for Satan *not* to be discontented. He is preeminent among the other angels; he is "great in Power," and "In favour" (v, 660b–661a). In short, he has a good situation, and it is against the fact of that situation that a single small word measures the unlikelihood of his apostasy. That word is "yet": "yet fraught / With envy against the Son of God" (v, 661b–662a). Why "fraught with envy"? When the answer comes, it only provokes questions all over again. He "could not bear / Through pride that sight, and thought himself impair'd" (v, 664b–665). That is, seeing the Son exalted and anointed, Satan takes offence and considers himself slighted and mistreated. Obviously this is an elaboration of "yet fraught with envy," not an account or explanation of it. A kind of account is provided in line 665 when we realize that in our experience of the verse "that sight" – the sight of the Son's exaltation – is seen "through pride." It's not that Satan sees the sight and chooses the response of envy; rather, his way of seeing is prideful; he only gets to the sight through the corridor as it were of pride. What this means is that there is nothing inherent in the sight to provoke this or any other response, including the response of joy evidenced by Satan's peers. The sight will take on the hue and shape and meaning already internal to the seer.

And so the question becomes, where does the pride come from, and the answer is brilliantly given in the second half of the line, which we can now read with a different emphasis, "and thought himself impair'd" (v, 665b). That is, not only thought himself made lesser, but made himself lesser by so thinking, i.e., thought himself into a state of impairment, of pride, of envy. Raphael notes that before this moment Satan was known by another name which has now been erased. That is because he has in a copulation with his own thought – recall again the birth of Sin – generated a new self with a new name. The answer to the question: "Where does evil come from?" is that it comes from nowhere, at least insofar as the expected answer would point to some external source, or rather evil comes from the only place it could come from, an agent free to nominate its own loyalties and purposes. Like Adam and Eve, Satan is free and, like Adam and Eve, when he exercises that freedom in the act of embracing envy, he becomes another person just as in embracing joy the other angels remain the loyal persons they have heretofore been. As is often the case, Milton provides an immediate gloss on Satan's self-generation in the very next line: "Deep malice thence conceiving and disdain" (v, 666). That is, Satan here conceives himself as a new creature made up in equal parts of envy, pride, malice and disdain, and it can hardly be an accident, although an occasion for wonder, that this account is reported in a line whose number is 666, the number of the beast.

If Satan's self-generation is a perfect illustration of what it means to be sufficient to stand but free to fall on the negative side, another figure is the perfect illustration of what that freedom means on the positive side and that is Abdiel, the only angel in Satan's legions who dissents when the new doctrine of rebellion and independence is proclaimed. In the midst of the first diabolical council Abdiel rises "in a flame of zeal" and declares Satan's words to be "blasphemous, false and proud" (equivalent terms if properly understood), and leaves the rebel camp with the intention of warning the loyal angels of the enemy about to attack them (v, 807, 809). Book VI opens with a description of Abdiel hastening back to the precincts of the faithful, but the very first line of the description alerts us to something: "All night the dreadless Angel unpursu'd" (VI, 1). This last word "unpursu'd" operates to undercut the urgency of the angel's journey, an urgency which depends on two factors at either end of the journey: someone pressing at your back and someone in need of your aid and agency ahead of you. Indeed the unfolding of this passage operates in a number of ways to remove the point and purpose from what Abdiel is doing or thinks he's doing. Even the syntax undermines the importance and efficacy of his action. The second line, "Through heaven's wide Champaign held his way, till Morn," seems simply to be a comment on the steadfastness he here displays, not stopping for a second through an entire evening (VI, 2). The phrase "till Morn" is read at the end of line 2 as an adverbial of time – how long did he continue in his flight? – "till Morn." But in lines 3 and 4 the syntax changes and "till morn" becomes the subject of the verb "unbarr'd." "Till morn / Wak't by the circling Hours, with rosy hand / Unbarr'd the gates of Light" (VI, 2b–4a). It is a small effect but a significant one. "Morn" takes over the agency of the passage, and is presented as performing an action that will occur independently of anything Abdiel does or doesn't do. This is a preparation in miniature for the more dramatic usurpation of his agency that occurs when he reaches his journey's end; for what he finds is the camp of loyalists already preparing for battle even though he has not yet warned them of its imminence: "all the Plain / Cover'd with thick embattled Squadrons bright, / Chariots and flaming Arms, and fiery Steeds / Reflecting blaze on blaze, first met his view" (VI, 15b–18). The word "first" is a tremendous rebuke to his ambition. It was his intention to be first, to be the first to tell them, but they are first in their preparations; his view is superfluous, and he knows it: "War he perceived, war in procinct, and found / Already known what he for news had thought / To have reported" (VI, 19–21a).

Notice that structurally this is the same kind of moment that leads Satan to be fraught with envy. It is a personal disappointment, the dashing of an ambition, the performance by others of something he had hoped himself to perform. What does Abdiel do? We must go back to line 21 and complete it. "Already known what he for news had thought / To have reported: gladly then he mixt" (VI, 20–21). The brilliant stroke in this line is the word "gladly," which goes with two different constructions: he wanted to report the news and would have done so gladly had he been given the opportunity; in this construction, "gladly" goes with "reported"; but in another construction, "gladly" goes with "mixt": "gladly he mixt." The point is that Abdiel's gladness is independent of either outcome; he would have been glad to have rendered a service. He is glad when the service he rushed to render proves unnecessary. The two possibilities which in Satan's analogous moment make all the difference – presumably Satan would have been glad had he and not the Son been exalted – make no difference at all to Abdiel, who is not changed by external circumstances, but fills all external circumstance, no matter what their narrative shape, with his serene confidence and steadfast faith. What is most remarkable about Abdiel's response to the disappointment of his personal ambition to have reported the news is that he has no response. It's not that he pauses and says to himself: "Well, this hasn't turned out as I hoped it would; what am I going to think about it?" Rather, like Satan, he does not see the already prepared squadrons unmediated by any point of view or attitude; he sees them "through" something, but not "through pride" – rather, through a faith so deep that it is not even named, only slightly registered in the wonderfully free-floating syntactic status of "gladly." The true action here occurs not as Abdiel rushes through the night, with, as he thinks, time's winged chariot at his back, nor in the realization of anti-climax that meets him, but in the interior precincts of his inner loyalties and commitments where nothing happens, and because nothing happens, he, unlike Satan, remains faithful, remains, through thick and thin, through hope and disappointment, God's servant, and that is what God says to him immediately: "'Servant of God, well done, well hast thou fought / The better fight'" (VI, 29–30a). What I hope you see is that Abdiel won the better fight by not knowing there was one, by remaining unchanged in relation to events that might have provided another response and therefore produced another person of whom it might have then been said: "He thought himself impair'd."

Abdiel's victory then is to remain who he is despite the opportunity provided by circumstance to change his loyalty, and his performance is matched by all the good angels in the great battle that is narrated in the rest of Book VI. That battle begins with the loyalists being provided with an expectation of a certain kind of victory. God tells his troops at the outset to drive the rebels out of heaven "Into their place of punishment"; but as it turns out they are unable to do so, because God himself limits the might of both armies and thereby produces a stalemate and an opportunity for the Son to mount the heavenly chariot and do the job they failed to do (VI, 53). In short, the battle is staged, and the loyalists find themselves again and again exactly in Abdiel's position – confronted with both the inadequacy and superfluousness of their own efforts. Just as Abdiel finds the news he had thought to have reported already reported, his comrades find the victory they had been promised given to another, to the Son, who says to them, "The punishment to other hand belongs," even though it had been said to them that the hand was to be theirs (vi, 807). They react not with disappointment or chagrin or resentment; they do not think themselves impair'd. They respond instead with joy (line 774), and thus exemplify the same steadfastness displayed by Abdiel and in the same non-dramatic way.

Again, the point is that the events of the external world will bear the shape and meaning configured on them by whatever faith or lack of faith informs the observer. No matter what physical actions the combatants engage in, their more important actions are interpretive, as we see when Satan and Michael dispute the meaning of what is happening. Michael says: "'Author of evil, unknown till thy revolt'" (note that "unknown" refers simultaneously to the evil, to the revolt and to the author – Satan – all of whom come into being at the same instant) (vi, 262). Satan replies: "The strife which thou call'st evil, but wee style / The strife of Glory" (vi, 289–290a). That is, "You and I, Michael, are in different epics because we begin with different basic assumptions about the nature of the universe and the nature of heroic action. You talk endlessly about obedience which we call servility. You call evil what we see as the struggle for independence." And Satan is right; everything does depend on what the interpreter makes of it, but that does not mean, as he implies, that one can make up reality as one likes; for in Milton's view, some interpretive acts are in touch with the real while others are not, even though there is no *independent* mechanism for determining which faith is true and which false. That again is what faith means, an act of affirmation that has no support other than itself – "on other surety none" – an affirmation that creates its own evidence, which then can be retroactively invoked to support it. Nothing that happens, no external sign, can alter a faith which transubstantiates all external signs into its essence. Throughout the three-day battle, both sides refuse to draw conclusions that might possibly have been drawn "from the evidence." The loyalists never conclude, from the fact that they are being used by God as mere props for the Son's dramatic intervention, that they serve an unworthy God; the rebels never conclude, from the fact they now first experience pain and military humiliation, that it is God they fight against and that they are therefore insane. Both draw the conclusions that flow from and extend their respective faiths.

Raphael both sees this and doesn't see it; he sees the rebels standing firm even in the face of what seems to him to be incontrovertible evidence of the hopelessness of their cause. He says "to convince the proud what signs avail / Or wonders move th'obdurate to relent?" (VI, 789–790). He is making the mistake of believing that, like him, the devils should recognize the irresistible authority of God's might and power; but in his innocence he forgets that the devils are precisely not like him; they are without his faith and filled with a faith in their own self-sufficiency. They can no more see what he sees than he can see what they see, and he might as well have asked: "To convince the faithful what signs avail?" For in both cases the answer is: "No signs whatsoever" because what avails in one direction or the other is the internal constitution of the interpreting agent. It is the error of empiricism to believe that accumulated evidence will eventually add up to the truth; it is Milton's belief that one must begin with the truth and that in its assumed light the evidence will fall into the place it has always had. What do you believe, not at the end of the sequence, but at the beginning and at every moment? This is the only issue. That is the issue here and everywhere and it is the issue, as we shall see, in the Fall.

WOMEN AND THE DANGER OF DISOBEDIENCE

Throughout these lectures I have occasionally referred to the question of Milton and women, and noted the anti-feminist tradition in which Milton is necessarily placed. In that tradition, women are seen as an after-the-fact supplement or addition to the original act of creation by which God makes man in his image. Woman is created as the Bible says to be a helpmeet, and the mistake, made possible by her surface attractiveness, is to forget her subsidiary status and elevate her to the status of an equal or perhaps even to the status of a superior. In the psychology of both Platonism and Christianity, this translates into an opposition between the mind and the body, the spirit and the flesh – the spirit and mind being understood as masculine and the body and the flesh being understood as feminine.

There is ample evidence that Milton subscribes to this constellation of views – "Hee for God only, shee for God in him" – but there is also evidence that in some of his own thinking the reversal of priorities he warns against is a reversal he himself is tempted by and sometimes seems to endorse. In short, Milton's relationship to issues of gender is extremely complicated, and most of the complications are on full display in the invocation of Book VII, where Milton addresses Urania, his female muse. The passage begins by imagining Urania, along with the allegorical figure of Wisdom, playing and singing "In presence of th'Almighty Father" (VII, 11a).

What Urania and Wisdom are said to be singing is a "Celestial Song" (VII, 12). In the Renaissance this phrase would have had a very precise meaning. It refers to what was called "the music of the spheres." It was thought that the entire universe as informed by God – the full panoply of planetary and heavenly bodies – was in continual movement and produced a divine sound. What is important about this sound, this celestial song, is that it is sung by no one, because it is sung by everyone. As the music produced by the *uni*verse, no one singer either stands apart from it or can be said to be responsible for it in the sense of being able to take credit for it. Throughout his career, Milton returns again and again to this image of a corporate ensemble of universal singers, each of whom receives an identity from the corporate effort and no one of whom is known or marked apart from that effort. What draws Milton to this musical image is its representation of union with divinity so total that the individual cannot be said to exist. It is this state of absorption into deity which Milton praises at the end of an early poem called "At a Solemn Music." In that poem the Fall is equated with the moment when some voices broke away from the ensemble, when "disproportioned sin / Jarred against nature's chime and with harsh din / Broke the fair music that all creatures made." Regeneration and salvation are then imaged at the end of the poem as that time when God will "To his celestial consort us unite, / To live with him, and sing in endless morn of light."

Traditionally, however, in Milton's time as well as in ours, the image of absorption and the loss of discrete identity in a harmonious community is marked as feminine, while the posture of aggressive independence, the posture in which one stands out from the crowd rather than being submerged in it, is marked as distinctly masculine. To put it oversimply, when Milton imagines the condition he most desires, he imagines himself as a woman, totally subsumed in a larger structure, but his own sense of moral and artistic superiority leads him often to place himself in quite another scenario, one in which as a lone heroic figure, he fights the good fight and says things that are distinctive, original and, he hopes, personally efficacious. There is a tension therefore between what Milton hopes for himself in the future, when "God shall be all and all," and the role he assigns to himself in the present, when he strikes the stance of the beleaguered hero. It is this tension that structures his troubled and ambivalent relationship to the muse he here invokes. In the same line that names Urania's song as celestial, that is, as universal and absorptive, her action in relation to him is described in ways that figure her as a threat. He says "Up led by thee / Into the Heav'n of Heav'ns" (VII, 12b–13).

In modern parlance we would say "she's leading him on." That is, Urania appears here as someone who is bringing the poet into a realm of danger, and in the following lines that danger is precisely specified. As "An Earthly Guest" in the heaven of heavens, he is like a fish out of water, there's no air for him to breathe; his consciousness, that is, his sense of self, is in danger of being extinguished and that is why he calls to Urania, "Return me to my Native Element" and compares himself to the mythological figure of Bellerophon, who presumed too high and fell from his horse when Jupiter, angry at his presumption, sent a fly to sting it (VII, 14a, 16). Milton may also be recalling, with half his mind, that Bellerophon's unhappy career begins when he resists the seductive overtures of the king's wife, who in retaliation tells her husband that she was the victim of unwanted advances. The angry king sets out in pursuit of Bellerophon, who flees from one disaster to another. I mention these details – not in the text, but behind it – because they contribute to the most persistent pattern in this passage, the pattern of the young man of talent in danger from an aggressive woman. When he says "Up led by thee," Milton adds Urania to the roll-call of threatening women, even though on the surface he is praying to her and celebrating her (VII, 11b).

The nature of the threat she poses becomes unmistakable when he describes his present task. He notes that this is the beginning of the second half of his poem and that in this half he will sing no more of the heavens, but of things that happen on earth: "Half yet remains unsung, but narrower bound / Within the visible Diurnal sphere / Standing on Earth, not rapt above the Pole, / More safe I sing with mortal voice" (VII, 21–24a). "Narrower bound" marks a diminishing of his claims, but also marks the movement toward safety. No longer operating in the thin atmosphere to which Urania has led him, he can talk about things he knows. More importantly for him as a poet, his voice will be heard since it will not have been incorporated into the celestial harmony from which he is now safely distanced. As the verse says with the usual Miltonic precision, he is no longer in danger of being "rapt." This word surfaces the sexual fears that give this passage its energy. To be "rapt" is to be taken out of oneself, to be in a rapture; it is to be carried away by force, to be ravished, possessed, raped. Lest you think that Christian theology sits oddly with this notion of being sexually assaulted by divinity, listen to John Donne as he implores his God: "I / Except you enthrall me, never shall be free / Nor ever, chaste, except you ravish me." Donne prays to be raped by God. Milton fears – the fear is the dark side of his fondest hopes – that he may be. That is why he describes his escape from Urania and the state of being "rapt" as a return to the "mortal voice." What is a mortal voice? A mortal voice is precisely a voice that has been detached from the ceaseless and circular rhythms of the eternal song, sung by the universe in cosmic concert. Mortality after all means the capacity for dying, which is also, paradoxically, the capacity for living, for having a story with a beginning, a middle and an end. If you live in the rhythms of eternity, every moment is the same moment, the flow of time is irrelevant to the emergence of meaning because meaning is always and already present at every moment: that is, at every moment you are already at the place – in harmony with God's will – to which linear time would bring you. A mortal voice is possible only because the singer is not where he finally would wish to be; but that also means that he has somewhere to go and something to do. Although a mortal voice is shadowed by its sense of temporality and finitude, that same temporality and finitude gives it consequentiality. If you are not yet at your final rest, what you now say or do will matter insofar as it either brings you closer or takes you further away from your goal.

We approach here the paradox I identified earlier as the tension between Milton's feminine desire for absorption and his masculine impulse to stand out from the crowd. A mortal voice wishes to arrive at the place where it will once again be enfolded in the rhythms of eternity, but what it wishes it also resists because the reaching of the goal will simultaneously be its own silencing in the corporate harmony it finally joins. What's nice about a mortal voice is that it can leave a mark – "Kilroy was here," "Milton was here"; a mortal voice can have a career, and if Milton's religious hopes were for incorporation into divinity his personal hopes were for artistic greatness. It's as if he's saying here to Urania, "No, no, it's too soon; don't rapt me yet; I've still got a lot of things to say. Don't overwhelm me; leave me some room. Let me be me – a distinctive, independent, if frail and narrow mortal voice." In the remainder of this passage Milton continues to play this double game with Urania, ostensibly deferring to her and imploring her aid and yet at the same time pushing her away and saying as we might now say, "I need my own space."

The game is played once again when Milton asks Urania to find him a fit audience, but to drive off the barbarous dissonance of those who would silence him, whom he imagines as the band of Thracian women who tore Orpheus to pieces. The Orpheus legend is one to which Milton repeatedly refers; it obsessed him and you can see why. It is the story of a poet with extraordinary powers, a poet whose song was uniquely efficacious, who could make rocks and stones move and could, in imitation of Christ, even rescue souls from hell. It is also the story of how these powers were stilled by a group of women angered when the poet resisted their sexual advances. In short, the Thracian women are the last of the threatening females who populate this passage and the explicitness of their threat to the mortal voice of the poet makes unmistakable the threat posed to that same voice by the muse he ostensibly invokes.

The surface rhetoric of this passage distinguishes Urania from the Thracian women and from the scorned wife who revenged herself on Bellerophon, but underneath the surface all of the fears that were the underside of Milton's attraction to absorption were in full play, and here at least the energies of his own poetry slip from his control. It is important to say this because up to now it's the poet's extraordinary control over the reader's experience that I have emphasized, but Milton should not be imagined as standing outside the human fallibility he demonstrates again and again on our pulses. He is himself an heir to the sin of our first parents and his ego no less than any of ours resists extinction even when the agent of extinction is divine.

In the account of creation that follows this invocation, the tension I have here identified – between the all-embracing vision of a universe everywhere informed by God and the desire of particular creatures to break away and stand on their own – is played out in the relationship between the Creator and what he creates. In this part of the book, Milton's voice sides with authority and the suppression of individual difference almost as if he were overreacting against the fears and ambitions that jostle against one another in his address to Urania. In passage after passage the primacy of omniscience is reasserted and the claim of fecundity, multiplicity and variety is denied even when it appears to be acknowledged. Raphael, speaking to Adam, says: "Male he created thee, but thy consort / Female for race" (VII, 529–530a). That is, "Don't forget that God first made you in his male image and that he created women only so that the same male image could be reproduced in your sons." Later in the century Andrew Marvell voiced a perennial male complaint that God didn't find a better way to do it: "Such was that happy garden state / While man there walked without a mate / . . . Two paradises 'twere in one / To live in paradise alone." In Book x Milton's fallen Adam will ask why couldn't God "find some other way to generate / Mankind?" (x, 894–895a), or, as Henry Higgins puts it, "Why can't a woman be more like a man?" All of these later wishes for a masculine Utopia are anticipated in the phrase "Female for race" – for procreation and for nothing else, and certainly not for adoration (VII, 530a).

In the very next line, Raphael rehearses God's famous command: "'Be fruitful, multiply and fill the earth'" (vii, 531). "Earth" has always been gendered female and that is what gives the next two words of the following line their force: "Subdue it" (vii, 532). Throughout the creation scene the forces of dispersion and individuation are let loose only for an instant and are then reined back in with a vengeance. The entire pattern reaches its climax as Raphael concludes his narration and advises Adam once again of his duty, to worship God, and in reward to rule over His works, which of course include women as well as ants and elephants. Man's reward for cleaving fast to God is a world in which inferiors will cleave fast to him; the agent faithful to the patriarchal order gets to play the patriarchal role. Line 630 says it all: go out "And multiply a Race of Worshippers" (vii, 630). For a second "multiply" suggests expansiveness, variety and diversity, but the word "worshippers" tells us that the apparent multiplicity will in fact be an endless reproduction of the order of the same. In short, the command is to clone perfect replicas.

As the story he's telling gets closer and closer to its fatal centerpiece, Milton clamps down more and more on the feminine impulses to dispersion, softness and difference. What I have been calling the poem's official morality becomes more and more insistent as the moment of the violation of that morality by our first parents draws nearer. That is why Raphael expresses such distress at Adam when, at the end of Book viii, he praises Eve in terms that the angel finds excessive. When I am in her presence, Adam says, she seems "so absolute" "And in herself complete" (viii, 547b, 548a). That is, she seems totally self-sufficient, excellence embodied, the acme of perfection. She seems, in short, a god, or as Adam says, "wisest, virtuousest, discreetest, best" (viii, 550). He knows what he is saying; he knows that he is making the mistake of valuing the creature above the Creator. He knows that he is in danger of regarding her "As one intended first, not after made / Occasionally," that is, as something incidental (viii, 555–556a). Raphael here is in the terrible position of someone who knows the end of a sad story and thinks that he sees here the fatal flaw which will bring that unhappy end about. He rebukes Adam with a force that seems harsh and even crude. What you admire and respond to, he says, is the mere delight of sense, "the same vouchsaf't / To Cattle" (viii, 581b–582a). This is not "worthy to subdue / The Soul of Man" (viii, 584–585a). It is the familiar voice of the older male who says to his younger friend, "Don't let those women get to you; they'll do you in every time." If, at the beginning of Book viii, Urania is the danger unacknowledged by the poet, at the end of Book viii, the danger is unambiguously named. It is woman, and as the evening before the Fall comes to a close, Milton and his characters are firmly ensconced in the world of misogynist fears and anxieties that still envelops us today.

It is in Book IX that everything finally happens, and it is in Book IX that the paradoxical relationship between the poem's plot and its central event reaches its curious non-climax. You will remember that the event in question is the choosing *by a free will* to disobey God. This inheres in the fact, as I observed in an earlier lecture, that if the freedom of Adam and Eve's will is maintained, then antecedent events or a succession of events cannot be seen as compromising. What this means is that every scene previous to the Fall is irrelevant to a causal analysis of the Fall. If the will is free, the Fall can have no cause in the sense of an external pressuring event that *produces* it. If we read the poem correctly (an increasingly difficult thing to do as the anticipated and foreknown disaster draws closer), we shall resist the invitation, issued by the verse itself, to link events in a chain of inevitability. Milton is here playing a dangerous game with us, one that reflects his commitment to the strategy of the good temptation as he describes it in the divorce tracts. He is literally daring us to make the kind of inferences which will disable us as interpreters of the poem's moral structure, at the same time hoping that we will refuse his dare, reflect on the attraction it has for us – the attraction of self-extenuation in the extenuation of our first parents' crime – and become wiser by experience.

He makes it all the more difficult by preceding the Fall with a scene in which Adam and Eve engage in the first domestic quarrel, the mother of all quarrels. What makes this penultimate test of our understanding so hard is that the quarrel, in all of its aspects, is so close to experiences most readers would have had in the past twenty-four hours. By showing Adam and Eve entrapping themselves in a web of mutual misunderstandings, Milton once again invites us to see them as just like us – that is, as fallen and therefore as incapable of the act of obedience to which God has enjoined them. There are then two perspectives to keep in mind when reading this scene, but they work against each other. The first perspective is psychological; more deeply than any other scene in the poem, this one anatomizes the psychology of Adam and Eve and of any domestic relationship. But the more convincing the psychological rendering (and it is entirely convincing), the more difficult it is to detach the scene from the question first posed way back in Book I: "Say first . . . what cause / Mov'd our Grand Parents . . . to fall" (I, 27–30).

For a long time Milton was thought to have no understanding of human psychology, but his depiction of the morning quarrel simply will not support any such assessment. As the scene unfolds it becomes clear that he is acutely aware of the three important facts about any domestic argument: (1) You are already in the middle of it before you realize that it is occurring. (2) Since you have reached the place of unhappiness by producing words the other has unaccountably misunderstood, you now think that you can get back to the original state of harmony by producing more words; these of course turn out to be new forms of self-justification which serve to extend the quarrel whose course you would reverse. (3) Quarrels cannot be resolved; they can only be walked away from.

Like all quarrels, Adam and Eve's begins innocently and even benignly. Eager to perform as the good helpmeet, Eve suggests a way of improving the efficiency of the task assigned them, the tending of the garden of Eden. She notes that the garden's growth outstrips their labors and reasons that the casual and affectionate conversation they enjoy gets in the way of the job, and that if they were to separate and work in different sectors of the garden, they would be more productive and would not be in the situation of having little to show for a day's work: "'and th'hour of Supper comes unearn'd'" (IX, 225b).

Adam, hearing this, also begins well by giving a "mild answer," one that praises Eve for thinking in a responsible way about the situation. But he notes, without exactly telling her so, that she has misconceived their situation in ways that are potentially distressing. She seems to imagine their task as a burden rather than as another field of labor in which they can affirm their loyalty. Even worse, she seems to regard the garden as a place of threat, the threat both of being overwhelmed by a fertility they cannot check and the threat of punishment on the part of a taskmaster who might dock their pay or withhold their supper if they don't meet a quota. God isn't like that, Adam wants to tell her. He hasn't made them to be his slaves; indeed, he could do the gardening himself in a stroke. Eve should understand that by not giving them a perfectly manicured self-regulating environment, God has given them the gift of participation in the construction of their own world. And finally Adam sees correctly that a fear of the garden's unchecked fertility implies a lack of faith in the benevolence and solicitude of God. As Adam says pointedly, "doubt not but our joint hands / Will keep from Wilderness with ease, as wide / As we need walk, till younger hands erelong / Assist us" (IX, 244–247a).

That is, don't worry, trust in God who did not put us here either to be overwhelmed or to act as his drones.

At this point the conversation is going well, and moreover, it is an illustration of another form of gardening in which they are engaged. Earlier, in Book v, Raphael explains what will happen if they remain in the garden and remain faithful, i.e. don't eat the apple. They will, he says, become more and more refined in spirit, "Improv'd by tract of time," and perhaps in time achieve an angelic state (v, 498a). In short, they are placed in paradise with the double imperative of cultivating the garden and cultivating themselves. They are, or are invited to be, their own best crop. The medium of their cultivation is conversations like this one in which they put forward not buds or shoots, but thoughts about themselves and their situation, and then they nourish some, prune others, lop off some others entirely, all the while nurturing themselves (or so the hope is) into strong, growing plants.

Of course, and here we return to the poised nature of the Edenic state – "Sufficient to have stood, though free to fall" – it is possible that they will fail to prune or allow to grow thoughts that should be lopped and that they may in their own lives exhibit the disorder Eve fears when she worries about a garden "Tending to wild" (IX, 212a). Will they tend to wild or will they grow in a good straight line? Here an important caveat though: in paradise, tending to wild, making mistakes in your conception of yourself and your situation, has as its bad consequence the retarding of the growth into angelhood predicted by Raphael. It does not have as its consequence the Fall, which can only occur if they eat the apple, and they could make every mistake under the sun and still decline to make the fatal one; a free will that has gone down erring paths is still a free will.

That said, we can pick up the conversation where we left it, with Adam replying in a helpful way to Eve's helpful offering of her "first thoughts." Everything is going as God and Raphael might wish, and then suddenly Adam says something wholly surprising: "But if much converse perhaps / Thee satiate, to short absence I could yield" (IX, 247b–248). Or, in terms all of us will find familiar, "If you're tired of me, maybe we should go on separate vacations." The question, of course, is: "Where does this come from?" The answer, as I hope you by now see, is that it comes from nowhere, just as Satan's "fraught with envy" in Book v comes from nowhere. Remember, a free will is free to originate its own conception of its situation, and here Adam comes up with a conception that in an instant projects a new understanding of their relationship, which, if allowed to stand, will in time alter that relationship. When Adam says in effect, "If you are tired of me . . .", he is characterizing himself as someone that someone else might be tired of, and he is positing Eve as the kind of fickle person who might get tired of someone else. That's the way it is in domestic quarrels. Everything you say about yourself implies something about the other; everything you say about the other implies something about yourself. Quarrels are performances of personality creation; they have the power of producing the defects of which each party accuses the other. The crucial moments are the early ones, before the path of mutual mischaracterization has been pursued too far.

Adam has chosen to project an unflattering picture of both himself and Eve. Eve has the choice of responding in a way that will disarm the danger of what he has said. She can, as the saying goes, "be bigger than he is." Obviously he is asking for reassurance; she's supposed to say: "Of course I'm not tired of you; you're the most wonderful man in the world" (a statement that would necessarily be true). In short, she could play the role often assigned to women in these situations: the role of someone who must be tender in the face of a self-bruised male ego, but she doesn't. Instead, she replies, "As one who loves, and some unkindness meets" (IX, 271). The important word in this line is "as" for it indicates that what this moment offers Eve is a choice of roles. How is she going to play the situation? She might have responded "as one who deals gently with her love's anxieties," or "as one who for the sake of harmony lets something pass." Instead she takes offense, and wonders how he could think such thoughts of her, "Thoughts, which how found they harbour in thy breast, / Adam . . . ?" (IX, 288–289a). Or, in other words, "I didn't think you were the kind of person who would think I was the kind of person implied by your thoughts." Again the spiral is one many of us will recognize. The aggrieved party asks: "What kind of person do you think I am?" and the other, now-aggrieved party asks, "What kind of person do you think I am?" and all the while they are making themselves into the kinds of persons they will be when the altercation ends. They are thinking themselves impaired.

The scene goes on for many lines, all of which are as psychologically acute as those we have examined, and when it is over, or rather when both disengage from it, wrapped in the now impenetrable armor of their respective self-justifications, they agree to part, giving Satan the opportunity he had not thought to have, the opportunity of getting Eve alone. "He sought them both, but wish'd his hap might find / Eve separate; he wish'd, but not with hope" (IX, 421–422). The fact that Satan is gifted by fate with an opportunity he did not expect to enjoy is another one of those hooks on which Milton invites us to hang the wrong conclusion, the same conclusion that we want to reach when we listen defensively to God in Book III and think to blame him for not stopping Satan from getting to Eden. Again the lesson that is so difficult to maintain: no set or succession of circumstances can force a free will. Even though Satan now finds himself in what he considers to be the most advantageous of positions, alone with Eve, we should not fall in with his way of thinking that alone she is vulnerable or more vulnerable than she would have been had she and Adam not separated. The free will is always poised between the sufficiency to stand and the freedom to fall, and could just as easily fall when there are no circumstantial pressures in the neighborhood.

Suppose Adam and Eve had negotiated their morning conversation more successfully and decided to stay together in the garden. The following conversation could possibly have taken place:

ADAM: "Well, what do you want to do now?"
EVE: "I don't know. What do you want to do?"
ADAM: "I don't know. Why don't we go and eat the apple?"
EVE: "OK."

That imagined moment of choice is structurally no different from the moment in which Eve is found alone. Even when Satan, now in the form of a serpent, piques Eve's curiosity by speaking and leads her to the tree whose fruit he claims gave him that new power, she is no closer to falling than she was when she awoke that morning; for as Milton says of her as she stands in front of the tree in conversation with a talking snake, "Eve yet sinless." But a few lines later she sins (IX, 659). Why? How? Well of course there are the arguments of Satan which echo and amplify the arguments he rehearsed to himself back in Book IV. Here in IX he seizes on the name "tree of knowledge" and asks "What can your knowledge hurt Him . . . ?" Eve will not answer this question, but if we have exercised ourselves in response to the poem's cognitive demands, if we have lopped, pruned and cropped our own thoughts in the proper direction, we should be able to answer immediately that the knowledge embodied in the forbidden fruit cannot hurt God, but can hurt Adam and Eve, because in the act of acquiring it they would be preferring it to God, or making it their God.

All of Satan's questions imply that God is another character in a situation of mere strategy and power, rather than God. Once you forget that God is God and not just someone whose personal authority you might or might not acknowledge, Satan's arguments make persuasive sense. But if you remember that God is God, they all fall apart at the slightest touch. Thus to his question "can envy dwell / In heav'nly breasts?" (an echo of the *Aeneid*, where the breast in question is Juno's and the answer "yes") the appropriate response is "no," and therefore any account of the divine prohibition that roots itself in godly envy must be mistaken; and when Satan speaks of the need they have of "this fair Fruit," the proper response is to cite the greater need of obedience to the Creator who sustains them in more basic ways than any fruit possibly could (ix, 729b–730a, 731).

As I said, these are the answers we should be giving if we have become adequate to the poem's demands, but they are not the answers given by Eve, of whom it is said: "his words replete with guile / Into her heart too easy entrance won" (ix, 733b–734). The metaphor here is not only one of verbal seduction but of sexual yielding. The words which enter her are phallic; they ravish her; she copulates with them; she allows herself to be taken over by "his persuasive words, impregn'd / With Reason, to her seeming" (ix, 737–738). What follows is an internal speech by Eve to herself in which she repeats and amplifies the Satanic account of the matter. One of Milton's favorite biblical verses is 2 Corinthians 3:3, in which it is said that the message of God is "written not with ink, but with the Spirit of the living God; not in tables of stone, but in fleshy tables of the heart." At this moment, Eve has allowed God's message to be dislodged by the message of Satan who, as the pen-like and phallic snake, has written a new message on the fleshy tables of her heart and in so writing altered it forever. When this has happened she is, like Satan when first fraught with envy, a new person. Having forgotten what she only a few moments ago surely knew – that God's command is to be obeyed because it is God's and not because of other additional external reasons – she is a creature without moorings, a creature cut loose willfully from the source of life; as the verse says, "she pluck'd, she ate" "And knew not eating Death" (ix, 782b, 792a).

Adam, however, knows, and does it anyway. What is remarkable about *his* fall is that we never see it happen. Instead of the long drawn-out temptation scene that ends with Eve's eating, we have an Adam who has fallen before he says a word. When Eve blithely informs him of what she has done (after the first "Sorry I'm late" speech in history), he is described only as "Speechless . . . and pale, till thus at length / First to himself he inward silence broke" (ix, 894–895). When he delivers to himself the soliloquy that follows, it becomes obvious that he has already resolved to fall with her: "for with thee / Certain my resolution is to Die; / How can I live without thee?" (IX, 906b–908a). It is not a serious question, because if it were, Adam would take some time and begin to think perhaps of some answers to it. Instead, in an act of the will that we never witness – for if we witnessed it, we would be tempted to assign it a cause other than itself – Adam makes his free choice which he then justifies by characterizing it as "Submitting to what seem'd remediless" (IX, 919). The word "seem'd" here tells the whole story. It is the moment in which Adam becomes just like Satan. You will remember that in his original rehearsal of the arguments he would deploy against Adam and Eve, Satan had reasoned: "They taste and die: what likelier can ensue?" He literally cannot conceive of a God who is as merciful as he is just. His mind by definition is not capacious enough to imagine such a possibility and therefore he projects the action of God – swift and implacable justice – as it would be if he, Satan, were to perform it.

At the moment of fatal choice, Adam falls into the same way of thinking. He can only think that he submits to what is remediless if he limits the possible remedies to those he is able to think of, but in the act of doing that, he has re-characterized God as just the kind of narrow-minded and mean-spirited taskmaster half-imagined by Eve when she worries that their supper might be withheld if they don't cultivate enough acres. The large sense of faith he urges upon her when he says "doubt not" is the large sense of faith to which he is at this moment inadequate. By thinking of their present situation as remediless, he thinks into being a God diminished in his properties, and by doing that he thinks himself, and all the rest of us, impaired.

When Adam and Eve a little later awake from the first act of post-lapsarian coitus, they are indistinguishable in the meanness and pettiness of their attitudes toward one another. Eve says "It's your fault. You shouldn't have allowed me to go." Adam says "I ate the apple for you and you will rebuke *me*, 'I, / Who might have liv'd and 'joy'd immortal bliss' without you?" (IX, 1165b–1166). The last three lines of Book IX tell the horrible story of what their act has wrought not only for them, but for all their sons and daughters: "Thus they in mutual accusation spent / The fruitless hours, but neither self-condemning, / And of their vain contest appear'd no end" (IX, 1187–1189).

By thinking themselves impaired, and thereby turning themselves impaired, they are incapable of extricating themselves. Their wills, once free, have now been enslaved by a wrong choice, and there is no way out for them except by the intervention of another: "till one greater Man / Restore us, and regain the blissful Seat" (1, 4b–5). That merciful act of restoration is already beginning in the opening lines of Book x, which rehearse, at first in very strict terms, the inevitable and awful logic of the Fall. The epic voice reminds us that while God "Hinder'd not Satan to attempt the mind / Of Man," that mind was endowed "with strength entire, and free Will arm'd / Complete to have discover'd and repulst / Whatever wiles of Foe or seeming Friend" (x, 8–11). In short, they had their chance and were capable of making the best of it.

At this late date in the poem, the big question remains, "Why didn't they?", and here for the last time we are given the answer: "For still they knew, and ought to have still remembered / The high Injunction not to taste that Fruit, / Whoever tempted" (x, 12–14a). Of course this is not an explanation at all in the usual sense. It amounts to saying they fell because they forgot, and if you ask then, "Well why did they forget?" you yourself forget what remembering is. Remembering is the act of calling to mind something that is not present in your field of vision; remembering is an act of the will in which the present scene is overleapt, and brought within the sphere of something it does not contain. Remembering is just another name for faith, acting on the basis not of what seems remediless or attractive or persuasive or even reasonable, but on the basis of evidence not seen. All they had to do was reach for the memory not only of the high injunction, but of the agent who issued it. It was, as Milton says so often in the poem, "easy"; but of course if it is easy to remember – we usually do it with a snap of the fingers – it is also easy to forget. Remembering is a perfect emblem of the poised will – the will poised in its freedom – that forms the basis of the poem's moral structure. They could have remembered; they were sufficient to have remembered; but they were free to forget, and they did, and thus as the epic voice says, they "Incurr'd (what could they less?) the penalty, / And manifold in sin, deserved to fall" (x, 15–16).

This implacable judgment belongs of course to the relentless consecutiveness of the logic of justice, but that is only one half of the story in this epic and finally the less significant half. Even as Milton ends line 16 with the harsh phrase "deserved to fall" and puts a period to it, the first three words of the next line are "Up into heaven" (x, 17a). Of course it doesn't make any sense. How can you fall up into heaven? That is the question for which Adam seeks an answer in Books xi and xii, an answer he finds only when he understands the incarnation, the crucifixion, and the resurrection. It is to that long hard journey of understanding that we shall turn in our final lecture.

AFTER THE FALL

From the beginning of these lectures we have been observing the double structure of *Paradise Lost*. In one structure – dominated by what I have called the logic of plot-thinking – the poem's central characters default on an obligation they have accepted, the obligation to display loyalty to God by refraining from eating an apple, and face the consequence announced by God in Book III when, foreseeing their commission of the original sin, he declares "Die hee or Justice must" (III, 210a). In this structure the line of cause and effect is inexorable, but as I said at the end of the last lecture, that is only half the story, and the second half follows immediately in that same speech of God's: "unless for him / Some other able, and as willing, pay / The rigid satisfaction, death for death" (III, 210b–212). It is at this moment that God's only begotten Son offers himself as that proxy payment and says "mee for him, life for life / I offer, on mee let thine anger fall" (III, 236b–237). Here then is the second structure within which the events of the poem must be seen, a structure not of logic and justice, but of mercy and redemption. In the context of the Christian vision it is the second structure which quite literally has the last word. As God Himself says, "But Mercy first and last shall brightest shine" (III, 134). By exalting mercy above justice, God inflicts on Satan his deepest wound, for as we have seen, Satan is counting on a God whose implacable decree leaves no room for maneuvering, and when instead God finds a way both to satisfy and undo the rigor of His own decree, Satan is fully routed.

God then, as Adam will say in Book XII, has been able to produce good out of evil, and Adam wonders whether or not he should repent his sin or rejoice in having committed it, since it gave God the opportunity to snatch victory and salvation from the jaws of defeat. This is known as the doctrine of the Fortunate Fall, and it in fact constitutes still another temptation in the long line of temptations Milton produces for us in his poem. For if we take the doctrine of the Fortunate Fall seriously, then we have found once again a back door way to excuse our first parents for their grievous fault; we can say: "Hey, they didn't obey and it was kind of wrong of them, but it turned out all right in the end, so perhaps it was a good thing after all." Milton is careful in Book XII not to endorse the doctrine of the Fortunate Fall, which is put forward by Adam at a moment when he is still in the process of learning how to think about his new situation. There is no response to what Adam says, but we are left to supply the response as we are in so many other cases. It is finally simple; the fact that God can turn evil into good tells us something about Him, not about the advisability or serendipity of the act. What Adam and Eve did was wrong, and its wrongness is neither mitigated nor dissipated by the fact that God is clever enough and gracious enough to find a way of allowing them to escape the penalty they deserved to incur. That way is the way of Christ, who satisfies the strict decree by performing the act of obedience Adam and Eve were unable to perform by dying in their stead on the cross. As Adam exclaims when he finally understands the crucifixion and the act of atonement it represents: "O goodness infinite, goodness immense" (XII, 469).

It is late in Book XII before Adam reaches this point of understanding, and the last two books are the record of his progress toward that understanding, a progress that is by no means easy or steady, but is rather marked by a painful succession of mistakes, corrections and more mistakes. The material of Adam's education is post-Fallen history, which unfolds before him in a panorama of scenes presented by the archangel Michael, who takes him to the highest hill in paradise and provides him with a long look into the future of the race he will father. That future, viewed from one perspective, is a long and dispiriting succession of evil deeds and unhappy events, beginning with the murder of Abel by Cain. It is Adam's task, and ours, to see in that depressing chronicle the hope and ultimate joy its surfaces do not display. Obviously what is required of Adam and of us is another act of faith, a faith that despite the dismal record of excess, crime, betrayal, idolatry, lust, avarice and envy, some grand and beneficent purpose is working itself out in what Michael calls the "race of time."

The mistake, and it is one that Adam makes again and again, is to attempt to generate that purpose from a focus on discrete events and actors. The mistake is once again the mistake of empiricism, of thinking that general truths can be derived from a close attention to objectively seen particulars. What Milton has Adam and us learn is that the general truths – the deep assumptions that make up belief – must come first, and that then the particulars will fall easily into the place already prepared for them.

In some sense Adam knows this before he begins his lessons. Early on in Book XI, he himself reads a lesson in faith to Eve, when he expresses a new confidence that the prayers he and she have sent up at the end of Book X have in fact been heard and that, despite the rigor of the divine prohibition, "we shall live" (XI, 158). Adam wonders at the improbability of God's bending his will to the prayer of two sinners: "Hard to belief may seem; yet this will Prayer" (XI, 146). It is a perfect formula for faithful seeing: "Hard to belief may seem; yet." That is what faith does, it breaks out of the confines of the seeming structures of appearance, and affirms against appearance, in favor of "The substance of things hoped for, the evidence of things not seen." The test of faith is always the same: will you allow the configuration of merely empirical circumstances to dictate your conclusions about God and the nature of the universe, or will you cling fast to a pre-interpretive conviction of God's goodness and benevolence and read that conviction into the things that are seen?

In Book XI, Adam fails the test again and again. When he, along with Eve, hears from Michael that although they will indeed live, they will no longer be allowed to live in paradise, Adam is aghast, not only because he must leave his home, but because he assumes that in leaving paradise he will be leaving the presence of God and be "depriv'd / His blessed count'nance" (XI, 316b–317a). Michael responds, as he will repeatedly, with a brusque rebuke: "Adam, thou know'st Heav'n his, and all the Earth, / Not this Rock only; his Omnipresence fills" and then he adds, making the lesson explicit and generalizing it: "surmise not then / His presence to these narrow bounds confin'd" (XI, 335–336, 340b–341). This is a precise analysis of Adam's mistake: he's reasoned from a limited empirical fact – that in the course of living in Eden he has seen and spoken with God many times – to the false conclusion that he will no longer be in God's presence when he leaves Eden.

His surmising has been narrow in more than one sense. It continues to be so. A little later on, after the unhappy fate of Cain and Abel has been revealed, Adam is shown another sight, a group of beautiful women, singing and dancing, who are wooed by and joined in marriage with a group of handsome men. Adam then says for the first, but not the last, time to Michael, "True opener of mine eyes ... / Much better seems this Vision ... / Here nature seems fulfill'd in all her ends" (XI, 598a, 599a, 602). In response, Michael does not mince words: "To whom thus Michael: / 'Judge not what is best / By pleasure" (XI, 603–604a). Adam is then described in the wake of Michael's rebuke as "of short joy bereft" (XI, 628). The phrase is precise in its dissection of what is wrong with Adam's joy. Where before he had generalized from the unhappy fact of his expulsion from Eden to the over-pessimistic conclusion that he was losing the sight of God, now he generalizes from the apparently happy fact of a lively wedding ceremony to the over-optimistic conclusion that all is well. His joy is short – without duration and without depth – because it is a response to a local particular rather than to some larger and sustaining vision within which local particulars could be given their true significance. It is only when he learns to rest in the bosom of that larger vision that his joy will be long.

Later in Book XI, Adam will be "of short despair bereft" when he once again falls into the error of generalizing from a present particular to the certain shape of the (in this case bleak) future. He has been shown a world sick with sin except for one righteous man, a "Reverend Sire" named Noah who, in anticipation of the godly vengeance he fears, builds an ark and places in it his family and two of every beast and bird (XI, 719). The deluge that follows covers the world and when Adam sees all of mankind afloat in one frail bark, he concludes that the end has come. He had hoped, he said, that men and women would cease their violence and learn to live with one another, "But I was far deceiv'd" (XI, 783a). There's none left except these few, and they "Famine and anguish will at last consume" (XI, 778). What deceives Adam is not the false signal sent by the surface features of historical events, but his reasoning from those features to a conclusion that should *precede* and order their appearance. What deceives him is his *way* of seeing. Adam's conclusion here is just as empirically narrow as every one of his earlier conclusions and has the exact structure of Satan's: "What likelier can ensue?" or of his own "submitting to what seemed remediless." He says in effect, "Well, I don't see how they could survive, and therefore they won't." The proper response, which he is not yet able to give, would be "Well, I don't see how they could survive, but God sees further than I and will find a way."

Adam becomes able to give that response after his despair, like his earlier joy, is taken away by events his empiricism could not anticipate. The waters recede, the ark finds firm ground, Noah and his family emerge and a rainbow appears in the sky. It is at this moment, after he has so many times reasoned narrowly from local details to general conclusions, that Adam finally gets it, and says to Michael: "what mean those colour'd streaks in Heav'n, / Distended as the Brow of God appeas'd? / Or serve they as a flow'ry verge to bind / The fluid skirts of that same wat'ry Cloud / Lest it again dissolve and show'r the Earth?" (XI, 879b–883) Adam could have read the rainbow in any number of ways: as a threat, as a show of power, as a physical phenomenon with a chemical and not a moral explanation. He chooses – there is no other word for it – a reading premised on a God who is benevolent and forgiving and relenting, and within the umbrella of that premise he reads the local detail. He has learned how to read faithfully and for the first time he hears a compliment from Michael: "To whom the archangel: 'Dextrously thou aim'st'" (XI, 884). That is, and there's a little pun here, "You've got it *right* this time; your aim was true, and it was true because you knew in advance where the arrow would hit." It is on this happy note of pedagogical success that Book XI ends.

The chronicle, however, continues, and while Adam has learned to move not from the particular to the general but in the other direction, he has not learned everything. The chief thing he has not yet learned is the meaning of history. Why is all this happening? What's it all about? A secular, empiricist view of history would have to answer "not much," or, as one historian/wit once put it, "History is just one damned thing after another." Christian history, however, is not "just one damned thing after another," as Adam begins to learn as he works out a puzzle that has been bothering him since the end of Book x, when, in the act of judging the fallen pair, God put this judgment on the serpent: "Her seed shall bruise thy head, thou bruise his heel" (x, 181). Several times Adam wonders exactly what this means and what it has to do with the historical panorama he has been viewing. In Book xii, he puts the puzzle together, when he is told of the birth of Christ, that is, of the greater man who will restore what he and Eve had lost. In response to this good news Adam is properly joyful, but his joy is the joy of someone who thinks that a hard and difficult time is finally over, that history has ended and he can relax. He says, as he has said before, "Now I finally understand." "Now I understand why woman's seed will bruise the serpent's head"; "now I understand how from my loins shall issue the Virgin Mother and from her, 'the Son of God most high'." He understands that God is so inclined to mercy that he will satisfy his own justice by paying its price with his only begotten Son. "Aha," Adam exclaims, in a moment of supreme realization: "So God with man unites" (xii, 382b).

Yet even here, at the moment of highest understanding, Adam falls into error when he expects the effect of the union of man and God in Christ to be climactic and instantaneous. "Needs must the Serpent now his capital bruise / Expect with mortal pain: say where and when / Their fight, what stroke shall bruise the victor's heel?" (xii, 383–385). Or in other words, "I see, there's going to be a final battle, the battle to end all battles, between the Son and Satan. Tell me where; I'd like a front-row seat; I want to be in on the end."

For the last time Michael produces the appropriate and unexpected rebuke: "To whom thus Michael: 'Dream not of their fight, / As of a duel'," and then the angel goes on to explain that Adam has entirely misconceived the nature of the moral life by projecting its responsibilities onto an external agent who fights a battle of which he could be the disinterested spectator (xii, 386–387b). "That's not how it's going to happen," says Michael; "in fact it's not going to happen at all, if by 'happen' you mean 'once and for all, never have to think about it again, just go home and sit on the beach with a margarita.' The Savior will overcome Satan, not by destroying him in single combat, but by destroying "'his works / In thee and in thy Seed'" (xii, 394b–395a). Once again Milton makes brilliant use of a line ending. Destroying Satan's works is a phrase that suggests some external field of action. The phrase "in thee" internalizes the field, makes Adam not the spectator, but the location of the struggle, and the addition of "and in thy seed" makes the struggle perpetual.

Adam here has fallen momentarily into what Milton always saw as the greatest temptation, the temptation of shifting moral responsibility to someone or some force outside the human heart and the human will. From the very beginning of his career, Milton thundered against reliance on external authority, whether it take the form of church fathers, or the edicts of bishops, or the proclamations of kings or even the Scriptures. The only authority one harkens to in Milton's view is the authority of God's message inscribed in the fleshy tables of one's heart; and since God is not the only inscriber seeking possession of the heart as a writing tablet, it is our obligation to seek and read His message and prefer it to all the other messages which falsely come in His name. The task is incredibly difficult in a fallen world where, as Milton puts it in the *Areopagitica*, "Good and evil in the field of this world grow up together almost inseparably ... and in so many cunning resemblances hardly to be discerned." The pun on "hardly" tells the whole story: you can barely discern the difference between good and evil; it is hard to do so. It is a never-ending obligation and one of whose success you can never be sure, because you are both the agent and the location of the struggle. That is what Michael tells Adam here, and at line 561, he finally, really finally, gets it right. "Henceforth I learn, that to obey is best" (xii, 561).

That is of course where we began in the first line of Book 1: "Of man's first disobedience." That's the sum of wisdom: obey God, an easier thing to do when the only action required was the negative one of not eating an apple, immeasurably more difficult to do when, as a result of that fatal disobedience, a clouded and infected will and intellect must labor to discern a difference between what is really obedience to God and what only seems to be – a difference that is "hardly to be discerned." Adam at least knows now what he's supposed to do, although he also knows how hard it will be to do and how the doing of it will take the whole of history and more. Still, he has at last graduated from Michael's hard school, and he is rewarded with what will pass in this circumstance for a diploma, and what is in effect a benediction. Knowing what you now know, says

Michael, you will not be sorry to leave this paradise, "but shalt possess /
A Paradise within thee, happier far" (XII, 586b–587). This is the final
rehearsal of Milton's great lesson, the lesson that however crowded and
variegated the landscape of external events, the true landscape – the one
whose composition really matters – is the landscape of the heart, the
landscape of belief and conviction, the landscape of faith.

There is no more to say on Michael's part nor on mine, and I leave you
with the last forty-four lines of the poem, which I will now read, as
I always do at the end of every Milton course I teach:

> He ended, and they both descend the Hill;
> Descended, ADAM to the Bowre where EVE
> Lay sleeping ran before, but found her wak't;
> And thus with words not sad she him receav'd.
> Whence thou returnst, & whither wentst, I know;
> For God is also in sleep, and Dreams advise,
> Which he hath sent propitious, some great good
> Presaging, since with sorrow and hearts distress
> Wearied I fell asleep: but now lead on;
> In mee is no delay; with thee to goe,
> Is to stay here; without thee here to stay,
> Is to go hence unwilling; thou to mee
> Art all things under Heav'n, all places thou,
> Who for my wilful crime art banisht hence.
> This further consolation yet secure
> I carry hence; though all by mee is lost,
> Such favour I unworthie am voutsaft,
> By mee the Promis'd Seed shall all restore.
> So spake our Mother EVE, and ADAM heard
> Well pleas'd, but answer'd not; for now too nigh
> Th' Archangel stood, and from the other Hill
> To thir fixt Station, all in bright array
> The Cherubim descended; on the ground
> Gliding meteorous, as Ev'ning Mist
> Ris'n from a River o're the marish glides,
> And gathers ground fast at the Labourers heel
> Homeward returning. High in Front advanc't,
> The brandisht Sword of God before them blaz'd
> Fierce as a Comet; which with torrid heat,
> And vapour as the LIBYAN Air adust,
> Began to parch that temperate Clime; whereat
> In either hand the hastning Angel caught
> Our lingring Parents, and to th' Eastern Gate
> Led them direct, and down the Cliff as fast

To the subjected Plaine; then disappeer'd.
They looking back, all th' Eastern side beheld
Of Paradise, so late thir happie seat,
Wav'd over by that flaming Brand, the Gate
With dreadful Faces throng'd and fierie Armes:
Som natural tears they drop'd, but wip'd them soon;
The World was all before them, where to choose
Thir place of rest, and Providence thir guide:
They hand in hand with wandring steps and slow,
Through EDEN took thir solitarie way.

CHAPTER 2

To the pure all things are pure

Law, faith and interpretation in the prose and poetry of John Milton

I.

Although the range of John Milton's concerns is enormous – stretching from politics to theology to literature to education to divorce to church government to interpretation to music to dance to cosmology to warfare and much more – central to every issue he considers is the relationship of written law or precept to a higher, deeper law that cannot be identified with what has been set down in formal terms.

Milton's unwillingness to accept positive law as an ultimate authority extends even to the first set of codified laws, the Ten Commandments. In a section of his *Christian Doctrine* titled "Of Good Works," he observes that "[s]ome theologians insist that the form of good works is their conformity with the ten commandments," but against this insistence he cites Romans 14:23 where Paul declares: "Whatever is not in accordance with faith, is sin."[1] "Notice," Milton says, that the Apostle does not say: "Whatever is not in accordance with the ten commandments is sin," but: "Whatever is not in accordance with faith." The difference between the Ten Commandments and faith is that the first have a visible, tangible form and the second exists (if it does exist; there are, after all, faithless men) in the interior recesses of the individual heart. Actions taken in conformity with the commandments can be assessed by placing them next to the text; actions in conformity with faith can only be assessed either by God (who is by definition inaccessible) or by the faith-claimer himself, which would make the process of validation entirely circular. (My faith compels me to do this; who are you or any written precept to say otherwise?)

Nevertheless, despite this circularity, Milton holds to the superiority of this interior measure: "Thus, if I keep the Sabbath in accordance with the Ten Commandments when my faith prompts me to do otherwise, my precise compliance with the commandments will be counted as sin or as unlawful behavior." The true form of law is hidden from carnal or (merely) empirical sight and can only be discerned by those whose hearts bear its inscription. (It takes one to know one.) "Ye are manifestly declared to be the epistle of Christ ... written not with ink, but with the Spirit of the living God; not in tables of stone, but in fleshy tables of the heart."[2] "It follows," Milton concludes, "that no work of ours can be good except through faith," for "it is faith that justifies, not compliance with the commandments, and only that which justifies can make any work good." When Milton then declares that "faith ... is the form of good works, because the definition of form is that through which a thing is what it is," he is playing on the word "form"; the true law is without form if by form you mean something you can hold in your hand (like a stone tablet) or point to. Faith *in*forms a work that is performed in its spirit, but whether or not a particular work is so informed cannot be determined by inspecting its outside.

Indeed, the "same" work in a merely physical sense of "same" could be good when performed by one person and bad when performed by another. The man informed by faith is not barred from complying with the commandments. Keeping the Sabbath if he does so prompted by faith will be a good work; breaking the Sabbath if he does so prompted by faith will also be a good work. And conversely, a man who keeps the Sabbath in a merely outward conformity will be committing a sin and performing unlawful behavior. As Milton puts it in his *Areopagitica*: "A man may be a heretick in the truth; and if he beleeves things only because his pastor sayes so, or the Assembly so determins ... though his belief be true, yet the very truth he holds, becomes his heresie."[3] In the same tract, he inveighs against a "rigid externall formality,"[4] and he cites Paul's "doctrine ... that he who eats or eats not, regard a day or regard it not, may doe either to the Lord."[5] The name of this doctrine is the doctrine of "things indifferent ... wherein Truth may be on this side, or on the other without being unlike her self," a self that has no fixed visible form but inhabits the inside of works (whatever they are) that proceed from faith. In Milton's theology, the category of "things indifferent" – of things not commanded by God, but left to the individual conscience – is expanded to include nearly everything. No action one takes or declines to take wears its merit or lack of merit on its face; the merit of actions depends on the spirit within which they are performed. "For the works of the faithful are the works of the Spirit itself"[6] and even if they "deviate from the letter ... of the gospel precepts," they "never run contrary to the love of God ... which is the sum of the law."

2.

It might seem that in these passages Milton is caught in a contradiction: he supports his case for the priority of unwritten over written laws with citations from a written law. How can he quote Scripture as he argues against its authority? Milton answers this question in another section of *Christian Doctrine*, "Of the Holy Scripture." He observes that the "requisites" for being able to interpret Scripture are "linguistic ability, knowledge of the original sources, consideration of overall intent, distinction between literal and figurative language, examination of the causes and circumstances, and of what comes before and after the passage in question, and comparison of one text with another."[7] But this perfectly conventional account of the abilities an interpreter should have is immediately complicated by one more "requisite": "It must always be asked, too, how far the interpretation is in agreement with faith." But how does one know that, given that the presence of faith cannot be verified by any outward measure?

The answer is that while public verification of the congruence of an interpretation with faith is unavailable, the faithfulness of an interpretation can be verified by the faith that resides within the interpreter. Again, this is circular, but it is a circularity Milton embraces and even formalizes (if that word can be used in such a context) in what he calls the doctrine of the "double scripture." There is, he says, "the external scripture of the written word and the internal scripture of the Holy Spirit, which he, according to God's promise, has engraved upon the hearts of believers."[8] Milton acknowledges that for the most part, or as he says, "generally speaking," the written word of the Scripture is a perfectly good authority – "it is the authority of which we first have experience" – so that in most circumstances keeping the Sabbath is a good thing to do. But when all is said and done and especially in matters of conscience, "the pre-eminent and supreme authority ... is the authority of the Spirit, which is internal."[9] Texts, he points out, can be corrupted because they have "been committed to the care of various untrustworthy authorities."[10] "But no one can corrupt the Spirit which guides man to truth and a spiritual man is not easily deceived." Indeed, the very fact that God "committed the contents of the New Testament to ... wayward and uncertain guardians" should itself "convince us that the Spirit which is given to us is a more certain guide than scripture and that we ought to follow it."[11]

Notice that the "it" we are supposed to follow is not something external to us – the true and narrow way is not marked out on a road map as Bunyan reminds us on every page of *The Pilgrim's Progress* – but something that lives inside of us (or doesn't, as the case may be). Nor can we put our trust in commentators, councils, or interpretive traditions to which the faithful man will always prefer "the guide of conscience, which as far as concerns himself he may far more certainly follow than any outward rule impos'd on him by others."[12] And by the same reasoning, the church itself can tell us neither what to do nor how to interpret; for "it is not the visible church but the hearts of believers which, since Christ's ascension, have continually constituted the pillar and ground of truth. They are the real *house and church of the living God,* 1 Timothy 3:15."[13] Once again Milton supports an argument against any reliance on the visible and tangible by citing a very visible and tangible passage in Scripture. But he would say that there is no inconsistency, for the verse he cites explicitly yields its own authority to the Spirit: "Thus ... on the evidence of scripture itself, all things are eventually to be referred to the Spirit and to the unwritten word."

3.

Once the logic of the superiority of the inner to the outer is fully grasped, nothing escapes it; no aspect of life is untouched by it. It is this logic that informs Milton's arguments in favor of divorce. He begins by defining marriage as a meeting of minds and souls: "In God's intention a meet and happy conversation is the chiefest and noblest end of marriage."[14] It follows that if a marriage is not marked by such a conversation, it is no longer truly in force. "If those whom God joyns, no man may separate,"[15] those whom God has not joined – those who inhabit only the form of a marriage – are already separate. "He who would divorce ... but for the law hath in the sight of God done it already." Moreover, if the link that holds a marriage together is spiritual, and if a marriage is no longer held together by that link, it is as wrong to maintain it as it is wrong for a man to keep the Sabbath when he is prompted by his conscience to break it. And wrong for the same reason: no outward form, no matter how hallowed, can be preferred to the inner reality. To remain in a marriage merely because some words have been uttered is "to make an idol of marriage"; "to advance it above the worship of God," to make the indissolubility of marriage a "transcendent command."[16] It is by a "divorcing command" (dividing the light from darkness) that the "world first arose out of chaos," and the chaos of a forced and empty union can be removed only "by the separating of unmeet consorts."[17]

Although Milton seeks support for these arguments in the word of God, he is well aware that some verses in God's book seem to tell against him. "What are all these reasonings worth, will some reply, when as the words of Christ are plainly against all divorce, except in the case of fornication?"[18] In short, how can I maintain my position in the face of Matthew 5:32?

Milton sets himself a tall order here. What he needs is an account of interpretation that will allow him to claim that a verse that seems to say that a man can only divorce his wife if he has caught her in the act really says that a man can divorce his wife for any reason approved by his conscience. He accomplishes this apparent "mission impossible" by making the priority of the inner over the outer the content of an interpretive method; that method then generates a reading that is the mirror image of its own tenets. That is, he takes the distinction between the spirit and the letter and makes it the basis of a procedure that always authorizes a reading that departs from the text.

First he declares that "we are not to repose all upon the literal terms of so many words," for Christ "meant not to be tak'n word for word."[19] Rather, he wants us to read him in the light of the spiritual sense from which his words proceed. We are to "expound him ... not by the written letter, but by the unerring paraphrase of Christian love and Charity, which is the summe of all commands."[20] What this means is that if an interpretation of a verse in Scripture does not reflect the primacy of charity – God's charity toward us and our charity toward each other – it is a wrong interpretation. Accordingly, the interpretation of Matthew 5:32 that has Christ forbidding divorce except in one bodily circumstance must be rejected because (1) it hangs everything on the physical act of an "impetuous nerve" and (2) it implies an uncharitable unconcern on the part of Christ for man's natural infirmities. After all, the best of men can make a mistake, and can be misled by a mere "faire outside" into thinking he has found a helpmate when in fact he has found a thorn in his side. Should such a man, eager to experience that fellowship of spirit intended by God, be bound to the dead carcass of a loveless union? Charity as an imperative and charity as an interpretive principle demand that we answer no: "The way to get a sure undoubted knowledge of things, is to hold that for truth, that most accords with charity."[21] Milton here follows in the tradition of St. Augustine, who says in his *On Christian Doctrine* that, when a passage in the Bible seems to point away from charity, "What is read should be subjected to diligent scrutiny until an interpretation contributing to the reign of charity is produced."[22]

In this case diligent scrutiny and the search for an interpretation contributing to the reign of charity leads to this ingenious (some would say
strained) reasoning: Christ speaks these words limiting divorce after the
Pharisees had put to him a provoking and tempting question. Therefore
his strictures are directed at them and "according to his custom" he was not
concerned "to inform their proud ignorance." It was "seasonable," Milton
explains, that the Pharisees "should hear their own unbounded licence
rebuk't, but not seasonable for them to hear a good man's requisit liberty
explained."[23] While the Pharisees do not "have eares to hear" the subtleties
of Christian liberty, those of us who are not Pharisees should not feel
constrained by statements of limitation addressed to others. So even though
the letter says that men may divorce only for the reason of fornication, good
men – men who live in the Spirit – are bound by no law but the law of
charity, which tells us that God would not insist on the "forcible continuing
of an improper and ill-yoking couple."[24] He would not wish us to rest in
the "alphabetical servility"[25] and "obstinate literality"[26] of the text. Rather,
it is our obligation as interpreters to penetrate to the charitable intention
informing it.

It makes sense that Milton would be an intentionalist, for the first tenet
of the anti-formalism he preaches is that without the quickening power of
the Spirit, the letter is dead, a mere husk or shell devoid of meaning.
And that is also the first tenet of intentionalism: marks or signs regarded
in and of themselves will point anywhere and nowhere. It is only when an
intention has been specified that meaning is stabilized and marks become
messages. The nice thing about biblical interpretation, at least as Milton
conceives it, is that the message is always the same: God's love for his
creatures and the obligation it places on us to love and take care of one
another. When the archangel Michael sends Adam on his solitary way at
the end of Book XII of *Paradise Lost*, he enjoins him to perform deeds that
are answerable to his knowledge of God. And what kind of deeds are
those? Deeds informed by "Charity, the soul / Of all the rest."[27] Michael
gives no list of properly charitable deeds, for charity is not a matter of
doing this or that particular thing, but of doing whatever you do in the
appropriate spirit – that is, with the proper intention. No deed, however
noble and grand its appearance, deserves to be called charitable simply
because of the figure it cuts in the world; and the meanest of deeds will
be truly noble and grand if charity informs it. George Herbert reads the
lesson perfectly: "All may of Thee partake, / Nothing can be so mean /
Which with this tincture (for Thy sake) / Will not grow bright and
clean."[28]

4.

The lesson holds also for matters aesthetic. If the goodness of a marriage can only be validated by an inner harmony and not by outward inspection, and if the goodness of a deed is a function not of its efficacy but of the intention (spirit) within which it is performed, then a piece of writing will not be good just because it conforms to some conventional measure of aesthetic decorum. In his *Apology Against A Pamphlet*, Milton scornfully describes his polemical opponent as "one who makes sentences by the Statute, as if all above three inches long were confiscat."[29] Milton is not here arguing for the superiority of long sentences (of which he is the virtuoso performer), but for the absurdity of composing sentences according to some formal rule, whether the rule requires sentences three inches long or three hundred inches long. The length of a sentence should not be prescribed in advance, but should emerge naturally in response to the insight of which it is a vehicle. As always for Milton, the inside comes first, and the outside follows. Later in the tract, he calls his opponent a "tormentor of semicolons," that is, someone who mechanically interrupts the flow of thought with externally imposed stopping points. (Three hundred years later, Gertrude Stein will make the same point in her *Lectures in America*.) The fissure a semicolon makes in the natural integrity of free-flowing utterance is then compared to the damage done to the bodies of those who dissent from church orthodoxy: he "is as good at dismembring and slitting sentences as his grave Fathers the Prelates have bin at stigmatizing & slitting noses."[30] In writing as well as in church discipline and in marriage, the flow of inward truth must not be impeded by the tyranny of set forms.

Milton anticipates the obvious objection: without some formal constraints will not writing (and thought) be chaotic and ugly? "The formalist will say," he predicts, "What, no decency in Gods worship?" His response is fervent and amounts to the announcement of an aesthetic credo: "Certainly readers, the worship of God singly in itself, the very act of prayer and thanksgiving with those free and unimpos'd expressions which from a sincere heart unbidden come into the outward gesture, is the greatest decency that can be imagin'd. Which to dresse up and garnish with a devis'd bravery ... addes nothing but a deformed uglinesse."[31] Just as the form of a good work is the faith that *in-*forms it – gives it form from the inside – so is the form of writing an effect of the inner state from which it issues. The more some external formal curlicues are applied (as if with a trowel), the more the result will be a *de*formation ("deformed uglinesse") of the true form, which is internal. The goodness or badness of the "outward gesture" depends on whether or not it issues from a rightly ordered heart. Outwardly fine language may be the "devis'd bravery" that hides a duplicitous and foul inside, and apparently mean and low language (of the kind Milton frequently employs in his prose) may be the effusion of a God-loving sincerity. It follows that a merely formal analysis of a piece of writing (like an inspection from the outside of a marriage or a deed) will tell you nothing about its value.

The point is made succinctly in *Paradise Regained* when Jesus contrasts the "swelling epithets thick laid"[32] of Greek poetry to the "majestic unaffected style"[33] of the prophets, whose writings, he declares, are "to all true tastes excelling."[34] What makes the prophetic style majestic is its unaffectedness; it is not put on or confected. But that essential fact about it is not visible to the naked eye (if it were we would be back to formalism), and to someone not capable of a "spiritual discerning" (like Mammon in *Paradise Lost*, who can appreciate only the gems of Heaven and hasn't the slightest idea of what Heaven is really about) the prophetic style will seem no different from the "varnished"[35] style of pagan poets. Since the difference is not in him, he will not be able to see the difference; without a "true taste" built into his perception, he will not know what in fact excels.

This means that you can neither write nor read a good poem unless goodness already lives within you and is the content of your every act. And that is exactly what Milton says in the most famous sentence in the *Apology*:

He who would not be frustrate of his hope to write well hereafter in laudable things ought him selfe to be a true Poem, that is, a composition and patterne of the best and honourablest things; not presuming to sing high praises of heroick men, or famous Cities, unlesse he have in himselfe the experience and the practice of all that which is praiseworthy.[36]

We are accustomed to separate the moral status of an author from his or her art; a bad person can be a great artist. No, says Milton, that would be to establish an aesthetic realm with no connection whatsoever to the imperative of always doing whatever we do in the name and service of God. Such a realm could be said to be ordered by laws – like the laws and rules of rhetoric Milton knew so well – but the laws would be entirely self-referential and adherence to them would win praise for nothing more than a technical proficiency that is as empty as it is (in Milton's eyes) contemptible.

5.

The problem with this vision of life and its ethical and aesthetic challenges is obvious. If deeds can only be evaluated by a measure they neither contain nor point to, if a marriage can be assessed only by the presence or absence of something that cannot be seen, if the merit or lack of merit of a piece of writing can only be established by a standard that has no formal correlation, is it not the case that one could simply declare his deed good, his marriage bad, and his writing great and defy anyone to say otherwise on pain of being called a mere formalist? Isn't the freedom from outward laws and measures a license to do anything one likes?

These are the questions that Milton takes up in the twenty-seventh chapter of the first book of his *Christian Doctrine*, "Of the Gospel, and Christian Liberty." The chapter begins with still another firm repudiation of an outward law in favor of the law of grace and faith. The covenant of grace "is much more excellent and perfect than the Law."[37] Once "the new covenant through faith in Christ is introduced, then all the old covenant, in other words the entire Mosaic Law, is abolished."[38] Given that the entire Mosaic law contains civil as well as religious prescriptions and proscriptions, this is a more expansive statement of the new covenant's scope than one would find in some of Milton's predecessors and contemporaries. However, the biblical citations he offers as a gloss leave little doubt that in his view the precedence of the inner law of grace over outer law is unqualified: "to the pure all things are pure"; "all things are lawful for me, but not all things are for my good"; "all things are lawful for me, but I will not let anything take control of me" (I will not fall into the idolatry of worshipping the things that as a man of faith I am entitled to use). "If you are led by the spirit, you are not under the law."[39] And if you prefer the law to the spirit, you are acting in an unlawful way. When "the spirit is at variance with the letter" it is only "by breaking the letter of the law that we behave in a way which conforms ... with our love of God."[40] This must also be the animating principle of interpretation: "Thus anyone with any sense interprets the precepts of Christ, not in a literal way but in a way that is in keeping with the spirit of charity."[41]

This unyielding account of what it means to live under the law of grace only intensifies the key question, which Milton poses himself. If "to the pure all things are pure" and if purity is an inner condition that can be neither validated nor invalidated by any outward act, isn't it the case that Christians under the new dispensation are entirely unconstrained and "owe no more obedience to the law"?[42] No, Milton insists, "this is not so at all." In fact, "it is not a less perfect life that is required from Christians but ... a more perfect life than was required of those who were under the law."[43] Whereas obedience to the outward law (if it were possible) would require no inward change, obeying the law inscribed in the fleshy tables of one's heart requires a total reorientation of being. One is enjoined to perform acts of the spirit, acts in accordance with God's will, rather than acts of the flesh; but one is not given a formula for telling the difference between them. He who obeys a written law can at least have the satisfaction (finally hollow) of being able to check off an accomplishment. But he who is called to obey a law that demands not a specific action but an orientation – away from the self and toward God – can never know with certainty that he has done the right thing. The "more perfect life" the Christian must lead is also the more anxious life. If "faith, not law, is our rule," there is no way of being sure that you are following that rule and not following instead a carnal impulse that you have mistaken for the impulse to do God's will.

6.

This anxiety is fully dramatized in *Samson Agonistes*, a play in which every character is an interpreter and where the task of interpretation is to specify the relationship between Samson's present situation and God's will. Was he following God's will when he married two Philistine women? Is it God's will that he labor in the mill, "eyeless in Gaza"? And, is it God's will that he tear down the Philistine temple and kill thousands of people who never did him any personal harm? It is this last question that has excited the passions of Milton critics, especially since the events of September 11, 2001 brought the issue of religiously inspired violence into the foreground of public attention. At the present time of writing, two strong readings of the play are locked in combat. In one, Samson is an antihero whose final act is to be regarded as a negative caution against confusing the brutish impulse of revenge with a command from God. In the other, Samson is a hero of faith (the status conferred on him in Hebrews 11:32) because what he does in the last moments of his life is an expression of his desire to perform God's will.

Those who argue the first position support it with statements from Milton's other works, with learned disquisitions on the many uses (some very negative) to which the Samson story had been put in the seventeenth century and before, and with praise of what they consider to be the better model of heroic faith Milton offers in *Paradise Regained*, where Jesus recalls contemplating the performance of "heroic acts" of warfare but determining finally that it was "more heavenly first / By winning words to conquer willing hearts, / And make persuasion do the work of fear."[44] Those who argue the second position support it with some of Milton's positive references to Samson and with an autobiographical analysis that has the poet projecting his own situation – defeated, endangered, isolated and blind – onto the situation of his protagonist.

For the record, I am of this second party. But I am less interested in defending that reading (which I have done elsewhere) than in pointing out that, according to the account of Milton's radical internalization of judgment offered in this essay, there is no firm basis for placing any value, positive or negative, on Samson's pulling down of the temple. It is surely the task of any interpreter to assess the significance of the play's key dramatic moment, but interpretation is complicated and made almost impossible by the fact that interpretation is itself a prime topic of conversation. Interpretation is what the play is about, and is about in a way that defeats the efforts to perform it.

The interpretive issue is first introduced in the context of a debate about Samson's marriages. The Chorus asks, why, Samson, did you "wed Philistian women rather / Than of thine own tribe?"[45] The question is structurally the same as the question events will later pose to Samson when he is commanded to appear at the Philistine temple in violation of Hebrew law. At first Samson answers firmly. He married the woman of Timna because God told him to. Those like his parents who protested "knew not / That what I motioned was of God."[46] But a few lines later, when he considers the marriage to Delilah, he reports that, in this instance, he was apparently mistaken about what God wanted him to do (a position his father, Manoah, had taken from the outset). "I thought it lawful from my former act."[47] That is, I assumed that the feelings within me were prompted by the same "intimate impulse"[48] from God that guided my actions initially, but given how things have turned out, I must have been wrong. At this early point, the relationship between the letter of the law and the claim of divine inspiration is already blurred. If Samson is no longer clear about the lawfulness of his previous actions, how will he be able to move forward when the choice between the letter and the spirit presents itself again, as it does when he is ordered to perform in the Philistine temple?

His first response to the summons from the Philistine lords is to cite the law and embrace it as the determinant of his actions: "Our law forbids at their religious rites / My presence; for that cause I cannot come."[49] But

then in an amazing sequence, he debates the points of law with the
Chorus in a back-and-forth that turns on definitions of "constraint,"
"outward acts," "outward force," "civil power," "obedience," "freedom"
and "command."

s.   Shall I abuse this Consecrated gift?
c.   Yet with this strength thou serv'st the Philistines.
s.   Not in thir Idol-Worship, but by Labor honest.
c.   Where the heart joins not, outward acts defile not.
s.   Where outward force constrains, the sentence holds.
       But who constrains me to the Temple of Dagon?

It would seem that the exchange is going to go on forever, when
Samson suddenly breaks free of it to report "I begin to feel / Some rousing
motions in me which dispose / To something extraordinary my
thoughts."[50] Whatever the thoughts are, the moment is certainly extraordinary, because it marks the point when Samson lets go of the (false)
security of the law and walks out into moral space with no safety net to
catch him and with no way of determining whether these rousing motions
have in fact been provoked in him by the Spirit. How can he know
whether what is rousing him is a message from the deity or a desire for
revenge?

       The answer is that he can't. What he can do is point out (as the Chorus
had earlier) that God himself may sanction a departure from his own
edicts: "... that he may dispense with me or thee / Present in temples at
idolatrous rites / For some important cause, thou needs't not doubt."[51]
The questions all remain. Is this a sufficiently important cause? Will God
relax his rules in this instance? There's no doubt that he *can* do it, but *is* he
doing it this time? In a world where action is enjoined but the guidelines
for action are unavailable – first, because the law can always be superseded
by a message from God, and second, because the fact of such a message
cannot be validated by any external measure – the only thing to do is what
Abraham is said to have done in Hebrews 11, hazard action in the hope
that it is in accordance with God's will. "By faith Abraham when he was
called ... went out not knowing whither he went." Samson obeys what he
takes to be God's call and he goes out, saying, "I with this Messenger will
go along."[52] Along to where and with what certainty? Whether he is doing
what God wants him to do he cannot know – and neither can we. That's
what it means to exalt the Spirit over the letter, to refuse the authority of
external laws, to insist that the conscience be followed wherever it leads.
Milton calls this precarious condition freedom, and it is; but, as he is well

aware, it is a freedom that is experienced as a burden, the burden of living up to a law that demands obedience but will not reveal itself, and will not reveal itself on principle.

It is with this burden (and opportunity) that Adam and Eve exit from Eden:

> The World was all before them, where to choose
> Thir place of rest, and Providence thir guide:
> They hand in hand with wandring steps and slow,
> Through Eden took thir solitarie way.[53]

Providence may be their guide, but not in a way that prevents them from wandering or feeling solitary. Providence may be what they can trust in, but its springs are not visible and they (and we after them) must somehow pick and choose between the alternative paths the world offers. How will they do it? The archangel Michael tells them to look within. Just obey God, depend on Him only, pledge yourself to faith, virtue, patience, temperance, and love and "then thou wilt not be loath / To leave this Paradise, but shalt possess / A paradise within thee, happier far."[54]

In short, put your inner landscape in good order and the outer landscape will take care of itself or, if it doesn't, it will serve as a foil for an integrity it can neither alter nor threaten.

Sounds simple, sounds hard.

NOTES

1 *Complete Prose Works* (New Haven: Yale University Press, 1970), VI, 639.
2 2 Corinthians 3:3.
3 See *Complete Prose Works, supra* note 1, at II, 543.
4 Ibid. at 564.
5 Ibid. at 563.
6 See *Complete Prose Works, supra* note 1, at VI, 640.
7 Ibid. at 583.
8 Ibid. at 587.
9 Ibid. at 587.
10 Ibid. at 588.
11 Ibid. at 589.
12 Milton, *A Treatise of Civil Power in Ecclesiastical Causes* (London, 1659), 9.
13 See *Complete Prose Works, supra* note 1, at VI, 589.
14 *Doctrine and Discipline of Divorce* (1643), *Complete Prose Works, supra* note 1, at II, 245–246.
15 Ibid. at 265.
16 Ibid. at 276.
17 Ibid. at 276.

18 Ibid. at 281.
19 Ibid. at 282.
20 See *Complete Prose Works, supra* note 1, at II, 678.
21 *The Prose of John Milton*, ed. J. Max Patrick (New York: Anchor Books, 1967), 183.
22 Augustine, *On Christian Doctrine*, trans. D.W. Robertson (Indianapolis, IN: Bobbs Merrill, 1958), 93.
23 See *Complete Prose Works, supra* note 1, at II, 307.
24 Ibid. at 277.
25 Ibid. at 280.
26 Ibid. at 279.
27 Ibid. at 584–585.
28 George Herbert, "The Elixir," *The Works of George Herbert*, ed. F.E. Hutchinson (Oxford: Clarendon Press, 1941), 184.
29 See *Complete Prose Works, supra* note 1, at I, 873.
30 Ibid. at 894.
31 Ibid. at 941–942.
32 Milton, *Paradise Regained*, in *The Poems of John Milton*, ed. John Carey and Alastair Fowler (New York: Norton, 1972), IV, 343.
33 Ibid. at line 359.
34 Ibid. at line 347.
35 Ibid. at line 344.
36 See *Complete Prose Works, supra* note 1, I, 890.
37 See *Complete Prose Works, supra* note 1, at VI, 521.
38 Ibid. at 526.
39 Ibid. at 526–527.
40 Ibid. at 532.
41 Ibid. at 533.
42 Ibid. at 535.
43 Ibid.
44 See *Paradise Regained, supra* note 32, I, 221–223.
45 *Samson Agonistes*, ll. 215–217.
46 Ibid. at 221–222.
47 Ibid. at 231.
48 Ibid. at 223.
49 Ibid. at 1320–1321.
50 Ibid. at 1381–1383.
51 Ibid. at 1377–1379.
52 Ibid. at 1384.
53 Milton, *Paradise Lost*, in *Poems, supra* note 32, at XII, 647–650.
54 Ibid. at 585–587.

CHAPTER 3

"There is nothing he cannot ask": Milton, liberalism, and terrorism

PREFACE

Since September 11, 2001, I have found myself the object of criticism from what appear at first to be different directions. From one direction I was chided (along with others) for holding certain philosophical views – labeled post-structuralist and postmodernist – that were said either to be responsible for the country's vulnerability to terrorist attack or to be corrosive of the country's resolve in the aftermath of terrorist violence. The reasoning was that since postmodernism and post-structuralism proclaim the unavailability of universally accepted standards by which actions might be evaluated, this form of thought eliminates the possibility of defending the superiority of the American way of life. According to what postmodernism tells us, some commentators complain, the terrorists' agenda and culture are in principle no better or worse than ours, and, therefore, the judgment that what they did was wrong or evil cannot be supported by reasons all rational persons would accept.

From another direction I was attacked for my reading of Milton's *Samson Agonistes*, and specifically for my contention that what Samson does in the climactic (although offstage) action of the play – tear down the Philistine temple and kill thousands of men, women, and children – must be considered praiseworthy because he believes (he cannot be sure) that it is what God wants him to do. Obviously, the link between the two criticisms of me is terrorism and especially the terrorism that takes the form of religiously inspired violence. Common to both lines of criticism is the worry that in the absence of an independent measure in relation to which judgments of right and wrong can be made, the moral life becomes a sham, for any act can be justified simply by claiming for it divine inspiration – not the devil, but God made me do it.

I. A LICENSE FOR ATROCITY

In the September 6, 2002 issue of the *Times Literary Supplement* John Carey published a piece entitled "A Work in Praise of Terrorism? September 11 and *Samson Agonistes*."[1] The essay is a complaint against what Carey takes to be the usual reading of Milton's play "as a work in praise of terrorism" and as "Milton's fantasy vengeance on his Royalist conquerors." In Carey's view, this reading turns the "subtle minded" Milton into a "murderous bigot." A better reading, he says, would pay attention to the many points in the play where Milton encourages us to question Samson's motivation and actions and render a negative judgment on them. Carey thus repeats and extends the analysis he offered in the preface to his 1968 edition of the play, where he calls the act of pulling down the Philistine temple "morally disgusting," and a "bloody act of vengeance" which, while it may be praised by the partisan Chorus and by Samson's father, is condemned "at a deeper level" by the "progression of imagery" and by much else.[2]

Carey's longtime conviction that Samson should be read as a negative model – a conviction shared by Irene Samuel, William Empson, Joseph Wittreich, Jane Melbourne, Derek Wood, and others – has been reinforced, he tells us, by the events of September 11, 2001. He explains that if we regard Samson's final action as one the play approves, then it could be said that Milton, were he alive today, would make no distinction between the Hebrew strongman and the hijackers who brought down the World Trade Center towers or, as they might say, brought down the Philistine temple of US capitalism. For, as Carey points out, "the similarities between the biblical Samson and the hijackers are obvious": "Like them Samson sacrifices himself to achieve his ends. Like them he destroys many innocent victims, whose lives, hopes and loves are all quite unknown to him personally. He is, in effect, a suicide bomber, and like the suicide bombers he believes that his massacre is an expression of God's will" (15).

In this last we find the real object of Carey's ire, not Samson or even the hijackers, but the idea that acts of violence could be justified by the conviction of those who perform them that they are doing the will of God. This "viewpoint," he says, is "monstrous," and he finds a particularly monstrous instance of it in my assertion that insofar as Samson's action is an expression of "his desire to conform to [God's] will, it is a virtuous action," and that, moreover, "*No other standard for evaluating it exists.*" "Samson's act," I go on to say (and Carey quotes this sentence too), "is praiseworthy because he intends it to be answerable to the divine will; whether it is or not ... he cannot know and neither can we; and in relation to the problem of judging him as a moral being, whether it is or not does not matter."[3] This line of reasoning, Carey complains, amounts to "a license for any fanatic to commit atrocity," and if "this is truly what *Samson Agonistes* teaches, should it not be withdrawn from schools and colleges ... as an incitement to terrorism?"

Before I respond directly to Carey's challenge, I should acknowledge that there is more than a little to be said for his linking of Samson and Islamic suicide bombers. (Whether this amounts to Milton's sanctioning of terrorism is a question that depends on the prior question of just what terrorism is, a question I shall take up later.) First of all, there are passages in the play that explicitly assert that what has happened has unfolded under the direction of God. God not only approves Samson's slaughter of the Philistines; he has engineered it, says the Semichorus: "While thir hearts were jocund and sublime, / Drunk with Idolatry ... / Chanting their Idol and preferring / Before our living Dread / ... Among them hee a spirit of frenzy sent, / Who hurt thir minds, / And urg'd them on with mad desire / To call in haste for thir destroyer" (1669–1670, 1672–1673, 1675–1678).[4] The key phrase is "drunk with idolatry," for it identifies those who die as persons who, quite literally, worship false gods and who therefore have set themselves up in opposition to the true one.[5] Hence, they deserve what they get and have, in the strongest sense, brought it on themselves. Indeed, because they are spiritually dead to the living God, they are in effect already dead; they are barely human beings, for the spirit of God does not live within them.

This demonizing and dehumanizing of the enemy, as Mark Juergensmeyer remarks, are standard features of religiously justified acts of violence: the foe is turned into a satanic figure "in the scenario of cosmic war."[6] And the report that such a foe died a violent death can be welcomed with joy as Manoa and the Chorus do in gleeful anticipation of the event: "What if ... / He now be dealing dole among his foes, / And over heaps of slaughtered walk his way?" asks the Chorus, and Manoa answers in a line that perfectly captures the frenzy and exultation of religiously inspired hate: "That were a joy presumptuous to be thought" (1527–1531). Manoa later declares that there is nothing to lament (1708) – certainly not the death of thousands of Philistines – and much to celebrate, for "Samson hath quit himself / Like Samson and heroically hath finish'd / A life Heroic, on his enemies / Fully reveng'd" (1709–1712).

Now, one might object – and the objection would have force – that these passages prove only that the idea of God-sanctioned violence is put

forward in the play and is persuasive to some of its characters. They do
not prove that the play, and by extension Milton, embraces the idea even
if the Hebrew Chorus and Samson's father, partisan and limited persons
after all, do. Still, it is worth noting, first, that *Samson Agonistes* does
display the justification Carey so dislikes – I am doing this because
I believe God wants me to – and, second, that the form the justification
takes is uncannily like the form it takes in modern instances of religiously
justified violence. In *Terror and Liberalism*, Paul Berman describes what
he takes to be a "new kind of politics" that has "come into flower" in the
last hundred years.[7] (We are concerned here with an earlier flowering.)
"It was the politics of slaughter – slaughter for the sake of sacred devotion,
slaughter conducted in a mood of spiritual loftiness, slaughter that led to
suicide" (110). In the course of the book, Berman traces the sources of this
politics and finds that one of them is the Book of Revelation, the message
of which he summarizes as follows: "The subversive and polluted city
dwellers of Babylon will be exterminated together with all their abomin-
ations … The destruction will be horrifying … Afterward, when the
extermination is complete, the reign of Christ will be established and will
endure 1000 years and the people of God will live in purity, submissive
to God" (47).

We recognize here a crude form of the millenarianism Milton entertained and at times professed in the 1640s, a millenarianism that led
Hanserd Knollys in "A Glimpse of Sion's Glory" (1641) to proclaim,
"Blessed is he that dasheth the brats of Babylon against the stones."[8] It
is this spirit that Berman finds in all of the twentieth century's destructive
movements – fascism, communism, radical Islam (and he might have
added Christian Identitarianism and Meir Kahane's brand of militant
Judaism). In each of these, he says, the story is the same: "The subversive
dwellers in Babylon were always aided by Satanic forces from beyond and
the Satanic forces were always pressing on the people of God from all
sides" (49). Always the majority of the people of God is complacent
and unaware of the imminent danger, and always the call to arms,
spiritual and physical, is issued by a "revolutionary vanguard who, by
embracing death, will awaken the sleeping nation" (119). ("Awake, arise,
or be forever fallen.")

Berman is horrified by the politics of slaughter and he recommends in
its place the kinder, gentler vision of Enlightenment Liberalism. The heart
of this liberalism, he tells us, "is the recognition that all of life is not
governed by a single, all-knowing and all-powerful authority – by a divine
force. It was the tolerant idea that every sphere of human activity – science,

technology, politics, religion and private life – should operate independently of the others without trying to yoke everything together under a single guiding hand. It was a belief in the many instead of the one" (37). It was, in short, the belief that the private and the public spheres should be distinguished and kept separate so that in each the appropriate obligations will be honored and neither will claim supervisory scope over the other. "Render unto Caesar . . ." Berman knows that it is precisely this doctrine that infuriates religious militants who are repelled by the idea that the obligation to do God's will can be relaxed while the business of the world is conducted by the man who, as Milton puts it in the *Areopagitica*, trades all day in his shop "without his religion."[9] But it is just such a sequestering of religion "in one corner, while the state does its business in a different corner" (79) that is necessary, Berman believes, if religious impulses are not to erode and overwhelm the commitment to public and general laws.

2. INTENTIONS AND CONSEQUENCES

With some of the pertinent issues now foregrounded, we can bring Carey back to center stage and listen to him as he throws down the gauntlet:

> From where does [Fish] derive his certainty that "Samson's act is praiseworthy because he intends it to be answerable to the divine will"? Faced with the horror of Samson's crime, on what does he base his assertion that "*no other standard for evaluating it exists*" apart from the perpetrator's desire to perform what he takes to be God's intention? To most people common humanity supplies "*a standard for evaluating*" mass murder. Why does it not do so for Fish? (16)

The first thing to notice is that Carey's language presupposes as obvious and unchallengeable the liberal worldview Berman champions, presupposes, that is, that in a civilized society, one in which religion has been safely quarantined, the only response to the death of so many is horror and condemnation. But to call Samson's act a "crime" and "mass murder" and to label the actor a "fanatic" from the beginning is to assume, without argument, everything that is in dispute both in the play – witness the exchange between Samson and Harapha on the nature of Samson's deeds – and in the criticism, which since the time of Sir Richard Jebb has been debating whether the spirit of *Samson Agonistes* is Hebraic and tribal or Hellenic and cosmopolitan. That is to say, Carey answers by fiat the question at the heart of Milton's interest here and elsewhere, the question of how one is to assess either actions or outcomes, given opposing interpretive perspectives on an event and in the absence of an uncontroversially authoritative pronouncement (an absence intensified by the condition of drama, lacking as it does a clear authorial voice).

Carey's answer to this interpretive question is simple: a lot of people whom Samson didn't know and who never harmed him died; therefore, it must be mass murder and he must be a fanatic. But Milton's answers to questions like this are never simple because he is acutely aware of the difficulty Carey slides by. We need only recall that extraordinary moment in *Paradise Lost* when, after he has heard Michael exclaim: "Author of evil, unknown till thy revolt" (VI, 262), Satan retorts, "The strife which thou call'st evil ... wee style / The strife of Glory" (289–290). By citing these verses, I do not mean to suggest that Milton intends us to understand that there is nothing to choose between these two accounts; rather, I think, we are intended to understand that we cannot make the choice – cannot say what kind of act the rebellion is – by simply pointing to what seem to be its empirical consequences; and we cannot do that because those consequences can be variously described ("we style it the strife of glory") and, depending on the description, the event will be given a different value. To base the judgment of an act on its consequences is to give over the responsibility of judgment to the shifting winds of the history of reception.

How, then, would Milton have us proceed if not by looking, as Carey does, to the "hideous consequences"? The answer I give, and here I am likely to be again the object of Carey's strictures, is that Milton would have us proceed by looking to the spirit within which an act is performed – to its intentional structure – rather than to what may or may not occur in its wake. My authority for this view is not my own moral or theoretical convictions and certainly not my conviction that the death of a lot of people is a good thing, but Milton's many pronouncements in his prose and poetry. One that is particular to our point is found in *The Tenure of Kings and Magistrates*, where in the course of justifying the execution of Charles I, Milton quotes with approval Sir Thomas Smith's assertion that in assessing such an act, "the vulgar judge of it according to the event, and the lerned according to the purpose of them that do it" (YP III, 221). That is to say, in a world where outcomes (but not intentions) are contingent, we should not, says Milton, justify our actions retroactively by waiting to see how they turned out and then reasoning backward to their virtue or vice, as Samson does when he decides that, given what has happened to him, the marriage to Delilah was a bad idea ("I thought it lawful from my former act"). Rather, it is a necessary and sufficient justification if the act issues from a desire to do God's will and to follow the path of obedience rather than the path of carnal impulse. (On this view of the matter, the road to hell could *not* be paved with good intentions.)

Of course, the distinction between the two paths is not always easy to discern, and one may come to doubt that it has been precisely observed either by oneself or by others; but it is, nevertheless, a real distinction and the exchange between Samson and Delilah turns on it. She says – in an anticipation bordering on parody of Don Adams's "Get Smart" tagline, "Would you believe *this*?" – I did it for this reason, no, for that reason, for the reason of civil duty, for the reason of religion, because the priests urged me to, because the maxims of "wisest men" urged me to, and on and on. In response, he says, that's "hypocrisy" (872), that is, "the feigning of beliefs, feelings or virtues that one does not hold or possess." He repeats the accusation when he declares Delilah to be not "sincere" (874). It is sincerity, the intention to do good and to be true to one's deepest loyalties, that justifies, not some confected heap of tried-on and cosmetically applied reasons. (The integrity and priority of intention requires that it be as independent of worldly pressures as it is of worldly consequences.) That is why Delilah's attempt to equate her action with Jael's, who "Smote Sisera sleeping, through the Temples nail'd" (990), doesn't work in Samson's or, I believe, in Milton's eyes: Jael acted under the direction of and in service to the Lord (at least that is what is said in Judges 4:15 and following), while Delilah acted from a mixture of jealousy, ambition, and the desire to keep Samson a prisoner.[10] On the surface, the two acts – Jael's and Delilah's – may be indistinguishable; indeed, Delilah's could be said to be the less culpable given that Samson, unlike Sisera, is left alive. But the surface – the world of measurable effects, of outcomes or consequences – is not what Milton is interested in; it is in the interior recesses of the willing and intending heart that he finds the true arena of moral testing.

This same internalization of value has an aesthetic equivalent in his thought, as we can see, for example, in *Paradise Regained*, where the superiority of the Hebrew prophets to the Greek and Roman orators is attributed in part to "their majestic unaffected style" (*PR* IV, 359). The question is: what is the difference between a majestic, unaffected style and a majestic affected style? The answer, Milton would say, cannot be found in a description of their respective formal features, for by that measure they will be exactly alike; one will just be the technically proficient counterfeit of the other. The true measure of the difference is interior. In one case, the words proceed from some calculated intention to deceive or impress; in the other, the words – the very same words in one sense but completely different in another – proceed "from a sincere heart" and "unbidden come into the outward gesture" (YP i, 941). And how can you tell the difference? Only if the difference is already inscribed within you. One cannot either recognize true virtue or praise it "unlesse he have in himself the experience and the practice of all that which is praise-worthy" (890). Whether the question is whose action, Delilah's or Jael's, is praise-worthy, or whose words are truly majestic, the answer will not be found by inspecting the outward signs. Only the intention, the unbidden and constitutive inward orientation, makes the difference, and the difference can only be recognized by one who is its (internal) bearer. It takes one to know one.

Everywhere one looks in Milton, one finds this preference (too weak a word) for the inner over the outer; everywhere one finds a refusal to mark crucial differences of judgment and evaluation on the basis of what can be observed and measured, on the basis, that is, of the letter. And this is true even if the letter is Scripture. There is, says Milton, a double scripture, "the external scripture of the written word and the internal scripture of the Holy Spirit which he . . . has engraved upon the hearts of believers"; and while "the external authority for our faith, in other words, the scriptures, is of considerable importance . . . The pre-eminent and supreme authority, however, is the authority of the Spirit, which is internal and the individual possession of each man" (YP vi, 587). Because it is an *individual* posses-sion, you can't borrow it from another; after all, "a man may be a heretic in the truth" (*Areopagitica*, YP ii, 545). And, moreover, when the prompting of the internal scripture inclines you to an action contrary to what the external scripture apparently commands, the internal scripture – the law written on the fleshy tables only you can see – always trumps. "Thus if I keep the Sabbath, in accordance with the ten commandments, when my faith prompts me to do otherwise, my precise compliance will be counted as sin," for it "is faith that justifies, not compliance with the commandments" (YP vi, 639). The faith that justifies is unavailable for inspection, and therefore no man can determine from the outside whether or not you have it.

In *The Doctrine and Discipline of Divorce*, Milton employs exactly the same reasoning to argue that no one except he who has experienced it can testify to the absence of the spiritual communion that makes a marriage a marriage. "*Paulus Emilius*, beeing demanded why hee would put away his wife for no visible reason, *This shoo*, saith he, and held it out on his foot, *is a neat shoo, a new shoo, and yet none of yee know where it wrings me?* [M]uch less . . . can such a private difference be examin'd, neither ought it" (YP II, 348). The marriage that "wrings" a man is already broken, is already no marriage, and the divorce the law will not grant him is already in effect, "for he that would divorce ... but for the law, hath in the sight of God don it already" (YP II, 348–349). Just as man is commanded to "break the Sabbath" if keeping it would be "unfruitfull either to Gods glory or the good of man," so must he not "injoyn the indissoluble keeping of a marriage found unfit" lest by doing so he "make an Idol of mariage" and "advance it above the worship of God" by making it a "transcendent command" (YP II, 276). The only command that is transcendent is the command of the Holy Spirit, of the "inward man, which not any law but conscience can evince" (YP II, 349).

Whether the question is what makes a marriage a true union, or what makes a line of poetry majestic, or what makes an action good, or what makes a law authoritative, or what makes a king legitimate, or what makes a regicide justifiable, the answer Milton gives is always the same: what is necessary is the indwelling presence of the Spirit. If the things you do are done in response to that Spirit – in response to faith – they are good, even if from some perspectives (perhaps the majority of perspectives) the result is an unhappy one. Conversely, things that are done in response to external promptings (of the kind that move Delilah) are inauthentic and therefore bad, even if from some perspectives (perhaps the majority of perspectives) the result is fortunate. The general rule is given in *A Treatise of Civil Power:* "I here mean by conscience or religion, that full perswasion whereby we are assur'd that our beleef and practise, as far as we are able to apprehend and probably make appeer, is according to the will of God & his Holy Spirit within us, which we ought to follow much rather than any law of man" (YP VII, 242). Note that the requirement is not that our practice is in fact in accordance with the will of God (a determination not within our power to make), but that insofar as we can "apprehend" or grasp the matter we are persuaded that it is (we may, after all, turn out to have been wrong). In short, what is asked of us is not a specific perform-ance, but a specific intention, the intention to do God's will: We "are justified by the faith we have, not by the work we do" (YP VII, 266).

3. THE INTERPRETIVE DRAMA

Here, then, is the not-so-short answer to John Carey's question: where does Fish derive his certainty that Samson's act is praiseworthy because he intends it as an expression of obedience to the will of God? I derive my certainty from the writings of Milton, including the argument of this very play where the poet describes Samson as being "persuaded inwardly" without passing judgment on the question of whether or not his inward persuasion corresponds to the truth of what God really wants him to do. I also find in those same writings a recognition of the dangers Carey correctly associates with the idea that one can justify deeds, no matter how "hideous" their consequences, by saying that they are a response to the will of God. The chief danger is that people who believe themselves to be acting in response to God's will may, in fact, be acting in response to the urgings of their own will, and may therefore clothe their commission of sin in the robe of self-righteousness. The point is made by Victoria Kahn in the context of a discussion of "reasons of state," which exceed positive law and claim the status of justified exceptions on the basis of a higher law. But, as Kahn observes, "this reference to a higher law is problematic since reason of state can be feigned to justify lowly considerations of expedience and self-interest."[11] "From the very beginning," she says, "Samson's task is to understand himself as an exception" (1078), but of course that is precisely the problem. Someone who understands himself or herself as an exception to positive law may feel licensed by that understanding to do anything he or she likes. Saint Paul poses the key question – "Shall we sin, because we are not under the law, but under grace?" (Romans 6:15). Does the belief that we are under grace mean that we can do anything we like? "God forbid," says Paul, and Milton amplifies: "It is not a less perfect life that is required from Christians but, in fact, a more perfect life than was required of those who were under the law" (YP vi, 535). The end for which the law was instituted – namely, "the love of God and of our neighbor" (YP vi, 531) – remains; it is just that the law no longer has residence in an external code (even the code of the Scriptures) but is written on the hearts of believers where it is legible only to them. And therein lies the difficulty; for the heart on which the law is written has its own desires and in the absence of an external authority or test the task of disentangling those desires from the pious desire to do God's will is arduous, never ending, and full of anxiety.

This is a perfect description of what Samson is doing at every moment. He is, as the Chorus says (the Chorus is not always wrong), "laboring" his mind (1298). That is, he is trying to figure out the relationship between his present situation and God's will, and he is trying to determine whether and in what circumstances he might once again be an instrument of that will. The drama of the play is thus an interior one; the drama, as many have said, is interpretive, and the interpretive stakes are as high as they get, eternal life or spiritual death.[12] The big question – and everyone in the play has a go at answering it – is how can one identify the true path to obedience amid all the conflicting agendas, guides, rationales and rationalizations? The action of the play, at least as I describe it, consists of the discovery, made again and again by characters and readers alike, that the world's visible signs do not provide an authoritative answer to that question in the form of a recipe or a test or an algorithm.[13]

This is all I mean by the judgment that so incenses Carey: the judgment that, insofar as Samson's act is the outward gesture of his interior desire to do God's will, "it is a virtuous action" and "no other standard for evaluating it exists." I should add – although I wouldn't have thought it necessary – that no other standard exists *in the play*. Carey seems to think that by giving this account of what Samson does, I endorse it and endorse too the reason – "me hungering . . . to do my Father's will" (*PR* II, 259) – I assign to it. But I endorse nothing except my reading – I am doing literary criticism, not morality – and the basis of that reading is not any personal view I might have about religiously inspired violence, now or then, but the repeated de-authorization *in the play* of every external sign – of every other standard – that might serve as a guide to interpretive certainty. Interpretive certainty (or at least interpretive confidence) could be achieved if a relationship of cause and effect could be established between the return of Samson's strength, the rejection of Delilah's several appeals, the recovery of his spirits in the form of some "rousing motions," the pulling down of the temple, and, most importantly, the return of God's favor (which assumes it has been lost, an assumption Samson makes but not one the play ratifies). But while the elements requisite for the determination of a cause and effect relationship are present in the play – Samson's strength does return, he does resist Delilah, he does experience rousing motions, he does pull down the temple – they are not arranged (as they are in other versions of the story) in a way that encourages or allows us to draw a straight line from them to the return of God's favor. It is not that there are no answers to the question "What is the meaning of what happens at the temple?"; it is, rather, that there are too many answers – given by the Chorus, by Manoa, by Harapha, by Delilah (not, however, by Samson) – and that not one of them is unambiguously confirmed.

This refusal to provide interpretive guidance leaves readers and critics where it leaves the characters, arguing about the significance of Samson's actions present, past and future and finding no independent and visible measure by which they could be assessed. In his exchange with Delilah, Samson's measure is sincerity, or purity of intention, something one can claim but hardly demonstrate. In the exchange with Harapha, the Philistine giant plays the role of John Carey by confronting Samson with the empirical measure of visible (and hideous) consequences. What God, he asks, will accept a champion who is "A murderer, a revolter and a robber" (*SA* 1180)? "How dost thou prove me these?" (1181), Samson replies, and the giant answers by pointing to specific acts: you did this, and then that, and then committed this other outrage, all while you were "subject to our lords" (1182). Samson first responds by invoking the traditional argument that deeds, otherwise suspect, are allowable in times of war – "force with force / Is well ejected when the conquered can" (1206–1207) – but then he turns to his true and stronger (in the sense of more deeply believed) position: "I was no private but a person raised / With strength sufficient and command from Heav'n" (1211–1212). Or, in other words, what you call robbery, murder and revolt I style as the effects of obedience to God. It is because I do these things in response to heaven's command that they are justified, and no other standard for evaluating them exists.

4. ANTINOMIANISM

Of course, the fact that the account Samson gives of the motive for his actions perfectly accords with mine does not render that account the right one or the one Milton would approve. It does, however, allow us to give a name to Samson: he is an antinomian, as, I believe, was Milton. That is, he prefers to any outward justification of his actions the internal justification of the Spirit of God working within him (with due allowance always for the difficulty of telling the difference between that Spirit and promptings less noble). "From the Middle Ages on," says Norman Burns, "the antinomianism implicit in the law breaking of Old Testament heroes was usually tamed by asserting that they acted on divine commands."[14] Burns is convinced, as I am, that Milton "reconceived the character of Samson found in the Book of Judges and ... presented Samson ... as an antinomian hero of faith" (28).[15]

To be sure, calling Samson an antinomian does not clear him of the charge of terrorism, for there remains the possibility that "antinomian" is just another word for terrorist. This is certainly the view of J. MacBride Sterret, who in a dictionary of theology describes antinomianism as the doctrine of "extreme fanatics who deny subjection to any law other than the subjective caprices of the empirical individual," and goes on to say that "all moral sophists are antinomians, all who pervert the principle that the end justifies the means into a disregard for established moral laws, so that some personal or finite end be attained." Sterret's distress at the argument implicit in antinomianism – I do it under the command of the Spirit – is more than matched by the anonymous author of "An Answer to a Book Entitled 'The Doctrine and Discipline of Divorce'" (1644), who complains that if Milton's view of divorce were accepted, "it would be an occasion to the corrupt heart of man without any just cause at all, merely to satisfy his lust, to pretend causes of divorce." "Who sees not," he exclaims, "how many thousands of lustfull and libidinous men would be parting from their Wives every week?,"[16] a question answered amusingly in 1646 by Thomas Edwards when he reports a conversation with a Mistris Attaway who, after having read *Doctrine and Discipline*, "hath practised it in running away with another womans husband."[17] This is how it is, says the anonymous respondent to Milton's tract, with those who go around doing anything they like and justifying it by saying, "We live in Christ, and Christ doth all for us; we are Christed with Christ and Godded with God."[18]

Obviously, "antinomian," like "terrorist," is not a name one gives oneself, and indeed in this same *Doctrine and Discipline of Divorce*, Milton lumps the doctrine with anabaptism and other "*fanatick* dreams" (YP II, 278). Nevertheless, by all the signs, Milton is an antinomian, although, as we have seen, his version of antinomianism, far from relaxing the requirements of morality, tightens them and makes them more difficult to live up to. What links antinomianism with terrorism, at least on the surface, is the doctrine (decried by Sterret) that the end justifies the means, the doctrine that no action is to be recoiled from if God commands it, or (and here is where all the interpretive troubles come back in) you are persuaded inwardly that God commands it. Milton, says Joan Bennett, agreed with the Ranter Laurence Clarkson that "there is no single commandment that literally and absolutely must not be broken" in the service of faith, although those not informed by that faith or informed by another will see what you do differently.[19] Milton himself "advocated in the regicide tracts what royalists called murder, in the divorce tracts what clergy called adultery" (*Reviving Liberty*, 110), just as, she might have added, Harapha would call what Samson is about to do, were he to know about it in advance, mass murder and atrocity by suicide.

The antinomian hero stakes everything on a faith that no sign in the external world confirms, a faith that many signs in the external world point away from. That is why, as Bennett observes, the paradigmatic antinomian hero, one to whose example Milton often returns, is Abraham, the first in the catalog of the heroes of faith in Hebrews 11, who is resolved

to kill his son because God has told him to. Bennett quotes Christopher
Fry's version of the story in which Isaac asks, "Is there nothing he may not
ask of thee" and Abraham answers "nothing":

This is the illumination of antinomian Christian liberty: There is nothing he may
not ask ... At stake is not whether one suffers or dies, but whether one suffers in
faith, trusting, as Abraham does, that the seeming contradiction of a law is
accounted for by the highest purpose of the whole law, God's love. Abraham ...
is prepared to kill his son, not in spite of the fact that he loves Isaac, but *because*
he loves him. This is the purest antinomianism. (*Reviving Liberty*, 156)

If so, it is easy to see why many want nothing to do with it. While the
argument may have a theological cogency – were Abraham to disobey God
for the sake of Isaac, he would make Isaac into an idol or "transcendent
command" by preferring him to the Creator – the price of its cogency may
seem too high, a licensing of the license performed by those who need only
say I act according to the inner promptings of the Spirit. Going down that
path legitimizes people who, hearkening to inner voices or to rousing
motions, commit what certainly looks like mass murder. Would it not
be better, one might ask, to put to one side the question – unavailable to a
public answer – of what God commands and settle (if that is the word) for
what is commanded by the imperative to live in peace and (possible)
prosperity with one's neighbors, an imperative that requires obedience to
procedural and published rules no matter what inner messages one believes
oneself to have received from on high? To that question, liberalism, the
political philosophy that honors the procedural means above the substantive end and preaches the priority of the right over the good, will answer
yes in thunder and will supplement that answer with a sidelong glance at
negative examples such as Samson and Jim Jones, who illustrate the danger
of following the light of conscience wherever it leads. Samson, or perhaps
the more reflective Milton, might reply that there are worse things than
death and that the destruction of cities or civilizations informed by the
spirit of Sodom and Gomorrah is a necessary prelude to the building of a
better, purer world. One might even argue that in destroying or extirpating
evil, the faithful hero follows or anticipates the example of Christ, who
will, says Milton,

> dissolve
> Satan with his perverted World, then raise
> From the conflagrant mass, purg'd and refin'd,
> New Heavens, new Earth, Ages of endless date
> Founded in righteousness and peace and love,
> To bring forth fruits, Joy and Eternal Bliss. (*PL* XII, 546–551)

5. THE QUESTION OF TERRORISM

There we must leave the question of what law we are to follow and by what signs we are to know it in the confidence that (a) there will be no end of answers to it; that (b) no answer will be independently authorized, and that (therefore) (c) interpretive challenges of the kind put to Samson will always be with us. But perhaps we can take one last stab at the question or questions that brought us here. Is the Samson of *Samson Agonistes* a terrorist? Is Milton a terrorist? Is Stanley Fish a terrorist? Well, to take the last first: Stanley Fish is a literary critic (a worse thing in some eyes than being a terrorist), and while the readings he gives of literary texts, including this one, may be right or wrong, no reading he gives commits him to terrorism or to becoming an apologist for terrorists, or to any other political or moral stance, for that matter. (There is, as I have argued elsewhere, no relationship whatsoever between one's performance as a literary critic and one's performance in any other area of life.)[20]

That said, what about Samson and Milton? Are they terrorists? They are certainly, on my account, antinomians, but does this make them terrorists? Well, it depends on what you take the hallmarks of terrorism to be. If terrorism is the willingness to violate civil law in the name of a higher commitment, Samson and Milton (as Charles I would attest) are terrorists, as is the Abraham who is willing to sacrifice Isaac, and the Jael who smote Sisera sleeping through the temples nailed, and the Martin Luther King, Jr., who urged his followers to break laws he and they considered oppressive.

But this answer settles the question too easily by identifying as a terrorist anyone who cares more for the end than the means. If this is what terrorists are, there are an awful lot of them — every proponent of affirmative action, for example, is one — and the word would seem to have lost its edge when it is taken to refer to activities recognized by everyone as being beyond the pale. The current literature tries to give the word "terrorist" back its edge by associating it with the performance of violence in a certain mode. For Mark Juergensmeyer, terrorist acts are "public acts of destruction, committed without a clear military objective, that arouse a widespread sense of fear."[21] In a similar vein, Jessica Stern defines terrorism "as an act or threat of violence against noncombatants with the objective of exacting revenge, intimidating or otherwise influencing an audience."[22] But that covers the bombing of Dresden, the destruction of Hiroshima and Nagasaki, the invasion of Afghanistan, and the Nuremberg trials. Defined that way, terrorism is simply the name you give to whatever your enemies do.

If we want the word "terrorism" to stand for something recognized as such by all parties, we shall have to reserve it for a form of activity that no one would want to claim because it would be repugnant even as a sanctified means. The way to do this is to remember that, strictly speaking, terrorism is the name of a military tactic, one that is to be distinguished from more traditional tactics in which gathered armies fight pitched battles according to the rules of the Geneva Convention. Terrorism, as we now know too well, involves hit-and-run skirmishes, covert operations, activity that is intermittent and therefore productive of surprise and anxiety, and theatrical excess. (This is not a complete list, but it will do.) Those who employ these tactics do so in the name of a cause that supposedly justifies them, and it follows that what they are committed to is not the tactics but the cause. The militants interviewed and discussed by Berman, Juergensmeyer and Stern explain what they do in just those terms: It is because we are dedicated to the work we have been called to, they say, that we must perform these actions. Terrorism is not for us a career choice, but a means to an end. No one says: "I just love violence and inflicting pain and I'll go anywhere and do anything just to get that rush."

But suppose there were someone like that, someone who killed women and children, burned cities, spread plague because he liked to, because it was what he did, because it was what he was. That would be a terrorist, pure and simple, someone for whom the tactics we call terrorism were not a means in the service of a larger goal, but the goal itself. In Milton's work, there is only one such being, and he identifies himself in this line from *Paradise Lost*: "Only in destroying [do] I find ease" (IX, 129). Satan is the arch-terrorist, inflicting pain and inspiring fear because that's what keeps him going, and he does have disciples – wanton serial killers, despots who love the cruel exercise of power more than they love its results, anyone devoted to destruction as an end in itself. This does not describe either Milton or his Samson, either of whom may be many things – regicide, misogynist, elitist, bully, boor – but they are not terrorists. This does not mean, however, that it is safe to have them walking around in the world. In the course of a conversation with Mir Aimal Kansi, who is in prison for having opened fire on commuters waiting to enter the headquarters of the CIA, Jessica Stern discovers that he has a master's degree in literature. "What kind of literature?" she asks. The "poetry of Milton," he replies (179). Score one for John Carey.[23]

NOTES

1 John Carey, "A Work in Praise of Terrorism? September 11 and *Samson Agonistes*," *Times Literary Supplement*, September 6, 2002, 15–16.

2 John Carey and Alastair Fowler, eds., *John Milton, Poems* (London: Longmans, 1968), 335, 341.

3 Stanley Fish, *How Milton Works* (Cambridge, MA: Harvard University Press, 2001), 426, 428.

4 Quotations of Milton's poetry are from *Complete Poems and Major Prose*, ed. Merritt Y. Hughes (New York: Macmillan, 1957).

5 This is the view held by Michael Lieb: "Through a misplaced allegiance to an idol that ultimately fails them, they are destroyed by ... a power whose impact they never for a moment expected to encounter." See "Our Living Dread: The God of *Samson Agonistes*," in *Milton Studies* 33, *The Miltonic Samson*, ed. Albert C. Labriola and Michael Lieb (Pittsburgh: University of Pittsburgh Press, 1996), 13.

6 Mark Juergensmeyer, *Terror in the Mind of God: The Global Rise of Religious Violence* (Berkeley and Los Angeles: University of California Press, 2000), 173.

7 Paul Berman, *Terror and Liberalism* (New York: Norton, 2003), 110.

8 Hanserd Knollys, "A Glimpse of Sion's Glory": *Puritanism and Liberty*, 2nd edn., ed. A.S.P. Woodhouse (Chicago: University of Chicago Press, 1950), 233.

9 *The Complete Prose Works of John Milton*, 8 vols., ed. Don M. Wolfe et al. (New Haven: Yale University Press, 1953–1982), hereafter designated YP and cited parenthetically by volume and page number in the text.

10 See on this point Alan Rudrum, "Milton Scholarship and the *Agon* over *Samson Agonistes*," *Huntington Library Quarterly* 65 (2002), 478. "Dalila's pleas of, 'Civil duty, religion, and public good' ... serve to define the nature of an idolatrous state, in which religious duty represents no more than the wishes of the priests and elders of her tribe." See also David Gay, *The Endless Kingdom* (Newark: University of Delaware Press, 2002), 137: "[Samson] is, Milton suggests, 'persuaded inwardly that this was from God,' ... Dalila, in contrast, is continually pressured by voices outside of her."

11 Victoria Kahn, "Political Theology and Reason of State in *Samson Agonistes*," *South Atlantic Quarterly* 95 (Fall 1996), 1068.

12 See Anne K. Krook, "The Hermeneutics of Opposition in *Paradise Regained* and *Samson Agonistes*," *SEL* 36 (1966), 129–147; Victoria Kahn, "Political Theology"; Gay, *The Endless Kingdom*, 99–184; John Shawcross, *The Uncertain World of "Samson Agonistes"* (Cambridge: D.S. Brewer, 2001). Interpretive conflict, as an organizing theme, is, I would argue, the key to answering the question of just how *Paradise Regained* and *Samson Agonistes* are related to each another. Are the figures of Samson and Christ to be linked by typology, or opposed as bad and good examples, respectively? It seems to me that the two productions share a single plot even though the differences of genre might tend to obscure the basic similarity. In both the poem and the play, the hero is presented (by one character in *Paradise Regained* and by

many in *Samson Agonistes*) with a succession of motives and reasons for action – wealth, military success, art, domestic ease, pride, despair, quietism, nationalism, political reform, the responsibility of leadership – and in both the hero rejects these reasons and motives in favor of the trumping reason that one must strive to be faithful to God without forcing or limiting ("appointing") his will. The value of the actions each takes is measured by the actions refused, actions that would nominate alternative loyalties and alternative obligations. The actions refused are specific and knowable in their likely effects; the actions taken find no immediate confirmation in the world, but stand as testimony to the substance of things hoped for and the evidence of things not seen. Samson and Christ are alike heroes of faith despite the enormous differences of personality and affect. The fact that one performs a spectacular but problematic act, while the other is problematic in his refusal to act should not lead us to think of them as opposing figures; rather, they jointly illustrate the truth that faithful action – action taken in response to God's will, however imperfectly known – can take any form, including the form of just saying no.

13 See Fish, chapter 13, "The Temptation of Intelligibility," *How Milton Works*, 447–455.

14 Norman Burns, "Milton's Antinomianism, and Samson's," in *Milton Studies* 33 (1996), 29.

15 On the question of Milton's antinomianism, see Joan Bennett, "Milton's Antinomianism and the Separation Scene in *Paradise Lost*," *Reviving Liberty: Radical Christian Unionism in Milton's Great Poems* (Cambridge, MA: Harvard University Press, 1989); and Alan Rudrum, "Milton Scholarship and the *Agon* over *Samson Agonistes*," *Huntington Library Quarterly* 65 (2002), 484: "Milton's radicalism was generally antinomian."

16 "An Answer to a Book Entitled 'The Doctrine and Discipline of Divorce'" (1644), reprinted in W.R. Parker, *Milton's Contemporary Reputation* (Columbus: Ohio State University Press, 1940), 8.

17 Thomas Edwards quoted in Parker, *Milton's Contemporary Reputation*, 77.

18 "An Answer to a Book," in ibid., 36.

19 Bennett, *Reviving Liberty*, 110.

20 Stanley Fish, *Professional Correctness: Literary Studies and Political Change* (New York: Oxford University Press, 1995).

21 Juergensmeyer, *Terror in the Mind of God*, 5.

22 Jessica Stern, *Terror in the Name of God: Why Religious Militants Kill* (New York: Harper Collins, 2003), xx.

23 One of the things John Carey says in his *TLS* essay is that *Samson Agonistes* has changed since September 11, 2001. That cannot be true. What is true is that in the aftermath of September 11, arguments, already in full career, about the meaning of *Samson Agonistes* – and especially arguments as to whether Samson's act was meant to be approved or condemned – acquired a new relevance as readers came quickly to see parallels between the moment the play dramatizes and the moment the nation had just lived through. But this

new relevance, while it may have added spice and even a contemporary urgency to the search for Milton's meaning, could not have altered the object of that search. If a text were to alter with every change in the circumstance of its reception, the work could not be said to have a meaning, but rather would have as many meanings as there are circumstances and receivers, would have, in effect, infinite meanings. And if that were the case, *disagreement* about the text's meaning would be impossible, and literary criticism would not progress beyond the assertion and counterassertion of "it means this to me" and "maybe so, but it means something else to me." The very activity in which Carey engages – criticizing my account of Milton's meaning – commits him to believing that *Samson Agonistes* does have a meaning and that it is our business as critics to figure out what it is.

CHAPTER 4

Why Milton matters; or, against historicism

To the question assigned us – why does Milton matter? – I would add two additional questions: Matter to whom? And matter as what? The second – matter as what? – is the crucial one, for I take it to be true that things matter in particular ways – nothing matters in *every* way – and I also take it to be true that the particular way a thing matters is a function of what it is intended by its maker or author to be. That is to say, when evaluating a human production (as opposed to a natural phenomenon) one must begin with a precise understanding of its purpose. What was it meant to do? What task was it fashioned to perform? Once these questions have been answered, you are equipped with a framework from the perspective of which you can identify the relevant features of a performance. And once those features have been identified, you can go about the business of determining what they mean, all the while keeping in mind that the meanings you seek to establish will be meanings specific to the purpose of the agent or agents who set out to do something, not everything. (Here I reaffirm C.S. Lewis's assertion that, "The first qualification for judging any piece of workmanship from a corkscrew to a cathedral is to know *what* it is – what it was intended to do and how it is meant to be used.")[1] It is in relation to the something purposive actors set out to do that the end result must be evaluated. If the evaluation is strongly positive, you say: "That's a really good instance of X or Y or Z – a really good song, or a really good wine, or a really good automobile, or a really good movie." And if this positive evaluation is transmitted to, and shared by, generations subsequent to the initial appearance of the something someone set out to do, you can then say, "This really matters," by which you will mean that in the history of the effort to do that kind of thing, this is a shining and lasting and exemplary contribution.

With these general speculations (to which I shall return) as background, I can now answer the question "Why Milton matters" by posing and answering the secondary (really primary) question, "Matters as what?"

Insofar as Milton matters, he matters as a poet, for it is poetry he set out to write; and, moreover, if this is so, then it seems to me that the best scholarship now being produced by the most intelligent, learned, acute students of Milton is designed, not self-consciously of course, to ensure that in time he won't matter. No one will care.

How can this be? How can a scholarship at once be best and be (at least potentially) responsible for the diminishing of its object? There is no puzzle or paradox here: the scholarship I refer to is best because it is scrupulous, well informed, wide-ranging, illuminating, full of insights, pathbreaking. But its very virtues are likely to have the negative effect I predict because in the exercise of those virtues the authors of this scholarship pick up the stick from the wrong end.

It's time for an example, and remember, it's an example of something excellent in many respects except for the one respect that counts. The year 2002 saw the publication of an important (and award-winning) collection of essays entitled *Milton and the Terms of Liberty*, edited by Graham Parry and Joad Raymond. In the introduction to the volume Parry identifies it as the report of the International Milton Symposium, a conference assembled "to discuss the current state of Milton studies" and declares that "the collection of papers presented here reflects the predominance of interest in Milton's constant adjustment of his political ideas to the changing circumstances of the nation" (xv). This predominance is reflected, he points out, in the fact that "many of the conference papers considered the larger question of Milton's place in the history of political thought in early modern Britain and Europe." "This bias," he concludes, "seems likely to continue to influence the future direction of Milton studies." That's just what I'm worried about, for although Parry mentions, in passing, that there was some attention paid at the conference to "the interconnections between linguistic register, literary form and ideas in the expression of political concerns," it is clear that in his mind and the mind of his fellow contributors, political concerns came first, their expression in linguistic and literary form second.

That is what I mean by picking up the stick from the wrong end. If what is important is Milton's place in the history of political thought, the form taken by his political reflections will be a matter of (at most) secondary interest. If you think of Milton as being in competition with Thomas Hobbes, John Harrington, John Locke, John Lilburne, William Prynne – a competition he would most likely lose – the fact that he wrote in verse will no doubt be noted, but it will not take center stage, and the history of poetic conventions – along with the imperatives for performance encoded in those conventions and the meaning-making recipes they provide – will first become background and then, after a while, fade from sight; and fading with them will be any recollection of why – as an instance of what general purpose – Milton wrote these things in the first place. In short, if Milton's value – the degree to which he matters – stands or falls on his contribution to English and European political thought, it will fall. After all, the only reason anyone would care about "Milton's constant adjustment of his political ideas" is because he's the guy who wrote *Paradise Lost, Paradise Regained, Lycidas,* and *Samson Agonistes,* and if those poems are quarried for political or economic or agricultural or military views, the collection and analysis of those views *as* politics or economics or agriculture (as if those disciplines named the arena of Milton's ambitions) will displace any interest in their status as poems, and as a result we will have lost our grip on what kind of accomplishment they are.

I here give voice to a concern that has been expressed with some frequency in recent years. Michael Clark, commenting on the recent tendency to subsume literature in "a more general symbolic determinism," observes that when "the system as a whole, rather than anything specific to the literary text" takes front and center stage, "Literature as such simply disappears against a general background of material action or symbolic determination." Richard Strier is making the same kind of argument when he declares that in giving up formalism, we "give up both the question of value and the conception of 'the literary.'" Ellen Rooney is even more pointed when she insists that, "For a critical reader bereft of the category of form, the subject matter of literary and cultural analysis loses all standing as a theoretical object." Once the category of form has been attenuated, she concludes, every text is reduced "to its ideological or historical context," and "reading has been displaced by a project of sorting by theme."[2] Of course, themes can be found embedded in any form whatsoever, and if you make themes the focus of your analysis, the particular form that gives them experiential life will receive no attention whatsoever.

I can imagine at least two objections to the arguments I have just rehearsed: (1) Why couldn't it be the case that the inventorying of Milton's views on a number of subjects illuminated rather than overwhelmed the poetry? and (2) Isn't the idea of a distinctively literary performance a relic of a long-since-rejected aesthetic idealism with its built-in alibi for a poetic genius floating free of the entanglements of the world? The inventorying of Milton's views on history, politics, theology and so on will indeed have a chance to illuminate the poetry, but only if those views have been tabulated in response to a literary question: that is, you notice, as everyone since Addison has, that the God of *Paradise Lost* is a puzzlingly unsympathetic figure and you look in Milton's writings on theology and kingship for a key to the puzzle. If, on the other hand, you simply ask and then answer the question, "What did Milton think about x?" you will have marshaled a good deal of information, but there will be no way to get from it to the poetry you want it to illuminate. Let me illustrate with another example, again a scholarly work that is in many respects impeccable: Jeffrey Shoulson's "Milton and Enthusiasm: Radical Religion and the Poetics of *Paradise Regained*."[3] Early on, Shoulson identifies his project by posing it as a question: "Is it possible to determine from *Paradise Regained*, a poem so deeply engaged in the matter of messianic salvation and its relation to history, Milton's attitudes toward these various enthusiastic movements?" (3). The answer is: "Sure it's possible," and in fact Shoulson does it for the rest of an elegantly constructed and argued paper. But when it comes time for him to make good on his subtitle – "Radical Religion and the Poetics of *Paradise Regained*" – he has nowhere to go because nothing in his framing of the essay's question and therefore of its agenda is in touch with any poetic or aesthetic concern. The pages he devotes to *Paradise Regained* as a poem at the end of the essay are interesting and incisive, but they don't grow out of the longer exposition that precedes them. That exposition was the exposition of a historian of theology, and while it is certainly possible and indeed likely that the history of seventeenth-century theology will be relevant to *Paradise Regained*, that relevance will not emerge if you simply lay the exposition next to the poem. Rather, the relevance must be elaborated and *argued* for, and argued for in specifically literary terms. There is, to be sure, an argument in Shoulson's paper, but it is not, until the very end, a literary argument, and its materials will not transform themselves into poetically significant materials without the intervention and controlling guidance of the literary interrogation Shoulson never sets in motion. What he does set in motion is an interrogation that proceeds from quite a different angle, and as that angle takes over his paper any sense of *Paradise Regained* as a poem, as a production of a particular and distinctive kind, pretty much disappears and the aesthetic object is absorbed by the cultural materials that now surround it.

But isn't that just the point (and here I take up the second obvious objection). After all, it has been the project of cultural studies to achieve just such an absorption by denying to the literary object its splendid but irresponsible and historically impossible isolation. Raymond Williams stands in here for the innumerable proclaimers of the same sentiments: "We cannot separate literature and art from other kinds of social practice, in such a way as to make them subject to quite special and distinct laws. They may have quite specific features as practices but they cannot be separated from the general social process."[4] Well, yes and no. While it is true that no discourse occupies a privileged, self-defining, independent and autonomous place, and while it is also true that all discourses are both culturally constituted and constitutive of culture, participating in and productive of a "general social process" they affirm and modify, it can nevertheless be said of a particular discourse that it is separate and distinct; not distinct in the impossible sense of being freestanding, but distinct in the sense that it inflects the general and shared set of discursive practices in a way appropriate to its claimed function. Writing a sermon and writing a history and writing a poem are all conventional activities enabled by and feeding back into the same social conditions of articulation, and no one of them is finally independent of the others. However, "finally" is a very abstract measure, and short of it the differences that attend different purposes are operationally real and result, despite what Williams says, in "quite special and distinct laws," the law, for example, that a sermon must have a homiletic and hortatory point, or the law that histories must offer explanations of the events they report, or the law that poems must at once utilize and display the resources of language, or the law that fictions can set aside the requirement of verisimilitude. To be sure, it is always possible to focus on the set of generally enabling conditions and to discover its traces in particular performances, but if you only do that and always do that you will lose sight of the conventional – not essential – differences that make things what they are; you will fail to ask the right questions and you are likely to be distracted by the wrong ones.

The lesson is simple and it is the one I began with: in the act of assessing a performance you must always be in mind of its point, of what it is trying to do. This was a lesson forgotten by those moviegoers who in 1967 criticized Mike Nichols's *The Graduate* because in a crucial scene the hero, played by Dustin Hoffman, drives his Alfa Romeo across the upper level of the Bay Bridge in a direction prohibited by the traffic laws. It was said that Nichols spoiled the movie by making this mistake, but it wasn't a mistake at all; it was a cinematic choice that had to do no doubt with the position of the sun, the quality of the light, the panorama available to the camera, and the relation of all of these to the film's dramaturgy. It was to those conventions and conventional resources – the conventions and resources of movie making – that Nichols was being responsible; he was not responsible to the conventions of the documentary or the conventions of news broadcasting or the conventions of history or the conventions of driving practices. Those viewers who held him to the decorums of another practice got hung up on something that was irrelevant to his achievement, and so they missed it.[5]

I would say the same about Raymond Williams's famous thesis about the pastoral, the argument that if we focus only on the formal and genre aspects of poems like *Lycidas* and *To Penshurst* we miss the fact that, by perpetuating the myth of an "enameled" country life, such productions functioned as screens and apologies for the reality of oppressive agricultural practices – enclosure, eviction, conditions of near-slave labor.[6] The accusation is that both the poets and the critics who follow the standard line of analysis are accomplices to the outrages they fail to address. They don't bring to light what was really going on at Appleton House or Tintern Abbey. My response is, right, they don't, and that wasn't what they set out to do. They set out to write poetry in a particular genre.

This doesn't mean that the poetry they produced is without any connection whatsoever to issues of agricultural reform, peasant labor, foreclosure, enclosure, and the like. Virgil's *Eclogues*, a model for would-be pastoral poets in the Middle Ages and Renaissance, are explicitly concerned with all of these matters, and after Virgil the formal/conventional properties of the pastoral genre are understood to include them. In his influential and authoritative *The Art of English Poesie* (1589), George Puttenham says of the pastoral that "under the veil of homely persons" it glances "at greater matters and such as perchance had not been safe to have been disclosed in any other sort." Thus, when Milton begins *Lycidas* with the words, "Yet once more," his readers know that the pastoral poet's lament will touch on matters greater than the "rustical manner" (Puttenham) the representation suggests. In short, substantive concerns are built into the formal signatures of the genre.[7]

What is not built into the formal signatures of the genre, however, are the concerns of the Marxist/materialist critics who, following Williams and others, focus on what the genre, at least in its classical instantiations, leaves out. Poems leave out many things – indeed the vast majority of things – but an account of what a poem leaves out cannot be an account of the intention of the author (and of the poem's meaning) unless it can be shown that the author wanted the reader to notice the exclusion and to make something of it. In general, anything *can* count as relevant to meaning (even an exclusion, if, for example, an allusion to a mythical hero leaves out half of his story) so long as it can be linked up to the author's intention. Something in the present, something in the past – it doesn't matter. Historical proximity to the act of composition is neither a requirement for nor a guarantee of relevance. The fact that an author said or did something does not make that something part of his intention, even if what he did was causally productive of the object of interpretation.

This is a point missed, I think, by Stephen Dobranski in his learned and illuminating *Milton, Authorship, and the Book Trade*.[8] Dobranski forcefully argues that an overemphasis on the picture of Milton as a solitary genius (a picture, as he notes, Milton himself sometimes draws) has deflected attention away from "the material conditions of Milton's authorship" (3). Dobranski is particularly interested in the transactions between Milton and his printers and booksellers, and it is his project "to reconstruct such relationships based on his publications and personal letters, as well as documentary evidence about the book trade" (3). This project is organized, he tells us, by three questions: "What role did Milton play in the production of his texts? What can we learn about the author by examining his practices of writing and publishing? How does the material creation of Milton's books affect their meaning?" But if you will allow me a Sesame Street moment, question three is not like the others. Questions one and two are historical and empirical questions and are interesting in their own right. Question three is an interpretive question; it assumes that there is a relationship between the details of composition and publication – How long did it take to write? To whom were various drafts shown? What were Milton's negotiations with his printer? – and what the published product *means.* There is no such relationship, or, rather, there isn't any except in the case of two special circumstances: (1) When the history of composition and publishing is incorporated explicitly into the text or is rehearsed in a prefatory note; (2) When there is a question of attribution that requires an examination of compositional practices and the identity of booksellers or printers in order to determine who the author actually was, a determination neces-sarily preliminary to any specification of his or her intention. In any other circumstance, information about the "practices of writing and publishing" will stand to the side of the interpretive effort, for while those practices are surely part of an author's biography, they are not evidence of what he or she set out to do, even if they are evidence of the route pursued in the doing of it.

Again, it is not that information about compositional habits and publishing practices can never be relevant to interpretive concerns. Rather interpretive concerns must be in place *first*; otherwise, one could never establish relevance and one would be in the position (as many historicists, in fact, are) of considering relevant any and every fact that came one's way. It may be, as Jerome McGann contends, that authorship "takes place within the conventions and enabling limits that are accepted by the prevailing institutions of literary production," but those conventions, even if they are necessary to the production of meaning, are not what the literary work means; they are not the author of the work; they do not have intentions. Dobranski's claim that by "analyzing Milton's books as physical objects we gain new insights into the circumstances of their production" is certainly true and even tautological, but the assertion that follows in the same sentence is certainly false: "and thereby improve our understanding of the individual texts' meanings."[9] An understanding of a text's meaning can only be achieved by first understanding the purpose – literary or otherwise – that animates and impels its unfolding. In Milton's case, that purpose will *not* have been to contract with a certain bookseller or secure the services of a certain printer.[10]

Critics like Dobranski draw a wrong conclusion from a correct premise. The correct premise is by now a commonplace and I have already alluded to it: literature is not a privileged, uniquely complex and transcendent discourse, but is rather "one of many culturally productive discourses susceptible to critical analysis"[11] and on that level no different from any of the others. The wrong conclusion is *any* conclusion that follows from the premise, for all the premise tells you is that literature is historically situated and produced. But so is the sermon, the political pamphlet, the encyclopedia, the catechism, the rhetorical handbook, the formal oration, the eulogy. In order to take the next step, or any step, you have to attend to the specificity of the discourse that has solicited your attention, and that means attending to its history, not to history in general (there is no such thing) but to the history of a form.

Here we come, I think, to the crux of the matter. The mistake polemical historicists often make is to think that there is an opposition between criticism that attends to history and politics and criticism that attends to aesthetic forms. But as I have already argued, aesthetic forms have their own histories and those histories are almost always more than "merely" aesthetic. The debates in the period about stressed and unstressed verse, writing in Latin and writing in the vernacular, the virtues and defects of the Senecan and Ciceronian styles, the merits of rhyme and blank verse are unintelligible apart from the issues of nationalism, political authority and public morality thought to hang on the choice between these forms, and we cannot understand the force and meaning of literary forms without first understanding their implication in such issues. A criticism that focuses on aesthetic form is no less historical than any other, and, therefore, there can be no opposition between historical criticism and aesthetic criticism; rather, the opposition is between different kinds of historical criticism, and to the question which of the various histories is the one appropriate to the description and evaluation of literary works, the obvious, and indeed tautological, answer is the history of literary forms, so long as we remember that far from excluding social and political concerns, literary forms are, more often than not, their vehicles. As Ellen Rooney puts it, formalism, properly understood, "is a matter not of barring thematizations, but of refusing to reduce reading entirely to the elucidation, essentially the paraphrase, of themes – theoretical, ideological, or humanistic."[12]

It is the tendency of much criticism that labels itself historicist to go directly for those themes and to bypass the particular forms in which they are expressed. But when this happens no pertinence whatsoever is given to the fact that the discourse in question is a poem, and, therefore, there is no possibility of gauging (because one does not even recognize) the particular effectivity of poetic representation. Moreover, if one keeps in mind the laws of poetic representation – the assumptions and requirements that are part and parcel of a fully developed genre like the pastoral – one knows what questions to put to the materials that present themselves for incorporation into an interpretation. That is to say, literary criticism has the advantage of actually having a direction and a point (provided by the intentional structure of its object) while the historical criticism that has no method except to proclaim loudly, "We're historical and you're not!" often has neither. Informed only by the conviction that if it's a historical item, it's relevant, such a criticism, as Richard Strier has observed, ends up being nothing more than a series of mentionings. The mention in the text of any "item ... taken to be politically or culturally significant ... is sufficient to get the machinery of 'archeology' and archive-churning going."[13]

That machinery does, of course, generate things to notice. As Strier declares, "Much that is rich and strange is turned up"; but what is turned up cannot settle anything, cannot determine or even help you to determine what the text means. The moral is not that historical investigation is to be opposed "as such." Rather, as Mark Cousins points out, "All that is opposed ... is the claim that such investigations can *resolve* problems within the human sciences."[14] Of course, such investigations can indeed resolve problems within the discourse of history because it is within the framework of that discourse – a framework that defines the object of study and the appropriate means of studying it and identifying what is and is not relevant – that the problems are set and present themselves for consideration. What historical investigation as such cannot resolve are problems in other disciplines, for those other disciplines – literature, theology, anthropology, political science and so on – come equipped with their own stipulations of what is relevant and noticeable. There is no *general* transferability of observation from discipline to discipline and, therefore, it is a mistake to assume that conclusions reached in historical investigation as such are relevant to investigations undertaken in other domains. The question one most always asks is: What is pertinent to this particular production of the human mind undertaken in response to a particular disciplinary agenda and purpose? A criticism that does not ask this question and then guide itself by the answer is a criticism that can say nothing because it can say anything.

I began by observing that the best minds of our profession are attracted to this kind of criticism and indeed believe not only in its methodological superiority – despite the fact that it is without method – but in its moral superiority. Why? The answer is politics. The practitioners of cultural studies or cultural materialism generally situate themselves on the left and for them the rejection of formalist criticism is a political act that demonstrates their political virtue. As Mark Rasmussen puts it, it is a "tendency of contemporary academics to find their own post-modern alienation mirrored in the anxieties of works produced at the inception of modernity."[15] If you can link the so-called literary work with revolutionary sentiments, or with the crisis of the nation state, or with the emancipation of the liberal subject from the hegemony of religion and political tyranny, you're doing the Lord's, or rather the proletariat's, work. And it follows then that you must enroll your poet in the same standing and marching army. That's why so many critics have a stake in demonstrating that the Milton they admire professionally has the right political values – their values – and believe that if he were alive today he would be against the war in Iraq and for multiculturalism. Actually, Milton probably would have been a cheerleader for the war in Iraq and he would have been horrified, I think, by the tendency of multiculturalism in its stronger versions to forgo judgments of right and wrong in favor of an ever-expanding ethic of mutual respect. Not that any of that matters, at least for the question of why Milton matters; for as I have said over and over again, any answer to that question must be a literary answer in relation to which historical and political matters matter chiefly as the material of an aesthetic achievement. Describing and evaluating that achievement, which while it is often inconceivable apart from histor-ical and political concerns cannot be identified with them, is the proper business of literary criticism. It is not the proper business of literary criticism to pronounce grandly on the substantive issues an author chooses to raise in the course of implementing the intention to write a poem.

One last example, from popular culture. Jody Rosen has written a book entitled *White Christmas: The Story of an American Song.*[16] Rosen's inter-ests are broadly cultural and sociological. He discusses the shift from the urbane popular sound of Cole Porter to the more nostalgic and sentimen-tal music that began to appear in the early years of World War II when "White Christmas" was written and recorded, and he makes much of the fact that Irving Berlin, a Jewish immigrant from the Lower East Side, produced not only "White Christmas" but also "Easter Parade" and "God Bless America." But Rosen is a careful enough historian to note that Irving Berlin's thoughts about his music were of another kind. When Berlin finished "White Christmas" and showed it to his manager, he said, "Not only is it the best song *I* ever wrote, it's the best song *anybody* ever wrote." Or, in other words, I have soared above the Aonian Mount and written something the world will not willingly let die. That's his perspective on things, and it is also Milton's and it should be ours. If I might quote or misquote from the gospel according to James Carville, George Stephano-poulos and Bill Clinton, "It's the poetry, stupid."

NOTES

1 C.S. Lewis, *A Preface to "Paradise Lost"* (Oxford, 1942), 1.

2 Ellen Rooney, "Form and Contentment," *Modern Language Quarterly* 61 (March 2000), 19, 26, 28; *Revenge of the Aesthetic: The Place of Literature in Theory Today*, ed. Michael Clark (Berkeley and Los Angeles, 2000), 5; Richard Strier, "How Formalism Became a Dirty Word," in *Renaissance Literature and Its Formal Engagements*, ed. Mark Rasmussen (New York, 2002), 209.

3 Jeffrey Shoulson, "Milton and Enthusiasm: Radical Religion and the Poetics of *Paradise Regained*" (unpublished).

4 Raymond Williams, "Base and Superstructure in Marxist Cultural Theory," *Problems in Materialism and Culture* (London, 1980), 44.

5 It is not that fidelity to historical fact can never be pertinent to the evaluation of a film as film. If, for example, verisimilitude is a part of the director's claim, if he or she signals us that his or her intention is a documentary one as well as a narrative one, the question of responsibility to fact will be relevant to the cinematic achievement. That is why the objections put to Oliver Stone's movies about JFK and Richard Nixon are to the point, while objections to Mike Nichols's flow-of-traffic error are not. To some extent it is a question of

historical distance. The recent TV biopic about Ronald Reagan was criticized because some words spoken by the former president were obviously made up, or, at the very best, composite versions of what he might have said on one or more occasions. There was a feeling that there was something wrong about taking factual liberties with a still-living person. But when Reagan, early in his acting career, played George Custer to Errol Flynn's Jeb Stuart, no one seemed bothered by the fact that the two were far apart in age and had never actually met.

6 Raymond Williams, *The Country and the City* (New York, 1973), 15 ff.

7 See Douglas Bruster, "Shakespeare and the Composite Text," in Rasmussen, *Renaissance Literature*, 44: "New Formalism could be defined as follows: A critical genre dedicated to examining the social, cultural, and historical aspects of literary form, and the function of form for those who produce and consume literary texts. The New Formalism sees language and literary forms – from the single-lettered interjection 'O' to the stanza, the epic battle, and epic itself – as socially, politically, and historically 'thick.'" There is a danger that by arguing for the substantive content of literary forms, those forms are rendered merely instrumental in relation to that content. In this scenario, attention to aesthetic form is legitimized, but at the cost of denying it a value of its own, a value we traditionally take note of with words like "beautiful," "powerful," "stunning," "ingenious," "innovative," and "wow." See on this point Heather Dubrow, "Recuperating Formalism and the Country House Poem," in ibid., 85: "The assumption that formalism may once again become respectable simply because it can serve the needs of its host, historical and political criticism, relegates the formal to a secondary, supplementary role that neglects the depth and range of its contributions to style and meaning."

8 Stephen Dobranski, *Milton, Authorship, and the Book Trade* (Cambridge, 1999).

9 Ibid., 181; Jerome McGann, cited in ibid., 105.

10 See on this point Edward Pechter, "Making Love to Our Employment; or, The Immateriality of Arguments about the Materiality of the Shakespearean Text," *Textual Practice* 11 (1997), 54: "They [materialist accounts] demonstrate merely that Shakespeare's texts *may* be studied as an aspect of the history of printing ... and that if they are examined from within the assumptions of this discipline, Shakespeare will be produced not as an author ... but as a product of the early modern printing industry." This is a materialist version of one thousand monkeys pecking away on typewriters for many years and accidentally producing *King Lear*.

11 Stephen Cohen, cited in Rasmussen, *Renaissance Literature*, 26.

12 Rooney, "Form and Contentment," 29.

13 Richard Strier, "How Formalism Became a Dirty Word," 213.

14 Mark Cousins, "The Practice of Historical Investigation," *Post-Structuralism and the Question of History*, ed. Derek Attridge, Geoff Bennington and Robert Young (Cambridge, 1987), 128.

15 Rasmussen, *Renaissance Literature*, 2.

16 Jody Rosen, *White Christmas: The Story of an American Song* (New York, 2002).

CHAPTER 5

Milton in popular culture

What exactly does one do when one studies the presence of Milton in popular culture? What pleasures and/or illuminations does such study promise to provide? What's the point, finally, of a volume like this one? One answer to these questions is given several times in the volume itself in the twined form of a complaint and a claim. The complaint is that Milton's presence in popular culture has been "overlooked" (4) and the claim is that these essays will at least begin to redress this slight. But the notion of an "overlooked presence" is an odd one. Overlooked by whom? Not by the authors who have embedded it; they, after all, knew what they were doing and that they were doing it, in some sense, with Milton. Nor is it readers and viewers who overlook Milton's presence, for in the examples analyzed here the allusions to Milton are foregrounded and flagged. It must then be the scholarly community that has been insufficiently attentive to the continuing influence on popular culture of Milton's prose and poetry, perhaps (and this is more than hinted at) because too much attention has been paid to the influence of Shakespeare. One could say then (although it would be ungenerous to say it) that the spirit informing this collection is "popular culture-envy": our guy's presence is just as big as yours. If that's what's at issue, I am only too happy to grant the point: everywhere you look in popular culture Milton is there, and it's time for a movie titled *Milton in Love.* (Actually, it is.)

But of course more is at stake than bragging rights, and just what is at stake in individual essays and in the collection as a whole is a matter I would like to explore in this chapter. Let me begin by saying (and this is an assertion I will not argue for here) that there are three questions one can put to a text (verbal, iconic, filmic, historical, anthropological, etc.): (1) What does it mean? (2) What has it been taken to mean? (3) What has been done with or to it? (I borrow this tripartite formulation from Professor Andrew Koppleman of Northwestern Law School.) Only the first is an interpretive question. The second is a question of reception history. The difference between the two is that one question has a right and a wrong answer (indeed many wrong answers), while the other has as many answers as there have been historical efforts of interpretation. The question "Is Satan the hero of *Paradise Lost*?" is an interpretive question to which the appropriate responses are "yes," "no," "yes and no," or "I'm not sure." Those who ask the question are trying to determine what Milton was getting at, what he intended. (To be sure, one might conclude that Milton intended Satan to be the hero, but failed in that intention, or, alternatively, that he intended an indictment of Satan, but failed in *that* intention; nevertheless, whatever one concluded, the conclusion would have been reached in the context of an attempt to fix Milton's intention.) But the question: "Did the Romantics think that Satan is the hero of *Paradise Lost*?" is a question about *them*, and not a question about Milton or *Paradise Lost*. One can answer "yes" without in any way being committed to the thesis that Satan is the hero of *Paradise Lost*. It would make perfect sense to say: "Yes, the Romantics did think that, but they were wrong," that is, to answer both the interpretive question and the historical question, as you would also be doing if you said: "Yes, the Romantics did think that, and they were right."

Either question is legitimate and the basis of a real project (interpreting a literary work and/or studying the interpretations offered for a literary work). It is important, however, to remember that they are distinct and independent of one another, which means, among other things, that answers to the historical question (what have people made of *Paradise Lost*?) are in no way answers or even parts of answers to the interpretive question (what does *Paradise Lost* mean?). It cannot be evidence for the Satanic reading that many have held it, even if among those many are Blake, Shelley, Empson and Philip Pullman. That's a piece of historical data, not an interpretive argument. When Stephen Burt tells us that "Pullman opposes institutional religion, takes the side of rebels in cosmic war against divine and civil authority, [and] endorses the temptation of his new Eve" (5), one cannot draw a line from his observations (assuming that you are persuaded of their truth) to some observation about *Paradise Lost*. What you can do, and what Lauren Shohet appears to be doing at times, is register your agreement with Pullman's reading or "engagement" (60) of *Paradise Lost*. But Pullman's agreement with your reading of *Paradise Lost* cannot be a reason for your having that reading, although it can provide reinforcement (of a psychological kind) for a reading you have come to on other grounds, the grounds appropriate to an interpretive conclusion, such as, for example, the grounds provided (at least argumentatively) by close readings or by statements of authorial intention ("justifie the wayes of God to men") or by quarrying *The Christian Doctrine.*

It follows, then, that the essays in a volume entitled *Milton in Popular Culture* are unlikely to be interpretive in their aim. That is, they will not typically offer answers to the question: "What does this or that production of Milton's mean?" and they will only occasionally refer to landmarks in the history of the effort to answer that question; they will usually not be doing reception studies. Rather, they will be doing what we might call "appropriation studies" and thereby offering an answer to the third question, "What has been done to or with Milton?" There are at least two things one can do with or to an author – compete with him or use him. (Or her, but because it is Milton we're talking about here, I'll stick with "him.") Someone who competes with an author may also be interpreting him, as Steven Brust does, according to Diana Benet, in *To Reign in Hell.* Brust's "version of events," Benet says, "offers a flat contradiction to the assumptions and items of faith that underlie *Paradise Lost*" (35). Of course you can only offer a contradiction to the assumptions of Milton's epic if you have already identified them, if, that is, you already have a reading of the poem. But the contradiction you then offer is not itself a reading: it is a departure. Nor is it, despite Benet's use of the term, an "anti-reading of Milton" (35). It isn't *any* reading of Milton. Brust is "anti" Milton only in the sense that he disputes Milton's account of theodicy. The relationship between the two is one of rival interpreters rather than one of interpreter to the object of his interpretation. Neither is it quite right to say that Brust's is a "dissident rewriting of Milton's rebellion" (44). It is a rewriting of the rebellion in Heaven in opposition to Milton's; it is another (not a re-) writing; it is an independent work.

To say this, however, is not to say that *To Reign in Hell* is entirely independent of Milton. Obviously Brust takes off from Milton, alludes to him, plays against him, appropriates him, uses him, all things that Milton does to others as Laura Knoppers and Gregory Semenza point out: "Milton courses typically begin with discussion of texts that Milton himself had appropriated: Homer's *Iliad* and *Odyssey*, Virgil's *Aeneid*..."(15). Knoppers and Semenza then cite Milton's appropriate practice as a justification for the present volume: "We are suggesting that it is equally useful and important to introduce students to some of the films, books, music, and digital materials that adapt and appropriate Milton in our own time" (15). But I'm not sure that the parallel (and the justification) quite works. We are interested in Milton's appropriations of earlier authors because we hope

that studying them will throw light on his achievement and help us identify his meanings; however we might value Homer and Virgil, our interest in them is, for purposes of this kind of exercise, parasitic on our interest in him. It is because we care about Milton that we investigate his sources. Do we care about Pullman, Brust, Billy Wilder, James Whale and Taylor Hackford in the same way? It may be the achievement of these essays to make us care, but even if this is so (as I think it is), it is still not obvious as a *general* proposition that introducing students to modern appropriations of Milton is "useful and important," and one must ask, useful to what end? (The question would not arise in the cases of C.S. Lewis, Malcolm X and Helen Keller, each of whom enjoys a status that automatically legitimates any effort to learn more about him or her.) The answer, as we have seen, cannot be "to the end of advancing our understanding of Milton," for understanding Milton is a normative project aimed at getting the right account of an event (purposive authorship) that happened in the past. Appropriations are made possible by that event, but they can't be read back into the event and made into an account of its meaning. (They use him, not the other way around.)

Unless, of course, one has a theory of meaning as something always evolving and never fixed. Occasionally the essays in this volume seem at least to flirt with such a theory. In their introduction Knoppers and Semenza declare that "the model of reading Milton in popular culture must necessarily move away from prioritizing authorial intention and original meaning to a more fluid model of production and consumption, in which new meanings are generated" (6). Meanings of what? They cannot be Milton's meanings – they are what is being moved away from – and therefore they cannot be the meanings of Milton's work. They can be meanings Milton's work has provoked, but that is another matter. There is a great difference between the question: "What does Milton mean?" – a question to which, as I have said, there can be only one right answer – and the question: "What meanings occur to people who are reading Milton?" – a question to which the answers are literally innumerable. It is certainly true to say, as Knoppers and Semenza do, that when "Milton's texts are detached from their initial authority ... they are open to a plurality of reinterpretations" (6). But "open" and "plurality" may be words too modest to describe what happens when a text is detached from authorial authority: "wide-open" and "infinite number" would be more accurate. There is no end to what can be made of a text untethered from the intentional context of its production. You can quite literally do anything you like with it, and then, if you get tired of what you have done, you can do something else, and on and on and on.

But that may be just the point. The justification for studying Milton in popular culture is not the light thrown on Milton (he can take neither blame nor credit for the fecundity generated by interactions with his work), but the light thrown on the workings of popular culture. Stephen Burt observes that popular appropriations of Milton can go "where more responsible (or intentionalist) readings of Milton may not go" (48). And Lauren Shohet gives his insight a colloquial turn when she declares: "Popular culture is promiscuous" and remarks on "the vast untidiness of interbreeding popular cultures" (69). There may be too much moralism in these statements with their implied binaries: responsible versus irresponsible, faithful (and monogamous) versus promiscuous, neat and orderly versus untidy. These distinctions would make sense only if popular culture were a form (or "model") of interpretation, if, that is, it were the purpose of popular culture to get Milton (or anyone) right. Popular culture isn't in the business of being faithful or responsible or orderly. Popular culture is in the business of being inventive, of showing audiences tricks (of plot, imagery, scenery, special effects) they have never seen before, and of (sometimes) employing as its vehicle the canonical texts it rewrites, parodies, eviscerates, and abandons as it wishes. The glorious thing about popular culture is that it has no rules (at least not rules of interpretive fidelity), and that is why it is not a form of interpretation and also why it cannot be to the point to say of a canonical work taken up by popular culture that it has been distorted. When Douglas Howard wonders whether *Animal House* is a "misappropriation" of Milton (166), he needn't have worried. In the context of what popular culture is and does, misappropriation – an accusation that assumes a normative project – is impossible. The act of appropriation always takes place from the perspective of the appropriator and what is appropriate is whatever he or she chooses to do. With respect to popular culture, the vocabulary of praise and blame is not right/wrong, accurate/inaccurate, appropriate/inappropriate, but fun/boring, ingenious/imitative, original/derivative.

Just as it would be wrong to criticize popular culture for being unfaithful to the canonical materials it appropriates, so would it be wrong to praise it for being transgressive. (Sometimes it is; sometimes it isn't.) If popular culture shouldn't be depreciated in relation to standards (like interpretive fidelity) it should not be held to, neither should it be romanticized, as Shohet romanticizes it when she claims that "popular culture may be uniquely positioned to maintain the vitality of the most important questions (reading, democracy)" (69), and when she credits popular culture in general and Pullman's novels in particular with keeping "dissenting reading alive" (60). First, I am not at all sure that I know what "dissenting reading" is. If it is merely another term for readings that disagree with readings already established, then there is nothing *generally* dissenting about such readings; they may dissent from a current orthodoxy but only with the hope of establishing a new one. If, on the other hand, dissenting reading is the name of a general project, the project is not interpretive but political. Its politics is rooted in the assumption that there cannot be a right answer – a right reading – and that therefore whenever a so-called right reading has established itself it can only have done so through an exercise of power that must be resisted. Dissenting reading supposedly performs that resistance. Its first principle is that there can be no first principle; therefore settled readings must be overthrown, not because they are wrong, but because the very idea of a right or wrong reading is an illegitimate imposition of a hegemonic authority. Popular culture, precisely because it is promiscuous and unfaithful to authorial meaning, is a particularly powerful agent of this revolutionary, destabilizing impulse. Or so the story goes.

There are two mistakes here. The first is to think that because interpretations are disputed and no independent measure for settling interpretive disputes exists, there is no right answer to the question: "What does a poem (or novel or film or painting or, for that matter, a sentence) mean?" But there is always a right answer – a poem means what its author intends it to mean – and the fact that there are various candidates for that answer and no mechanical way of choosing between them tells us not that the enterprise of figuring out the right answer is misguided or impossible, but that it is difficult and not always certain of success. So that when readers of popular culture become aware (as they sometimes do) of "previous readings" and are thereby "alerted to the possibility of disagreement" (60), there are no interpretive implications to their awareness. (The appropriate action in the arena of disagreement is not to throw up your hands, but to take sides.) Neither are there any political implications (this is the second mistake). The possibility (and even inevitability) of disagreement does not direct us to mistrust firm answers to the question: "What does a poem mean?"; we distrust a particular answer to that question because we have not been persuaded of it, and the judgment that we have not been persuaded of it makes sense only if there is an answer to which we might be persuaded. (Can there be a general rule of thought that says one shall never be persuaded?) There is then no obligation, interpretive or political, to keep dissenting reading alive. Now, as a matter of fact, some (perhaps many) works of popular culture have the aim of dissenting from established views. If that is so in the case of a particular work, the interpreter is obliged to note it, not because he or she is keeping anything alive, but because one should always tell the truth about the objects of one's interpretive efforts. This obligation is not unique to the objects to which we give the label "popular culture"; it is a general obligation in force whenever we turn our intention to a purposive or designed composition (of words, colors, stone, notes, etc.).

What I have been trying to do in the previous paragraphs is to free popular culture, first from the thralldom of its opposite (high culture) – it should be allowed to be what it is – and second from the imperative – a political imperative and one external to its forms – to be always dissenting. As I have already said, some popular culture is dissenting and some isn't, and the same can be said of the high culture artifacts (like *Paradise Lost*) of which popular culture often makes use, a use that has no necessary political direction, whether it be democracy or any other. My counsel would be to take popular culture on its own terms, and within those terms pose the usual questions: What are its aims? How does it work? What pleasures and/or illuminations does it provide? In general, the answers to these questions will follow from the designation "popular." The intended audience is large, the premium is on novelty (not of ideas, but of forms), the admired skill is experimentation, the media are multiple, and there is a willingness, though not a determination, to be ephemeral. Popular culture can have any content, any morality (or no morality) and any relation or nonrelation to the political issues of the day. Popular culture, in short, is a *formal* category, and it remains so even when the materials it quarries are distinguished by their moral, political, religious and philosophical content. The essays in a volume entitled *Milton in Popular Culture* are likely, then, to tell you more about popular culture than about Milton.

But as J.L. Austin often quipped, after having said it, I now get to the part where I take it back. These essays do tell us something about Milton. They tell us that in the popular imagination the Satanic reading of *Paradise Lost* is the right one. And they tell us, as Knoppers and Semenza predict they will, that Milton is a "vital living part of contemporary culture" (6). And at least four of them, in contradiction to everything I have asserted here, tell us something about the interpretation of Milton. The two essays on the 1954 and 1995 versions of the movie *Sabrina* are at once sophisticated analyses of different directorial styles and perceptive comments on the relationships between sex, marriage and commerce in *Comus*. Catherine Gimelli Martin poses the right question: "Does an unearthly stream deity really have anything to do with Fairchild's quixotic daughter, who unlike Milton's Lady, never confronts a truly treacherous, Comus-like seducer or requires two guardian brothers, an Attendant Spirit, and a water sprite to free her?" (141). The answer, she declares, reveals "surprising continuities not only between the moral vision of Milton, Taylor, and Wilder, but also between the Protestant ethic of seventeenth-century England and 1950s America" (141). Martin then proceeds to explain how in the film the Lady's brothers are turned into the two L'Allegro-like and Il Penseroso-like suitors for the hand of the magical Sabrina, a chaste nymph and a Paris-educated sophisticate, who is both the bridge and the prize between them. The result is a myth that is at once new and a Hollywood updating of the myth Milton and Spenser so powerfully promoted, the myth of "an idealistic cultural synthesizer" (149), the vehicle of whose magic is the bourgeois institution of marriage. In her essay, Julie Kim shows how, in Sidney Pollack's version of the story, Sabrina is ultimately controlled by men. Her "commodification" (161) is never challenged, much less resolved, and at the film's conclusion, Sabrina, always and already the object of desire, is returned back to her "'rightful owner' – as the Lady is returned to the proper guardianship/ownership of her male relatives" (161). It seems, muses Kim, that "Despite the lapse of over three hundred years between *Comus* and *Sabrina,* there is a "continuity of discourse on female sexuality deliberately fused with economic metaphor" (161). After reading these essays one wants both to see the movies again and to read *Comus* again.

One feels the same about revisiting *Paradise Regained, Samson Agonistes,* and Taylor Hackford's *The Devil's Advocate* when Ryan Netzley shows how the much-criticized "twist" ending of the film – the hero, flush from a successful resistance to temptation (if only in a dream), falls in what seems a moment of casual interaction with a reporter – is a critique of the film's more spectacular dramatic centerpiece in which our hero kills himself rather than submit to Satan's demand that he copulate with his sister. Anyone, Taylor seems to be telling us, can recognize the ethical imperative of not committing incest. A more acute and subtle morality asks us to recognize the ethical dangers residing in the most ordinary social occasions. One refuses the lure of forbidden sexuality and emerges triumphant; one agrees to talk to a reporter about having done the "right thing" and falls. The film, Netzley argues, "problematizes such confident ethical assurance" (122) in the same way that Milton does in the brief epic and the closet drama. Just as Milton rejects spectacle for quiet inner resolution in his work, so does Taylor undercut spectacle at its most spectacular (and remember that Samson's pulling down of the temple occurs offstage; the true moral drama is elsewhere) by daring to dissipate and undercut the theatrics of his cinematic climax. To the extent one is persuaded by Netzley's analysis, one is also persuaded to a reading of Milton. So too with Laura Knoppers' reading of *Bride of Frankenstein*. Alternating between discussions of the Satan of *Paradise Lost*, tormented by his loneliness, and by the sight of Adam and Eve emparadised in each other's arms, and the Monster searching vainly for a friend and a soul-mate, Knoppers traces the literary and filmic career of the "lonely Creature" and establishes the enduring power of "Miltonic language of loneliness" (106). Before reading Knoppers's essay, one might have thought that our poet of loneliness was Roy Orbison, not Milton, but now one knows better.

I realize as I conclude this chapter that there are more than a few essays I have slighted. Please do not regard my failure to discuss a particular essay as a judgment on it. The judgment should be directed at the personal obsessions (with certain theoretical questions) that have led me to a disproportionate (and at times churlish) account of a volume that is uniformly rewarding. To the readers of that volume I issue an imperative in keeping, I think, with the spirit and achievement of popular culture: Enjoy!

CHAPTER 6

How the reviews work

It is time to say aloud what I have always known: much of my work on Milton has been a gloss on a single sentence in Thomas Kranidas's *The Fierce Equation*: "Milton is accused of being improper, while Milton accuses his enemies of being wrong" (101). That is (and this is still more of the gloss), for Milton, merely external decorums – whether of style, sentence length, vocabulary, prayer, marriage, and anything else you can think of – are themselves *in*decorous if they do not issue from an inner decorum that is achieved only by being allied steadfastly to the source of being. This means (among other things) that one cannot judge an action – tearing down the Philistine temple, deciding to fall with and for Eve, rejecting an opportunity to feed the hungry – by its apparent virtue with respect to a system of public or domestic values. Instead, the only judgment that counts (and not everyone is capable of rendering it; it takes one to know one) is the judgment as to whether or not the action is an expression of a loyalty that is entirely interior and therefore not available to empirical verification. By this logic, Milton's "intemperate" language (and this again is part of Kranidas's point) is finally more decorous than the milder language of his opponents because its vehemence is an outward manifestation of the poet's commitment to a master and overriding truth; while, on the other hand, the commitments of his polemical opponents are (or so he would say and often did say) merely strategic and therefore cosmetic and therefore false. And since truth or falsity are here to be understood not as properties of objects or utterances but as properties of what we have come to call "subject positions" (the key question is the Augustinian one: whom do you love?), one cannot calculate the worth or propriety of anything by inspecting surfaces and appearances, a lesson the Satan of *Paradise Regained* never learns and never could learn so long as he remains Satan.

It is this Milton that I have described in *How Milton Works*, and it is safe to say that many have resisted my description and indeed recoiled from it. In what follows I will attempt to account for that resistance and to read it as an instance of something larger than mere disagreement with a single literary scholar. I do this with some trepidation, for an author who responds to the strictures of his critics risks sounding at best defensive and at worst pathetic. Nevertheless, I am going to court that risk, in part because the book in question is in all likelihood the last extended piece of literary criticism I shall publish, but mostly because, as a corpus, the reviews of that book constitute a cultural document that is interesting in its own right.

One thing that is interesting about the reviews is that often *How Milton Works* is only an incidental target of their criticism. They have – if I may avail myself of a metaphor I heartily dislike when others use it – bigger fish to fry, occasionally as big as America herself and everything she is thought to stand for. Here, for example, is John Carey, who, after wrongly attributing to me the thesis "that it is impossible to criticize the assumptions of any culture," instances as one assumption worthy of criticism "America's assumption . . . that it has a right to a disproportionate share of the world's resources" (*The Sunday Times*, June 24, 2001, p. 35). By implication – certainly not by anything like an argument – this assumption is one I at least approve and perhaps reinforce, and later in the review I am put into the same relationship of complicity with "America's self-righteousness" and its material vehicle, "its nuclear armory" (36). No one would want to defend an author who advocated nuclear warfare and applauded America for disregarding the rights and needs of non-Americans, but I am not that author and *How Milton Works* is not about American foreign policy.

Other negative reviewers have a smaller target, not America and its imperial ambitions but American scholarship, although perhaps the latter is regarded as a stand-in for the former: just as America is brash, overweening, domineering and basically vulgar, so are American literary critics, and especially Stanley Fish – or, rather, Morris Zapp, for a number of reviewers, after noting that David Lodge based his fictional character in part on me, go on to review Zapp and the American style criticism he supposedly incarnates. John Mullan in *The Guardian* in quick succession identifies me as "one of the big punchers of the academic world" in "the US" – here the image, barely below the surface, is once again of a pugilistic America where academic bullies like me flourish – and then segues to Zapp, described as "a ruthlessly professional professor from California," before returning to Stanley Fish, "the sharp publicity seeker," who in the years since *Surprised by Sin* has become "even more successful and even more like a creature from some satire upon academic mores." It is perhaps Mullan's habit of conflating the fictional character with the real-life academic that leads him to attribute my scholarly production to being "unhampered by too much in the way of teaching commitments." This is empirically false – my teaching schedule is a matter of public record – and perhaps libelous; it is also false to say, as Mullan does in the same paragraph, that, in my view, "there is no truth." If there is an unconcern for truth and accuracy here, it is Mullan's not mine.

In somewhat the same spirit, the anonymous reviewer in *The Economist* declares me to be "the most eminent provocateur in America's Eng-lit establishment" (June 16, 2001). It is clear from this and others of his or her observations that the villain in the piece is as much the American Eng-lit establishment as it is I. This is certainly the case for Alastair Fowler, who worries over the puzzle of a book that in his opinion is "hardly . . . worth reading" (*Times Literary Supplement*, August 31, 2001), yet nevertheless comes trailing clouds of blurbs from the likes of Stephen Greenblatt and Elaine Showalter. How to explain, he wonders, "Fish's extraordinary reputation on the other side of the Atlantic?" It may "have more to do," he explains, with Fish "having been a Professor of English and Law"; for since Americans are citizens of a "highly litigious country," and are burdened with a constitution "with . . . contradictory rights," they "are easily impressed by legal performance." There's a lot of huffing and puffing going on here and one doesn't quite know what is animating it, but a hint may be provided in another of Mullan's characterizations of Morris Zapp: "he is openly disdainful of his muddle-headed, shabbily dressed British counterparts, who are apparently incapable of publishing the necessary paradigm-shattering books." It all comes together: these British reviewers recognize and lament the fact – for which they and their colleagues on *that* side of the Atlantic are largely responsible – that Milton studies and indeed British literary studies in general have long ago been taken over by imperialist Americans who commit the unpardonable sin of being the better commentators on a literature not properly theirs by birth and nationality. This is of course perfectly true. Almost all literary criticism of British authors worth reading is produced by Americans and Canadians, and the few exceptions to that general rule emigrate to America and to American universities as fast as they can.

To be sure, there are reviewers who do begin by actually reviewing Stanley Fish rather than Morris Zapp or American hegemony, but more than a few of them have some difficulty getting around to Stanley Fish, the author of *this* book. They are more interested in Stanley Fish, the "guru of postmodern subjectivism" (Michael Potemra, *National Review*, August 6, 2001) or the "postmodernist gadfly" (Matthew Price in *Lingua Franca*, August 7, 2001) or the "Manichean Deconstructionist" (A.D. Nuttall, in *The London Review of Books*, June 21, 2001). Fowler puts a kind of statistical face on this characterization when he complains that while deconstructionist critics like Derrida, Herman Rappaport, Mary Nyquist and Marshall Grossman are indexed, his favorite critics – John Leonard (his student), Philip Gallagher (my one-time student, who is in fact indexed) and James Nohrenberg (his sometime colleague) – are not. In fact, Derrida is briefly brought into one chapter and is then sent away as a thinker relevant only up to a point, and the critics most prominently displayed (and celebrated) in the book are Leavis, John Crow Ransom, Donald Davie, Northrop Frye, Barbara Lewalski, J.M. Evans, B.A. Rajan and Rosemond Tuve, hardly a list of wild-eyed nihilists. The truth is that there is nothing particularly postmodern about the book or the Milton it presents, a Milton who, rather than rejecting master narratives and absolute truths, builds everything on the absolute truth of one master narrative and the obligations – for men and angels – that follow from it.

And finally – at least in this little subset of critics – there are those who almost get to *How Milton Works*, but first have to stop, as John Leonard (*The New York Review of Books*, July 18, 2001), for example, does, to tell a story about the career of its author. The story goes this way: once upon a time in a galaxy far away, a bright young man just setting out in professional life wrote a wonderful pathbreaking book everyone admired. Now he returns to the scene of his early success; but, infected with bad theoretical ideas and showing the signs of age if not senility, he has produced a volume only occasionally graced by flashes of his former powers. Would that at least the first half of this tale were true. But, again in fact, *Surprised by Sin* was initially met by the same mixture of praise and condemnation that characterizes the reviews of *How Milton Works*. Here, for example, is the evidence provided by Gary Olson, now provost at the University of Florida at St. Petersburg. Olson recalls a day in his graduate Milton class when the instructor came in brandishing a book and saying of it, "This . . . is an abomination! This is *not* how you read Milton, and it's *not* how you do literary criticism! Don't waste your time and money on such drivel!" Needless to say, Olson reports, he and all the other students immediately "ordered copies of this forbidden fruit to discover what magic resided there" (*Justifying Belief*, 2002, p.1). Even in the more favorable reviews of *Surprised by Sin*, there were occasional sentences that presaged some of the negative judgments on *How Milton Works*. Bernard Bergonzi, for example, spoke in *The Guardian* of the book as "a gleamingly efficient product of the best kind of American graduate school training," as if to say, "not only do they manufacture washing machines and big ice boxes, they write scholarly books of the same meretricious glitter."

It's time to get to the heart of things, to the account offered in the reviews of the book itself, and especially those accounts that are hostile. After all, there is little I can say about or do with reviews that announce "No one else could have written this book" (Dennis Kezar, *JEGP*, April 2003, p. 310) or, less ambiguously, "this book takes its place among the finest commentaries on Milton" (Albert Labriola, *Choice*, December, 2001), or "A masterful study, indispensable for anyone who reads Milton" (Bryce Christensen, *Booklist*, April 7, 2001) or (my favorite): "If St. Augustine were to come back from the grave … he could not have done better than Fish does here" (Edward T. Oakes, *First Things*, November, 2001, p. 26), or (and this is advice I would not give): "Any reader interested in tracking an encounter across time of one bottomlessly inquisitive, endlessly skeptical 17th century mind with a similarly oriented 21st century writer … would be advised to stash this book in their beach bag" (*Publishers Weekly*, June 25, 2001), or: "Fish reminds us he's a world-class Miltonist, brilliantly distilling a distinct vision of the great poet's thought for another generation of readers" (*Publishers Weekly*, "The Year in Books," November, 2001, p. 41).

But of course that's just the question: even if the vision is distinct – that is, sharply presented – is it answerable to Milton's achievement? Is it on the right track or is it just horribly wrong? Well, before a reviewer can answer that question he or she must understand what the distinct vision of *How Milton Works* is, and on that score a number of reviewers fail the course, usually by getting only one half of the thesis, the half that presents a Milton who insists on an absolute fidelity to a single obligation, the obligation, first, to discern the will of God, and then to do it. Here, for example, is the reviewer in *The Economist*. According to Fish, "For Milton, all value and all good action depend on obedience to the will of God. Those who seek to obey the will of God see the world in an entirely different way from those who do not … As Mr. Fish puts it, 'what you believe is what you see is what you are is what you do.'" The verdict? "This position is not itself interesting, nor could you imagine it producing great poetry." Right on both counts, wrong in asserting that that is my position or at least the whole of it. The half left out – although I rehearse it obsessively every few pages and at the beginning and end of most chapters – is the half that emphasizes the difficulty, both for fallen and unfallen creatures, first of discerning God's will in the midst of signs pointing in multiple directions, and the subsequent difficulty of determining what course of action among the many possible would be the appropriate vehicle of obeying that will if it in fact – a fact never perspicuous in mortal life – has been discerned. Absolute certainty about what is to be done, absolute uncertainty – in the sense that one's decisions will not be given an immediate grade by the world or by God – about how exactly to do it or about whether it has been correctly done, and therefore a life full of crisis, anxiety and provisionality, not because the world and its meanings are finally provisional and multiple and context-bound, but because we are.

What this means for the poetry is that the pressure of the single obligation is responded to in the context of a variegated world that is replete with many proffered obligations, each of which offers itself as the true one, and we are left with the task – impossible to complete but necessary to prosecute – of choosing the right one. It follows then that the "material" of every moment – in life and in the poetry – is the material of difference, of all the alternative paths and loyalties (fame, beauty, heroism, Eve) that beckon to us, but at the same time (not a phrase lightly intended) difference is not offered us to be embraced (in the name of pluralism or multiple values or natural fecundity) – as Satan embraces the ethic of multiple stories when he says of the War in Heaven, "We style it the strife of glory"; you live in your epic, we'll live in ours, thank you – rather, difference is offered as the unavoidable condition within which we must at least try to make our way toward the identification and worship of the One. Here is how I put it in one place: "The law is simply to do the will of God, to align one's actions with His great design. The difficulty is in knowing, in particular circumstances, what that will is" (500–501). And since it is in particular circumstances that we live and read, the difficulty will make up the bulk of our experience; the mistake would be to make a divinity of it, to honor it above the goal waiting for us on the other side of its landscape. Thus, as I say in another passage, Milton's is "a vision that unites monism and the proliferation of difference; there is only one Truth and it is everywhere the same . . . but its unmediated form is not available to us in our present state and we must rely on whatever state of illumination we may have reached while at the same time resisting the temptation to identify that state with the fuller one we shall know at our master's second coming" (501–502). That temptation is what impels the poetry forward; surrendering to it is the error made available to us in every line. The result is an experience informed both by a relentless sense of single obligation and an acknowledgment of everything that stands between us and the face-to-face encounter with that singleness.

This is what the *Economist* reviewer misses. He or she is correct to say that Milton "understood that people live each day within a variety of value systems," but it is a mistake to say that "the Milton described by Mr. Fish" is "hard as a rock, obsessed by a single, all-encompassing belief that obedience to God's will is the only value in the universe." No, it is not my thesis that Milton believes that there is only one value, but that there is one value that always trumps other values, even those that might command a quite blameless allegiance were they not being offered – as they are for instance at the moment of Adam's fall – as substitutes for, or as reasonable alternatives to, the value of being faithful to the source of being. And as a dramatist of our moral condition, Milton is interested in just those moments when such a configuration of choice – between a good or value that at almost any other time would be the proper object of our embrace and the good or value in the absence of which judgment itself would be unintelligible – offers itself. That is what I mean by the statement both John Leonard and John Carey deride: "In Milton's world, there are no moral ambiguities." Leonard, in *The New York Review of Books*, points out in triumph that I also promise at one point to discuss the ambiguities and dilemmas of the moral life. Gotcha! Well, no. The imperative to obey God's will and remain faithful to him is unambiguous and in competition with it, any other imperative, no matter how laudable it might be in moments less sharply poised, simply loses its content and value and in a sense does not exist. When Adam must decide what to do in the wake of Eve's disobedience, he is *not* enmeshed in a moral dilemma. What he does is not morally ambiguous, but simply morally mistaken. What *is* ambiguous, especially in the postlapsarian world, are the signs pointing to the location, in this particular situation, of the master imperative of obedience. Should I stay at the mill, laboring for my daily bread, or should I go to the temple and tear it down? Where does the path of obedience lie? Plenty of ambiguities there and elsewhere in Milton's work, but it is still true to say, and I say it again, in Milton's world there are no *moral* ambiguities.

What some critics miss, others see, but see as a contradiction. Eugene Hill complains that my view of Milton as an "Augustinian fundamentalist" – a view he regards as "a caricature of Milton's religion" – combines "oddly" with "an existential uncertainty that recalls Raymond Chandler's detective" (*Kritikon Litterarum*, 29, 2002, pp. 73–74). Nothing odd about it; that's what makes the whole thing work and be exciting and dynamic even though it is rooted in stasis. A.D. Nuttall observes that "in one place [Fish] writes that knowledge and truth are not, for Milton, linked to objects, but are 'inward dispositions . . .,' in another that Milton was 'a hard core objectivist.'" And again, "having argued for Milton's preference for stillness over journeying and action . . . very near the end of the book he suddenly allows, in a lucid interval, the poet's fierce interest in perpetual progression. A page or two later, however, he is once more reasserting Milton's monism." At the very beginning of the book I explain, and then re-explain at regular intervals, how monism – the argument that at bottom difference is the order of the same – is perfectly consistent with the insight that apprehending the sameness in difference – determining the still center of objectivity in a world of shifting perspectives – is an endless and difficult challenge and one that Milton is forever re-presenting.

If you don't see the centrality of that challenge to Milton's project and if you don't see the obligation at its heart, the obligation to affirm oneness in the face of a forever self-renewing diversity, you will miss some of the great moments in Milton's poetry, and thereby mis-recognize what counts for Milton as poetic beauty. And then you will say with Helen Vendler, that "Fish does not care much for the poetry of Milton's poetry" (*The New Republic*, July 30, 2001, p. 381). She means by that that I do not pay much attention to "sorts of different rhymes and line lengths" or to the "mixture of speeches and songs" in a production like *Comus*. Instead, she complains, there is "always a grim reduction to theme" and "always the same theme." That's right, for it is in the context of that theme – of the tension between the attractiveness of variety and the imperative of obedience – that the most powerful poetic moments occur. When Adam rehearses for nearly twenty lines the many and nuanced reasons for his decision to fall with Eve, the Son of God replies with four words: "Was she thy God?" The question cuts through everything Adam has said and does not so much respond to his points but declares them unreal in a gesture of almost unbearable clarity. Now that's poetry, Milton style, as is a similar moment in *Paradise Regained* when, in response to nearly thirty lines of Satanic sophistry, culminating in a request for access, the Son neatly and concisely steps out of the trap: "Thy coming hither, though I know thy scope / I bid not or forbid; do as thou find'st / Permission from above; thou canst not more." The quiet elegance of this performance – by limiting the scope of Satan's action, the Son limits his own, neither embracing Satan nor sending him away – is then matched by the even more concise elegance of the epic voice who says simply "He added not."

He didn't swerve in either direction; he didn't say one extra, and perhaps self-diverting word, and neither will I. *He* added not too.

Of course Milton is perfectly capable of other poetic effects, including the deployment of puns. But his puns are not like Shakespeare's, kaleido-scopic, exploding, ever expanding in their significance; rather they are tied to the theme of which Vendler complains, and rather than opening out return invariably to the lesson the poetry is always teaching. I devote some pages to these puns, and to my great surprise, a number of reviewers, including Vendler, have been unpersuaded and even upset by them. Two in particular have drawn the ire of my critics. I say that when haemony is described by the Attendant Spirit as an "unsightly root," unsightly means both unattractive and not available to sight. Thomas Wheeler objects that the *Oxford English Dictionary* (*OED*) does not recognize this meaning and, moreover, cites this very passage "to support the meaning *unattractive*" (*Sewanee Review*, Fall, 2001, p. 598). The same *OED* however glosses "viewless" as invisible, or incapable of being seen and cites as an instance line 92b of *Comus*: "I must be viewless now." I must be the opposite of viewable. The negative suffix reverses the root meaning. And the same *OED* again reports that the primary meaning of "sightly" in the period is "visible" which might very well suggest to Milton the possibility of using the negative prefix to reverse that meaning; un-sightly, not visible, incapable of being seen. My contention of course is that Milton intends both meanings: haemony is unattractive to those who are incapable of seeing its true properties, those for whom those properties are invisible, un-sightly. In my reading of Milton, this wordplay makes perfect sense given a moral aesthetic in which inner, secret meanings and values are always preferred to the meanings and values of mere appearances.

A second claimed pun has provoked even more consternation. It is the pun on rais'd, rased and razed – elevated, erased and destroyed – found, at least by me, in many lines of *Paradise Lost*, from "Satan exalted sat, by merit rais'd / To that bad eminence" to Satan's claim of being "self-begot, self rais'd," to God's promise to "dissolve / Satan with his perverted world, then raise / From the conflagrant mass, purged and destroyed / New Heavens" to the moment when Satan is said to have "gently rais'd" the fainting courage of his troops. It is this last that has been most fiercely resisted. Frank Kermode (in *New York Times Book Review*, June 24, 2001) merely says that it is "far-fetched" to claim that "rais'd" here means "not only what it seems to mean, but its opposite, raz'd" (12). Perez Zagorin avers that "all we need to do is to think of the alternate phrase 'gently raz'd' to see how improbable it is" (*Virginia Quarterly Review*, vol. 78, no. 4, p. 738).

Exactly! That is, in my analysis, the reason Milton would deploy the pun: he wants to disallow Satan the deep reality of the surface virtue he appears to display, just as later Gabriel will not allow Satan to claim the virtue of faithfulness: "O sacred name of faithfulness profaned! / Faithful to whom? To thy rebellious crew? / Army of fiends." That is, if the object of your faithfulness is unworthy – if you are faithful to fiends – then you lose the name of the virtue. And, by the same reasoning, if you are gently urging a course of action that will inevitably destroy those who take it, you have profaned the sacred name of gentleness and no longer have title to it. You are not raising your followers, but razing them in the guise of raising them, perpetrating a terrible violence on them that is anything but truly gentle. John Leonard writes: "Fish claims that Satan's speech has the effect of eradicating what little courage his troops have left. But the claim is false. Satan's army does not disintegrate; it rallies." But I say nothing about the effect of the speech within the logic of the linear narrative; in that logic, it is as Leonard reports: the troops do rally. So much the worse for them, for they are now animated by the false courage (the perfect product of the false gentleness) that attends an enterprise – rebellion against the Almighty – at once impossible and unworthy. By allowing themselves to be rais'd in rebellion, they participate in their own razing. In Milton's poem, the logic of the plot and the significance its actions appear to have are always in a relationship of counterpoint and contrast to the higher, more encompassing logic of the story of faith, obedience and redemption. Time after time we are prevented from "going with the flow" by some device that recalls us to the master narrative from which the events of the surface narrative receive their true meanings, if we can see them, if they are sightly to us. The "rais'd" in "gently rais'd" is such a device, puncturing the apparent gesture of leadership just as the same word punctures Satan's claim to be "self-rais'd" and reminds us of the awful truth of what happens to agents who cut themselves off from the center of being: they are self-razed. Leonard concludes that, "Fish's insistence on a pun is a cheap attempt to rob Satan of his charisma," that is, of his appeal. There is nothing to rob, because there is no appeal, except to those who, like Mammon, see only the glitter and not the reality beneath.

   I have saved the most frequently voiced objection to *How Milton Works* for last in part because it collapses almost immediately under its own weight. It is the objection (this is Leonard's version) that "Fish is routinely indifferent to history and politics." No, I am *militantly* indifferent to history and politics because it is my thesis – stated and elaborated again and again – that history and politics, while certainly the necessary vehicles of action, are for Milton the measure neither of an action's meaning nor its value. Milton, like the rest of us, must work in history and he must perform politically in the context of political hopes. However, if those hopes are not realized, the value of what he has done in an effort to obey God's will remains and is finally primary. That is why he often declares, as he does at the beginning of *Areopagitica*, that what he desires most is not to produce a trophy – a sign of victory – although that would be nice, but to perform a testimony. Testimony is to be performed in any and every situation, and while the differences between situations, between historical contexts are real, the important thing about situations and contexts is that they provide opportunities, forever renewed, to affirm in ever-changing circumstances the same loyalty and thereby to be continually enrolled in the army of the heroes of faith. History and politics are certainly not to be discarded and cannot be transcended, but in Milton's vision they cannot deliver their own meanings; rather, they must seek the meaning of their putative events in a narrative that is neither historical nor political.

To put it in another way and perhaps most provocatively, history and politics are for Milton and his readers temptations because they offer themselves as the repositories of an intelligibility they cannot possibly contain without claiming divinity. If idolatry, the substitution of the created and secondary for the creating and primary, is for Milton the chief sin – and I believe it is – then history and politics are that sin's most seductive forms. They say, believe in us; Milton says, no you must see through them to the truths they can point to but cannot generate; they are not, despite the claims made for them, self-begot or self-rais'd. It follows then that had I performed as a historical or political critic in a serious sense, had I regarded history and politics as the object to which I would be faithful, the dimension of Milton's thought and achievement that most interests me and is to my mind the dimension most crucial to him, would have been lost, and *How Milton Works* – a book that both critics and admirers agree is relentless in its insistence that it is the interior drama that matters – would never have been written. As Al Labriola sees, my "thesis could not have been effectively developed and deployed in another way"; detractors, he notes, "will fault its synchronic approach" (*MLQ*, vol. 16, no. 3, September, 2002, p. 385), but if I had employed a diachronic approach the distinctiveness of what I was attempting would have been fatally compromised. The book derives whatever authority it has, as Dennis Kezar observes, from "an almost constant obedience to its thesis," (312) an obedience that is both its method and its content.

Finally, I find some of the reviews simply puzzling. I am not puzzled because individual readers disliked the book or reported, at length, that they were unpersuaded by it, either by local moments or from the first page to the last. Such responses, after all, are what we let ourselves in for, perhaps even court, when we send our work out into the world. No, what puzzles me is the intensity of an animosity more than occasionally displayed, a hostility bordering on outrage but without any clear specification of the crimes committed by the author. That hostility has a life, indeed a life of its own, and persists even when the reviewer's preferred view of Milton seems indistinguishable from mine. One example will have to suffice. Perez Zagorin says of the book: "Fish's image of how Milton works seems to reflect a critical monomania. The Milton it presents is static, a man without difference or change" (737). But when, at the conclusion of his review, Zagorin offers his own characterization of Milton, it comes out like this: "Although Milton went through great changes of opinion on important subjects, he never acknowledged doing so or admitted to being wrong ... He possessed an astonishingly strong personality [which] neither reverses ... nor political defeat could undermine. Always and essentially a moralist, virtue was the one quality he sought and demanded" (742). I couldn't have said it better myself.

In Zagorin's view, the Milton he reports in these sentences is the bad Milton against whom the good Milton – the humanist, literature-loving, ambiguity-loving, kinder and gentler Milton – is always struggling. This, for a long time, has been the "plot" of much Milton criticism, especially criticism written by those committed in their non-academic lives to a progressive left-wing agenda. Such critics have a stake (which I neither understand nor share, although I pretty much share their politics) in claiming the poet they admire for the political causes they champion. They believe that a poet so obviously compelling as Milton is must be a good man, that is, must be on their side. (Milton of course would also declare, as he does in the *Apology*, that one cannot be a good poet without being a good man, but his definition of "good man" would not be theirs.) To these critics, *How Milton Works* brings a most unwelcome message: Milton is not the tolerant, proto-Rawlsian they want him to be. Rather, he is a man of hard edges whose art is powerful precisely because he refuses to soften those edges in moments of moral crisis.

CHAPTER 7

The new Milton criticism

If I were king, I would lay it down as a rule that no Miltonist could do theory, except for me. The reason is that Miltonists who do theory almost always make what I call the "theory mistake": They announce some grand theoretical truth (often a dubious one) and then claim to derive from it an interpretive conclusion, usually the conclusion that Milton is of the Devil's party with or without knowing it; or the conclusion that while the official orthodoxy of *Paradise Lost* tells one story – of disobedience, loss and possible redemption – the energies of the verse tell quite another story and it is the better one; or the conclusion that Milton has for too long been captured by an orthodox establishment that either ignores or aestheticizes or stigmatizes the radical forces at play in his work; or the conclusion that Milton's poetry and prose tell no single truth, but problematize issues of truth and fact to the point where the only message being sent is the message of instability, mutability and indeterminacy; or the conclusion that in a poem that celebrates freedom and condemns tyranny, the strongest image of tyranny is the heaven presided over by a God who demands mindless obedience for no good reason. In this essay I will not be considering these conclusions (which I find unpersuasive), but the argumentative logic by which they are supposedly reached.

Those who reach these conclusions and make these arguments are described or describe themselves as the forerunners of a "new Milton criticism" or as "guerilla Miltonists" (Herman, *Destabilizing Milton:* Paradise Lost *and the Poetics of Incertitude* [Macmillan, 2008], 20), a band of brave brothers and sisters thought to include, among others, Michael Bryson, Stephen Dobranski, Neil Forsyth, Peter Herman, William Kolbrener, Ronald Levao, Catherine Gimelli Martin, Lucy Newlin, David Norbrook, William Poole, John Rogers, John Rumrich, Elizabeth Sauer, Regina Schwartz, Jeffrey Shoulson, Victoria Silver, Richard Streier and Shari Zimmerman. More than honorable mention is often made of Joseph Wittreich, John Shawcross, Christopher Hill, Dennis Saurat, A.J.A. Waldock,

John Carey and John Peter, while fulsome tribute is paid to William Empson (who certainly deserves it). Michael Lieb is often referenced as someone who should be of the New Miltonist party, given his many analyses of a wrathful God who inspires dread and fear, but Lieb, it is lamented, finally remains within the conservative fold.

The tenets of the conservatism that will not relax its hold are listed by Peter Herman:

> Milton is a poet of absolute unqualified certainty
> *Paradise Lost* coheres
> The critic's job is to make the poem cohere

The chief villains in the story are C.S. Lewis, who at least had the honesty to admit that his purpose was to "prevent the reader from ever raising certain questions" and Stanley Fish, who, after forty years of a disabling and disastrous influence, just refuses to get off the stage, even when someone like Michael Bryson cries: "The time has come to say 'enough.'" (25)

My list of the conclusions the New Miltonists typically reach should tell you that what they are saying is no newer than Dryden, who early on opined that *Paradise Lost* would have been a better poem "if the Devil had not been his hero." But that is hardly a fatal criticism. Whether a particular account of Milton is old or new is beside the point. The point is whether or not it's right. That word, however, presents a problem for those New Miltonists who rest at least part of their case on a certain version of postmodern or post-structuralist theory; for their commitment to multi-vocality, perspectivism, infinitely plural meanings, the textuality of truth – not as features of a particular text, but as necessary features of any text – would seem to deprive them of a place from where they can coherently assert the rightness of their interpretation of Milton or the falseness of C.S. Lewis's and mine. It is one thing to say of a text – like Browning's *The Ring and The Book* or the film *Rashomon* – that it discourages the reader or viewer from coming to any conclusion about what it is trying to convey; that is merely to assert your view of the author's or film-maker's intention, an assertion that can then be supported or challenged by evidence. But it is quite another thing to say that no text could possibly convey something determinate, because all texts are radically indeterminate by nature. That is not a preliminary to interpretation, but an announcement of its impossibility, and an end, one would think, of the effort to specify what a text means. For if every text means everything, it means no single thing and anything you say about it cannot even rise to the level of being wrong. Nor can you intelligibly reject an interpretive orthodoxy by complaining that it has distorted Milton's text. By the logic of the celebration of infinite meanings, there is nothing to distort, and a meaning that puts God and obedience at the center of the poem's morality is as good as one that gives the primacy to Satan and rebellion.

In the face of this difficulty, some of the Miltonists who have fallen prey to theory take the desperate, but logically inevitable, course of disavowing their own readings in advance of presenting them. Carl Freedman does this in an essay ominously titled: "How To Do Things With Milton." (If you are an interpreter of Milton there is only one thing you should do with him – try to figure out what his words mean. Anything else you did might be interesting, but it wouldn't be interpretation.) "Every reading," Freedman declares, is "inevitably an *interested* reading that does not merely respond to but participates in the construction of its object" (*Critical Essays on John Milton*, ed. C. Kendrick, 20). If Freedman is saying that any account of what a text means is to some extent inflected by the interpreter's history, affiliations and commitments, his statement is both commonplace and harmless. But if he is saying that apart from its construction by interested readers there is no text and no meaning, and that, therefore, every reading is a unique, incomparable event, he has rendered whatever he then says about Milton without interest, except for the interest a friend or relative might have in the thought processes of Carl Freedman.

Freedman clearly intends the latter and supports his position by borrowing a vocabulary from J.L. Austin, who also gives him his title: "The critical utterance is less constative than performative." The trouble is that the distinction between the constative and the performative is undone by Austin in the course of *How To Do Things With Words* (Oxford University Press, 1962). The key moment in the book is when Austin declares that a constative – a speech act that describes or reports or predicates – is also a performative – a speech act that brings into being what it reports – and adds that the happiness or felicity of performatives depend as much on matters of fact as do constatives. So to say, as Freedman does, that "every act of criticism is a performative labor" is to say nothing that distinguishes criticism from any other piece of verbal behavior and is certainly not to say that acts of criticism cannot be evaluated by the normative vocabulary of right/wrong, accurate/inaccurate, on target/off the wall.

But this is what Freedman wants to say and he claims as his warrant a misreading of the theorist who gives him his title. So it is no surprise to find him declaring that in criticizing the readings of other commentators he does not want to give the "impression" that he is "implicitly contrasting them with the perfectly 'true' reading ... that I myself possess." He then immediately offers that reading: "Milton is to be read as primarily a revolutionary and regicide, as a prophet of liberty, as one whose deepest affinities across the ages are with such later antinomian revolutionaries as Blake and Shelley, as well as ... with Marx himself and the entire Marxist tradition" (23). Now that is a perfectly legitimate candidate for a reading of Milton, but it cannot be put forward seriously by someone who has just told us that he makes no claims whatsoever for it.

Later, Freedman turns from Austin to Pierre Macherey, whom he summarizes as saying that "literature tends to foreground ideological contradictions and gaps." He notes that Empson also reads *Paradise Lost* "in very much this way." But whereas Macherey's "method of analysis consists mainly of immanent textual ideology-critique," Empson is engaged in what Freedman calls "an unabashed intentionalism." That is, Empson actually thinks he is getting at the truth about what Milton intended; he doesn't realize that he is merely writing his own poem, one that happily coincides with the truth of theory. He accidentally comes up with the right reading – that is, a reading in line with what literature always does: foreground contradictions and gaps – but he claims too much for it; he claims it's right.

Catherine Belsey, in her *John Milton: Language, Gender, Power* (which should be titled *Language, Gender, Power: John Milton*), renounces any claim to be right by page 7: "My interpretation of Milton's plural, disseminated texts lays claim ... to no special authority." But she at least asks the obvious question. Why then offer it? Because, she tells us, the history of Milton criticism has been one of attempts to "take control of meaning, to fix it" and to outlaw "alternatives by making them literally unthinkable." It is her intention, she announces, to release "the plurality of the texts," the meanings and vindicate "the triumph of language in its creativity" (10). In this way she will be countering the repressive effort of those who wish to "extend their power by arresting the inevitable play of meaning." Belsey regards the arresting of the play of meaning as a crime. I thought it was the task.

Her project, then, is larger than the mere explication of a poem. In the course of her analysis, *Paradise Lost* is not so much read as it is made into an allegory of contemporary theory. Every moment in the poem is scrutinized until it delivers up an overarching truth about language and meaning. The points she makes most vigorously are theoretical, not interpretive:

Meaning is always an effect of difference between signifiers (23)
Truth cannot be sealed finally and incontrovertibly into words (26)
Meanings are made and remade, the signified is deferred and differed
with all the plurality and indeterminacy that that releases (43)

Belsey does not even pretend that she is interested in what *Paradise Lost* is
about in the traditional sense: "My interest," she says," is in "the plurality
of the texts and the contests for meaning played out within them" (9),
played out, of course, without resolution. "What is realized in . . . *Paradise
Lost*," she declares, "is not finally the Logos, but the primacy of textuality
itself, not the presence of God, but the triumphant presence of the
signifier" (43). The triumph of the signifier is not a thesis as to what the
poem means; it is not an account of what its author had in mind; it is a
thesis about what any word, line or image in *Paradise Lost* necessarily
means before it is contemplated or encountered.

Take, for example, the hoary issue of the "fortunate Fall." When
Miltonists argue about whether the Fall is fortunate, they adduce as
evidence lines in the poem, passages in Milton's prose, discussions of
the Fall in contemporary and patristic texts. But for Belsey the question is
determined not by evidence but by the demands of the theoretical
perspective to which she is committed. Before the Fall, she tells us, Adam
and Eve know only one truth as it has been promulgated by an unim-
peachable deity. But after the Fall, the "politics of truth," described by
Belsey as a "despotism" ("there is . . . an inherent authoritarianism in a
world where truth . . . constitutes the difference between right and
wrong"), is replaced by "a politics of interest, which is also . . . a politics
of difference" (84). Therefore – and it is a theoretical not an interpretive
therefore – the Fall is fortunate: "the fall is the condition of [Adam's and
Eve's] entry into the symbolic order. Knowing good and evil, they are
only now full humanist subjects, full participants in the order of language
and culture" (83). A plurality of meanings is good; God and his despotic
minions like Abdiel insist on a singleness of meaning in the name of a
single truth; rebellion from their tyranny – an epistemological tyranny – is
praiseworthy; the Fall is fortunate. The sequence makes sense, not as an
interpretation of the poem, of what Milton meant, but as a set of deduc-
tions from a philosophical linguistic premise.

That premise need not have brought her to that conclusion. The idea
that meaning is always plural and open to contestation does not *yield* the
reading of the Fall as fortunate. It does not yield any reading; it serves as a
permission to bypass reading entirely and go directly, as I have already

said, to allegory. Theoretical premises operate on a level entirely removed from acts of interpretation, and any relation between them – any interpretation supposedly derived from a theory – is entirely arbitrary. Given that the very point of a theory is to abstract away from particulars to a realm far above them, no pronouncement that issues from that realm has relevance for any particular we might encounter. The very generality of theory renders it irrelevant to any matter of mundane fact, including the facts that are asserted and disputed in the performance of interpretation. If I say that a line in a poem means such and such, and you respond by saying, "Meaning is always an effect of difference," your rejoinder is simply not to any interpretive point. The practice of theory – the practice in which you say things like: "Meaning is always an effect of difference" or: "Every reading is an interested reading"– flies so high above the practice of interpretation that there can be no commerce between them whatsoever.

Peter Herman's *Destabilizing Milton* engages in both practices, theorizing and interpreting, and his title hesitates between them. Is "destabilizing" an adjective that points to what Milton is doing – destabilizing meanings, certainties and values? Or is it a present participle that tells us what Herman will be doing in his book – destabilizing meanings, certainties and values? If it is the first, if he is presenting a thesis about Milton, it is one we can either reject or be persuaded by. If it is the other, if Herman is showing us how many types of ambiguity he can tease out of Milton's text, argument is beside the point, and we can only admire or be bored by his ingenuity. His analyses cannot be either right or wrong; they can only be entertaining – like a magician's tricks – or tedious.

Herman's theoretical gurus are Thomas Kuhn and Jacques Derrida, and it is from Derrida's "Plato's Pharmacy" that he derives his "method." A word like *pharmakon*, Derrida says, "is caught in a chain of signifiers," yet translators choose only one of the word's possible meanings and thereby "cancel out the resources of ambiguity." Herman pledges to follow Derrida's example and refrain from "privileging one set of meanings." Instead, he will recover "the mixed signals of Milton's metaphors, by taking into account both poles" of images that have been read too narrowly (27). This section of his book bears the title "Warring Chains of Signifiers" and the title tells us in advance what is going to happen. Herman will focus on an image or comparison that seems to cast a negative light on Satan, but then point out that in some traditions the figure of comparison is inflected positively. So, for example, while the linking of Satan to the Titans in an early simile is often regarded as damning, in some texts the Titans are presented as heroes who are simply "trying to reestablish [their] rights" (28). "Thus," he concludes, "what starts off as a simple negative comparison could also work to Satan's advantage and God's disadvantage, or to the disadvantage of both; or all four simultaneously. Certainty, thus, segues into uncertainty" (29).

Yes it does, and it always will, if all that is required is that one find a text or a tradition that complicates received wisdom. No matter how clearly an image or an allusion seems to point in an interpretive indirection, Herman is able to say (because he has decided so in advance) that its "meaning is far from self-evident" (42), and that a meaning one had not thought of is at least "arguable." "And how," he asks, "does one resolve these conflicting and equally plausible interpretations?" "My point," Herman responds, is "you don't"; and then after having declared irreconcilability as a general theoretical principle, he makes it, by fiat rather than argument, into an interpretive conclusion: "I suggest that irreconcilability is a constituent element of the poem itself" (42).

Destabilizing Milton does not always proceed in this mode. It does have a genuinely interpretive thesis that is presented in the company of evidence. In a chapter titled: "England A Free Nation," Herman argues that the concept of the Ancient Constitution "enshrined in English common law" should be understood as central to Milton's thinking both about monarchy and about the portrayal of heaven in his epic. The chief tenet of the concept, Herman reminds us, is that monarchy has a "human – not divine – origin" and that, consequently, "the monarch cannot change the nation's laws without the explicit consent of parliament." Herman then easily finds evidence in Milton's prose that he believes in the "contractual" not absolute "nature of kingship" (73), and concludes that "it is unlikely that Milton would find absolutism acceptable in Heaven and not on earth given his belief that absolutism contradicted the law of God" (85). Rather, "when Milton associates Heaven and God with absolutism, he associates the deity with a concept widely considered fundamentally antithetical to the English polity . . . and even antithetical to God Himself" (86).

Now that's a real argument, and one that enters a familiar interpretive conversation in which the key question is this: When Milton puts into Satan's mouth the very Republican principles he proclaims in his anti-monarchical tracts, does he intend us to see Satan as he sees himself – a rebel against illegitimate authority – or does he intend us to see the difference between an absolutism claimed by a mere mortal and the absolutism that belongs properly to the Creator and Sustaining Agent of all life? Answering that question requires the ordinary, humdrum methods of interpretive analysis – assessing and compiling evidence, both internal and external, and tying it to a plausible account of Milton's intention. It does not require a theory.

Michael Bryson has an answer to the question, and it is concisely given in the title of his book, *The Tyranny of Heaven*. *Paradise Lost*, Bryson contends, "forces its readers to stare directly into the face of God conceived in terms of military might and kingly power ... manipulatively defensive, alternately rhetorically incoherent and evasive ... in short, a God who is nearly indistinguishable from Satan" (25). Like Herman, Bryson argues from an account of the intention Milton must have had: "it is unlikely that the man who labored so hard to destroy the *Eikon Basilike* would set up a poetic *Eikon Theios* as if it were an absolute representation of the real thing" (24).

Well, that sounds like an interpretation – and one that could be disputed or agreed with. But Bryson believes that it is generated and supported by a theoretical point, which he promises to "repeat as often as necessary" (26). It is that "the Son and the Father are *poetic characters, works of fiction, constructions of a writer's imagination*" (26). And again, "What Milton presents ... is not God, but an *image* of God, a poetic character drawn from the human imagination – an instrument that is limited and thus inherently unable to create a personal deity in any but its own limited terms" (17–18). And a third time, "in the context of a 'fallen' world, a 'fallen' human poet could not present an all-good God even if that were his intention" (17).

This is an extremely curious argument which says that because the Son and the Father are fictional characters, they could not be representations of absolute virtue. But the test of whether a character is virtuous is not his or her fictionality, which, absent a special case of divine inspiration, is a condition of all characters. The real question, which Bryson glances at, is whether or not Milton intended the Son and the Father to be virtuous and therefore to be the poem's normative figures.

To be sure, you could answer yes to that question and still decide that Milton's notion of virtue is faulty. That is, you could decide that you don't like what Milton's intention produced, which would be quite different from saying that he didn't have the intention or couldn't have had it or couldn't have realized it. The determination of what a poem means is logically distinct from the judgment of whether the meaning is one you want to affirm. And neither has anything to do with the supposed problem of fictionality, which is a low-rent version of Belsey's problem of textuality. Belsey's argument is that since the truths we affirm are textually not immediately conveyed, none of them has its claimed authority. But the very scope of "textuality" – it includes everything – disqualifies it as a concept that could be the basis of evaluation, positive or negative. If everything is apprehended textually, then the textuality of an assertion cannot be a reason for either affirming or rejecting it. And by the same reasoning, if all characters are constructions of a writer's imagination, then saying that a particular character is fictional is to say nothing. Bryson might be right about the tyranny of Milton's Heaven, but whether he is or not has nothing to do with textuality or fictionality or any other theoretical notion.

John Rumrich's preferred theorists in *Milton Unbound* are Dan Sperber and Deirdre Wilson, and he draws from their work several theoretical points: first that "intention is fundamental to communication" and interpretation (148); second that human languages are "highly charged with chaotic potency"(28), and third "that the richest poetry is that which is most flexible, articulate and far reaching in its implications"(28). These three theoretical insights are then cited in support of Rumrich's contention that Milton's poetry is indeterminate, dynamic and open-ended (27, 37). I agree completely with the assertion that intention is the key to interpretation and I also agree that it is possible that it was Milton's intention to produce a work that would be open-ended and indeterminate rather than closed and didactic. The task is to demonstrate, by amassing the usual kinds of evidence (from the text, from letters, from a study of genre, from authorial statements), that that was in fact his intention. The mere assertion that intention is the key to interpretation will not further the task; it merely tells you what it is. The work remains to be done, and it will not be done or furthered by proclaiming either that human languages are charged with a chaotic potency or that the richest poetry is that which is most flexible. If it is true that language is charged with a chaotic potency, it is a truth that is of no interpretive help; for the question is, with what potency (if any) is *this* language – the language of *Paradise Lost* – charged, and again the answer will not be provided or even hinted at by some grand statement about language in general.

And as for the assertion that "the richest poetry is that which is most flexible," that is neither an interpretive point nor a theoretical one. It is a moral point and a point of taste. Rumrich is telling us that richly layered, indeterminate, relatively chaotic poetry is what he likes and approves or approves because he likes. That's fine, but he can't conclude that *therefore* Milton's poetry is like that. Any such conclusion would have to follow from an analysis of the poetry, and theoretical pronouncements will not be a part of such an analysis. What will and can be part of such an analysis are statements like this one: "From the mid-1640s on, [Milton] consistently maintained that indeterminacy and differences of opinion are inevitable among imperfect creatures in an unfinished world"(37). It does not follow necessarily that Milton wrote a poem that was similarly "unfinished" or open-ended, but there is at least a plausible connection between this fact, if it is a fact, about Milton's views, and an interpretive conclusion, while there is no plausible connection between an interpretive conclusion and a premise of theory.

If Rumrich foregrounds intention as the central and necessary element in interpretation, James Dougal Fleming makes intention the villain of his piece. Fleming's book, *Milton's Secrecy And Philosophical Hermeneutics* (2008), is the latest installment in the let's-rid-ourselves-of-Stanley-Fish project. Fleming has a historical/interpretive thesis. He announces in his introduction that most Milton scholars (I am the chief exhibit) "argue or assume ... that studying Milton's work entails a search for hidden meaning," the meaning we can divine by going behind the text to the poet's true and occluded intention. What the text presents the critic refuses to accept and subjects to a skeptical interrogation, asking what is *really* going on. This, Fleming declares roundly, is wrong. Milton, he argues, proclaims the virtues of openness and clearness; he believes that everything should be manifest, nothing hidden. Secrecy – the sequestering in some dark interior place of truth or meaning – is, he says, Satan's way and is so announced when he famously declares: "The mind is its own place." Satan is "psychologically secretive, inward to the point of solipsism"(9). Milton, in contrast, "insists on radical openness"; he "abjures hiddenness in itself and excoriates it in others"; he "correlates secret-keeping with damnation."

This account of Milton's views is supported by extensive historical analysis of key terms in Reformation theology and by numerous citations from Milton's work. On the basis of his analysis of these sources, Fleming arrives at some provocative, even counterintuitive, readings of Milton's poems. He contends, for example, that the Lady in *Comus* is morally wrong when she declines to explain to the villain the "sage / And serious doctrine of virginity" (785–786), on the reasoning that he couldn't understand it anyway; and he finds that rather than being guilty for giving up the secret of his strength to Delilah, Samson was right to do so because it brings everything out in the open and clears away the ground in a way that makes his final act possible. "The secret as *kept* is the very last thing Milton is interested in"(107). What he is interested in, according to Fleming, is

Samson's move from interior navel gazing and the endless splitting of hairs about everyone's intentions to genuine – that is surface, not hidden – expression in the destruction of the Philistine temple. "Samson rejects nonperformance" identified with interiority, intentionality and secrecy – "in favor of performance"; he makes "a concluding commitment to exoteric [outward, displayed] catastrophe" (99).

I am not persuaded by these readings, but at least they are readings, supported by the ordinary kinds of evidence that tell either for or against an interpretive thesis. But while Fleming does marshal that evidence, often to good effect, he spends more energy prosecuting a theoretical argument, which, he thinks, not only underwrites and generates his interpretations, but says something important and even cosmic about interpretation, meaning and truth. He is not content to argue that Milton rejects intentionalism – secret meanings – in favor of surface texts and openness of declaration; he wants to argue that intentionalism, as an account of meaning, is wrong and literally Satanic, not simply when it turns up in Milton's poems, but when it turns up anywhere in the world.

"Strong intentionalism," he tells us, "consists in an interpretive penetration from outward appearance to an underlying or inward reality, which wholly determines the appearance while remaining wholly discrete from it. In other words, strong intentionalism is esoteric and potentially Satanic. It is the interpretive theory of the mind as its own place" (67). What Fleming does in this and other formulations is make his reading of Milton dependent on – indeed, a function of – his theory of intentionalism. By his own terms, if you are not persuaded of the one – if you don't agree with his account of intentionalism – you won't be persuaded of his accounts of *Comus* and *Samson Agonistes*. That's the way he sets it up, and that is unfortunate because he is wrong on every point about what the intentionalist thesis is. He is wrong to say that intentionalists think of intention as separable from expression (62). He is wrong when he says that intentionalists relocate meaning in people's heads (117). He is wrong to say that intentionalism amounts to "a contempt for language" (116). And therefore he doesn't make it as a philosopher of language. But this shouldn't matter, or, rather, it matters only because he has made it matter. Fleming's and my disagreement about what Milton's poem means is logically independent of his and my disagreement about the structure of intentionalism. The two sets of claims and counterclaims have nothing to do with one another. I should be able to say "yes" to his reading of Milton and "no" to his critique of intentionalism because entirely different questions – What does this particular poem mean? And what is meaning in general? – are being asked and answered. But he won't let me. He wants me (and you) to assent both to his theory and to his reading. Indeed, he wants me and you to assent to his reading *because* we assent to his theory. But I don't, and a lot of others won't either, which means that his reading, which should be presented and challenged and defended in the context of literary critical norms, will be judged by the norms of philosophical hermeneutics. He is not offering me Milton, but Milton as Gadamer (his hero) would have written it. Like Belsey, he makes the poet's work into an allegory of a questionable theory. Too bad, because there's a really smart piece of literary criticism embedded in some not so smart theoretical speculations.

Theory doesn't have to be high, philosophical theory in order to be out of place and beside the point in the performance of literary criticism. Stephen Dobranski's version of theory is materialist. He wants to move from an account of the material conditions attending the emergence of a work to an account of its meaning. In *Milton, Authorship, and the Book Trade*, Dobranski argues "for the social orientation of Milton's writings and against the tradition of the poet as an isolated genius"(9). By social orientation he doesn't mean that Milton looked outward to the actual lives of men and women, but that he "benefited from the advice and assistance of acquaintances both during the imaginative creation of his works and during the practical process of putting his writing into print"(9). Dobranski calls these acquaintances "collaborators" and complains that Milton's "strong authorial voice has virtually drowned out" their contributions.

There are two arguments here: the first is that a given work couldn't have come to light without a lot of help, and that is certainly true. The second is that those who provide the help are the work's co-authors. But why stop there? What about those who helped the helpers, wives, suppliers, bankers? And what about all of those who supported them, and on and on until in the end you want to say that everyone and everything wrote the work, which would mean either that the work meant nothing because no intelligence designed it (only designed artifacts can mean) or that all of society (or its zeitgeist) was the controlling intelligence and we are back to what Dobranski calls the myth of the autonomous author. While the material conditions surrounding and leading up to the appearance of a work are certainly indispensable, they have nothing to do with the work's meaning because they didn't write it. The fact that the person who did write it "depended on others" for criticism and material support does not mean that those others are collaborators except in a metaphorical sense. The theory of material production may explain how artifacts come into being, but it has no interpretive force whatsoever except in those special cases (Blake, performance art) where the materiality of the artistic presentation is part of its content.

So there's my single, typically monomaniacal, thesis: interpretive issues and theoretical issues are independent variables, and the presence in a Milton book of a theoretical discussion is a sure sign that at least on one level the author is confused. But if there is no real connection between theoretical stances and interpretive conclusions, why is it that the theoretically inclined Miltonists I have been discussing tend to be of one interpretive mind? Doesn't this suggest that the theory they profess yields the interpretation they all arrive at? Actually, it is the other way around. Their interpretation comes first, and then they look around for a theory that can be said to support it. They presuppose a poem that is indeterminate, ambiguous and radically open-ended, and they then cite in support of their reading a theory according to which all uses of language are indeterminate, ambiguous and radically open-ended. But in doing that they leech the interest out of the text by making it into just one more example of the general truth deconstructive theory (in some versions) proclaims. The support theory seems to give to their interpretation is rhetorical rather than causal or fully explanatory, and this is necessarily the case because, as I have repeatedly said, there is no line of argument from a theory to an interpretive conclusion. The theoretical propositions favored by the New Miltonists – multi-vocality, textuality, the plurality of meanings – neither generate nor confirm any interpretive claim, and the fact that they think otherwise is an indication that they are making a familiar mistake.

The mistake is to think that the central postmodern insight – that all knowledge is mediated, textually produced, known only under a description, socially constructed – has consequences for what we can and cannot claim for our assertions. The reasoning is that the pervasiveness of mediation or textuality undermines judgments of right and wrong, true and false, factual and fictional because nothing can be said to be absolutely so. But it is precisely because mediation is a general condition that it has no implications whatsoever for judgments being made in particular contexts. If everything is mediated or socially constructed, then the fact that a judgment of truth or falsity is necessarily mediated does not tell against it. What might tell against it is evidence adduced in the context of inquiry within which the judgment has emerged. To be sure, that context and the evidence it yields will also be mediated and historically produced, and revisable, but unless you wish to relativize all judgments simply because none of them is rooted in the ground of absolute fact, that is of no consequence.

Relativizing all judgments is indeed what some of the New Miltonists wish to do; for if truth and value can be relativized, then anything a narrator or a character says is rendered suspect and non-authoritative even before it is heard or read, and Satan's pronouncements can be declared to stand on even ground with the pronouncements of the epic voice, not because the details of the poem direct us to that declaration but because a theoretical proposition – presupposed in advance of interpretation and rendering it superfluous – has commanded it. It is more than a little ironic that a brief against the tyranny of orthodoxy gets its purchase by surrendering to an orthodoxy of theory, and to a theory that cannot be made to do the work assigned to it.

But the fact that theory can do no interpretive work means, paradoxically, that its presence in the writings of the New Miltonists is in no way damaging to their interpretive claims, which stand or fall independently of the theories that neither generate nor support them. So it would seem that what I have called the theory mistake is harmless: no harm, no foul. And yet I cannot give it a pass because those who make it are likely to believe that they are doing something infinitely more important than reading poems. If you think of literary criticism not as a job of work (R.P. Blackmur's old phrase), but as an intervention in the epistemological, moral and political crises of our time, you will be tempted to inflate its importance and to believe that by offering this rather than that interpretation of *Paradise Lost* you are engaged in the toppling of hierarchy or in the defense of freedom or in the fight against the forces of repression. No, you're just trying to figure out what someone meant by these words, nothing less and certainly nothing more. It may seem odd that a chapter that began with my anointing myself king should end with a call for professional humility, but there it is.

Early modern literature

CHAPTER 8

"Void of storie": the struggle for insincerity in Herbert's prose and poetry

"OH THAT I ONCE PAST CHANGING WERE"

In a somewhat neglected poem of George Herbert's entitled "A Dialogue Anthem," two characters, Christian and Death, debate the shape of history, both personal and cosmic. Christian tauntingly asks, "Alas, poore Death, where is thy glorie? / Where is thy famous force, thy ancient sting?" and Death replies in kind, "*Alas poore mortall, void of storie, / Go spell and reade how I have kill'd thy King.*"[1] We are meant to see, of course, that Death completely misunderstands or misreads the situation: he thinks that because Christ has died, there is no longer any center to Christian's life, nothing in relation to which his actions could have meaning; however, Christian knows that meaning, and the continuation of his story, is assured by Christ's death, an act of self-sacrifice that rescues man from the death-sentence (separation from deity) earned by Adam and Eve in Eden. It is only because of Christ's death that man will live.

But live how? The answer to this question reveals a further irony in Death's accusation, "void of storie"; for, correctly understood, it is not an accusation at all, but a precise specification of the requirement that Christ's sacrifice imposes, the requirement that the Christian not have a story of his own, that he be, in that impossible and perhaps inconceivable sense, void of story. The logic is familiar in Christian thought. It is present, for example, when Milton reminds us that the taste of the forbidden tree was "mortal" and brought Death into the world. The point is profound, if tautological: mortality *is* death in the sense that it names a state which is finite, which has an end, a cessation, a conclusion. Once separated from the endless rhythms of eternity, from that "Grateful vicissitude"[2] in which change is "delectable" (*PL* v, 629) but not needed, man is delivered into a world where change always has reference to the pressures exerted by beginnings and ends. Mortal man always feels time's winged chariot at his back because as a creature whose mode of existence is linear every moment brings an opportunity that will not come again and also brings choices that are at once irrevocable and determining. When Milton says of our first parents that at the moment of the Fall they "knew not eating Death" (*PL* IX, 792), he might as well have said, they knew not eating narrative (story), that wandering and errant course which is theirs once they are no longer incorporate members of a choir who live with and in God and therefore "sing in endless morn of light."[3]

There is of course another way to put this point, and it is Satan's way when he sneeringly refers to the loyal angels as the "Minstrelsy of Heaven" (*PL* VI, 168) and contrasts their "servility" with the "freedom" (line 169) in whose name he claims to contend. If death is another name for mortality, then freedom is another name for both, for freedom, at least as Satan defines it, is the state of being separate from God, of not being enfolded in the ceaseless repetition of his praise, but, instead, exposed to the world of chance and hazard. In death, then, in mortality, in finitude, Satan finds life, by which he, and Adam and Eve following him, mean an independent story line. By breaking union, by disobeying – or, rather, *in* disobeying – they get to do it their way, and their way, in contra-distinction to God's way, is to be finite and to have a beginning, a middle and an end. It follows then that if fallen man is ever to repair the ruins of his first parents, he must somehow do it *no* way, have no story line, be void of story. We see then another sense in which Death is precisely wrong when he cries, "mortall, void of storie"; to be mortal is to have a story, to have a continuity, to be available to narration; to be void of story is to be enclosed in the story of another ("I live to show his power," "Josephs Coat," line 13), and it is this that Herbert's Christian voice desires, although that desire is itself self-defeating, since to have it is to envision a fulfillment which, if achieved, marks the end and point of a story of which the desirer will then be anything but void.

What to do? Or, rather, how to "do" doing nothing, how to a-void story? The answer to this question often appears in Herbert's poetry in the guise of a complaint. Here, for example, are the first four lines of "Giddinesse":

> Oh, what a thing is man! how farre from power,
>   From setled peace and rest!
> He is some twentie sev'rall men at least
>   Each sev'rall houre. (lines 1–4)

What Herbert laments here is the absence of continuous being; he bemoans the fact that life brings so many and so violent changes that at the end of an hour he is not the same person he was at its beginning; in effect he has no identity, and is a thing or a no-thing always on the move.

This is the master theme of any number of Herbert's poems. "The Temper (II)" begins by recording the loss of the resolution – of the state of being – achieved at the end of "The Temper (I)": "It cannot be. Where is that mightie joy, / Which just now took up all my heart?" (lines 1–2). The severity of the disjuncture is underlined by the fact that the speaker is not here recalling the moment of loss; he doesn't remember it; he only knows that at this moment he is not what he was a moment ago; and he knows too that what he now feels he may not feel in the moment yet to come. The world of nature, "The grosser world," he complains, "stands to thy word and art" (line 5); that is, once made by you (God) it abides; but the inner (and supposedly superior) world of consciousness, "Thou suddenly does raise and race, / And ev'ry day a new Creatur art" (lines 7–8). It is important to realize that this is not a reference to the Old Man who is made new – transformed – by the grace and sacrifice of Christ; this man is not made new, but newly made; *he* is "rac'd" or erased by a mark that simply writes over him. When Herbert begins "Affliction (II)" by crying "Kill me not ev'ry day," he might as well have pleaded, "make me not ev'ry day": for in relation to a self that would have its own story, killing and making are the same thing, and what they are is killing. In these poems, as Barbara Harman observes, the speaker comes to see himself "not as someone who grows, or fails to grow, 'in a straight line' but rather as someone who dies many deaths and experiences many renewals," as someone, in other words, who is not a some *one*.[4] The speaker keeps finding himself to be someone else, and this finding, in Harman's words "signals the end of coherence, the end of narrative, the end of *representational* life."[5]

Indeed in almost every one of these poems the moment of unhappiness (and sometimes of despair) is presented as a moment in which a promising story line had been broken off. In "Giddinesse" man is imagined first as fixed on heaven "as of his treasure" (line 5), but then "a thought creeps in" (line 6) – as if a switch on a railroad track had been turned by an unseen agent – and suddenly that same man is fixed on the pleasures heaven will require him to relinquish. In subsequent stanzas he is a soldier, a pacifist, a recluse, a miser, a spendthrift, until finally his mind is characterized as a "whirlwinde" (line 14), as something that continually alters (line 18) with "desires" (line 20) he cannot control and which, like the thought that "creeps in," are not finally his own. In "The Flower," that same variability, without transition and without pattern, leaves the speaker unable at any moment to make continuous sense of his existence: "It cannot be / That I am he / On whom thy tempests fell all night" (lines 40–42). "O that I once past changing were" (line 22), he cries in a line that itself marks a change from the achieved equanimity of the previous stanza, and it is clear that even when the change is from a "shrivel'd heart" (line 8) to one that "buds again" (line 36), from "tempests" (line 42) to "dew" (line 38), it is no less disconcerting than it would be if the direction were malign; for in either direction what the speaker (if he can still be honored by that appellation) is deprived of (a deprivation that leaves him with nothing) is, as the poem precisely says, a "straight line," a directionality that is sustained enough to afford material for a story, for a story of a someone. This speaker, like so many others, is continually discovering that he does not know himself, that there is no himself to know because the stances and attitudes he displays merely follow one another in a succession and do not follow from a set of motives and purposes that would confer on them a coherence.

Of course this is exactly the goal of Christian life, to lose the coherence that makes one's actions a career and gives them a shape independent of the shape imposed on everything by God's will. The variability of which Herbert's speakers so often complain, the sense they have of a story line continually interrupted by forces outside them, the sense of being the vehicle of so many conflicting and temporary voices that they have no voice of their own, is exactly the condition of their salvation. Even as they lament their distance from God, as evidenced by an inability to sustain a sense of his presence ("If what my soul doth feel sometimes, / My soul might ever feel?"), they testify to the annihilation of that distance when they are able to do nothing but helplessly record alterations of mood and understanding so violent and random that they resist intelligibility. "O rack me not to such a vast extent" (line 9), pleads the speaker of "The Temper (1)." The number and extent of the changes he suffers are too great to be accommodated within the canvas of the self which because it cannot contain – manage, order, relate, narrate – them is exploded, disintegrated, dispersed by them; as a result the self is not its own, but another's. "Those distances belong to thee" (line 10) the speaker says in a complaint that should be a celebration of the gain he enjoys in loss.

In some poems that celebration arrives, as it does here in "Temper (1)": "Yet take thy way; for sure thy way is best: / Stretch or contract me, thy poor debter" (lines 21–22); and in "The Flower" the achievement of insight is even more decisively announced:

These are thy wonders, Lord of love,
  To make us see we are but flowers that glide:
    Which when we once can finde and prove,
  Thou hast a garden for us, where to bide.
    Who would be more,
    Swelling through store,
  Forfeit their Paradise by their pride. (lines 43–49)

Or in other words: "I see now that what I have been complaining about is
nothing more or less than the strategy by which God brings us to the
realization that rather than being creatures that grow we are creatures
always in transit, never the same, always passing from state to state, never
in one place." But if this resolution is satisfying because it renders intelligible something that had previously resisted understanding (the apparently unpatterned succession of extreme mental and spiritual states), that
very satisfaction is the vehicle of its own undoing; for in this hard
economy, intelligibility undoes the spiritual benefit; gain – especially gain
of insight – is loss, since to acquire it is to have written and lived a story:
"Once I was perplexed and disoriented by the vicissitudes of my life; now
I see how to make sense of them; no longer am I disoriented, once again
I am an I, a someone whose struggles are the stuff of a spiritual *bildungs-
roman* which now displays (and can boast of) a beginning, a middle, and
an end."

We can see what is wrong with this by slightly rewriting another of
Herbert's poems, "The Holdfast," a short lyric in which the speaker
searches for an action, however small, that he can call his own. He
determines first to keep the law, but is told that it is beyond his power
and that he must trust not in himself, but in God. He then resolves to
trust, but this course too is denied him as his interlocutor explains,
"Nay, ev'n to trust in him, was also his; / We must confesse that nothing
is our own" (lines 6–7). Aha, the speaker says, then I will confess that
nothing is my own, only to hear in reply, "But to have nought is ours,
not to confesse / That we have nought" (lines 9–10). That is, philosophizing about having nought is not the same thing as having nought,
for the very act of philosophizing is a claim to possession and mastery
of one's own thoughts. Similarly, if the speaker of "The Flower" claims
to have realized that he is transitory, then by the inexorable logic of
"The Holdfast" that realization undermines itself because it can only
be the product of a consciousness that claims continuity in its ability
to sum and pronounce, to be reflective, to speak from a perspective, to
have a point of view, to have duration. "But," as the second voice of

"The Holdfast" might say, "To *be* transitory is ours, Not to *realize* that we are transitory." Harman would have it that the speaker here "acknowledges the *impossibility* of any full saying, when he acknowledges that our sentences, like our bodies and like our stories, are provisional";[6] but of course that acknowledgment is itself a "full saying" in which provisionality is domesticated and evaded by being made into a conclusion, an ending, the terminal point of a new (though ever more sophisticated) narrative.

The very action of having reached a conclusion is the "more" to which the last three lines of "The Flower" refer: "Who would be more, / Swelling through store, / Forfeit their Paradise by their pride" (lines 47–49). Richard Strier wonders about what he calls these "grim final lines."[7] They are to be explained, I think, as a reaction on the part of Herbert to the robustness of the lines that precede them, lines in which he becomes more by seeing through to the other side of his situation where he finds waiting the pride of successful intellection. "Store" means "increase" or "addition"; it is a motion exactly opposite to gliding or diminishing and here it is the motion of adding to one's stock of insight and therefore to oneself by reaching an extending resolution. You can't *be* gliding at the moment you become newly able to proclaim (indeed boast) that you are gliding. Herbert's requirements are always more severe than the achievements he records, because the basic requirement is that there be no achievement, nothing to report, no story to tell, not even anything to know.

The point is made at the end of "Gratefulnesse" when the speaker asks to be given a "thankfull heart" (line 27), but then immediately qualifies his request in a way that can serve as a comment on all of the poems we have looked at. I don't want a heart, he says, that is "thank-full when it pleaseth me," but rather "such a heart, whose pulse may be / Thy praise." That is to say, he doesn't want a heart that *knows* itself to be grateful and is therefore, in its knowledge, making a claim. He wants a heart that is just – without consciousness, without more – grateful, full of gratitude, its every beat speaking a praise from which it is indistinguishable. But even to have that want, to be conscious that your goal is to be without separate consciousness is to be separate from that goal, is to be too much, to be something in addition, is to swell through store. Neither Herbert nor his speakers can ever get quite thin enough, be sufficiently insufficient, sufficiently shallow, sufficiently without depth, to disappear.

SHOWING HOLY

The one exception to this statement, and therefore Herbert's one success – because it is a non-success – is the title figure of *The Country Parson*. Until recently this pastoral work has always been regarded as a model of sincere piety. In 1908 Joseph Blount Cheshire, then Bishop of North Carolina, praised its "simplicity and unaffectedness, its directness of purpose . . . its genuine humility and sympathy . . . its absolute fidelity to truth,"[8] and sixty-three years later W.A. Powell was still sounding the same note: "The simplicity and homeliness of style, the directness of tone . . . and the uses of images which unmistakably present a spiritual truth all combine to depict the simple faith and devout spirit of George Herbert's humble audience."[9] In every discussion of *The Country Parson*, the same words recur, "sincere," "direct," "simple," and "unaffected," and the praise is always for the "integrity" of the title figure, and, by extension, of Herbert, whose practice at Bemerton is presumed to be his model.

It is only in the last decade that critics have begun to complicate this pretty picture, usually by bringing *The Country Parson* into the ambit of the courtesy books it is now said to resemble. Cristina Malcolmson quarries both the courtesy manuals and the "character genre" in support of her thesis that "For Herbert, 'character' referred directly to the process of a public self-representation . . . To have a holy 'character' was not to be spiritually minded but to make that spiritual mindedness public."[10] It was for him as for others in these traditions, "a matter of performance."[11] Kristine Wolberg extends this argument and renders it even more pointed: "Herbert's manual in fact instructs the pastor in how to fashion a correct public image. The great bulk of Herbert's advice is not immediately linked to spiritual realities, but to the minister's appearances."[12] And, in what is surely the most nuanced and sophisticated version of this line of analysis, Michael Schoenfeldt finds that *The Country Parson* repeatedly "blur[s] the distinction between social and religious demeanor that it attempts to draw," and he substitutes for the benign and simple figure of an earlier criticism a parson who "imposes upon his congregation a regulation of body and behavior that is continuous with courtly self-control."[13]

I agree with the points made in these analyses but I find them made in ways that leave in place the same familiar oppositions – between surface and depth, artifice and substance, show and reality – that were assumed and honored by those whose view of Herbert and his parson was less critical and more benign. When Malcolmson says that the chief lesson of

The Country Parson "was not to be spiritually minded but to make that spiritual mindedness public," she assumes that the spiritual-mindedness is securely in place (in its *inner* place) and that the skill required is the translation of that interior condition into a public posture. In her reading, the public performance is anchored in and validated by the parson's private integrity; his life "links internality and appearance, inside and outside, ethical quality and visible behavior."[14] (One has no doubt as to which is the superior and controlling term in each of these phrases.) And in the same vein, Wolberg feels obliged at the end of her essay to detach Herbert from the courtesy tradition in which she has embedded him so that she can reassert his commitment to a higher aim: "[w]hile Herbert, like the secular courtesy author, emphasizes appearances rather than realities, he stands out in his final aims as well as in his confidence that appearances can have a profound mimetic effect upon one's spiritual realities."[15] I would argue, however, that Herbert's emphasis on appearances (and on performance and control) is not so easily domesticated, and that if one reads his little tract in the light of what I have identified as the poet's impossible project – the effort to be thin to the point of vanishing – something quite remarkable, and even disturbing, emerges.

Let me begin with a sentence that conveniently foregrounds the issues that will remain in play throughout *The Country Parson*. "The Countrey Parson, when he is to read divine services, composeth himselfe to all possible reverence; lifting up his heart and hands, and eyes, and using all other gestures which may express a hearty, and unfeyned devotion."[16] What strikes one immediately about this sentence is the tension between its two vocabularies – on the one hand the vocabulary of piety and sincerity – "reverence," "heart," "unfeyned devotion" – and on the other the vocabulary of artifice and theatricality – "composeth," "gestures," and "express." This latter set of words combines to emphasize the extent to which the parson's actions are superficial in the sense that they are "put on" much as one might put on a suit of clothes. The "reverence" is precisely "composed," that is, constructed or confected; the heart is not really lifted up; rather, a theatrical gesture stands in for the parson's heart of whose actual posture we know nothing, and as for the "unfeyned devotion," that is the triumph of the composer's art, to express, by means of some outward movement, an inward orientation defined precisely by its scorn of the external. The parson, in short, is skilled in feigning being unfeigned. He is the expert not at being devoted, but at expressing devotion, and in the sentences that follow, the tools of his trade are laid out and anatomized:

This he doth, first, as being truly touched and amazed with the Majesty of God, before whom he then presents himself; yet not as himself alone, but as presenting with himself the whole Congregation ... Secondly, as this is the true reason of his inward fear, so he is content to express this outwardly to the utmost of his power; that being first affected himself, hee may affect also his people knowing that no Sermon moves them so much to a reverence, which they forget againe, when they come to pray, as a devout behavior in the very act of praying. Accordingly his voyce is humble, his words treatable, and slow; yet not so slow neither, as to let the fervency of the supplicant hang and dy between speaking, but with a grave livelinesse, between fear and zeal, pausing yet pressing, he performes his duty. (*The Country Parson*, p. 231; ch. 6)

As this passage makes clear, not only does he perform his duty; performance *is* his duty, and what he must first perform is the spontaneity of the gestures he so deliberately orders; he must act as if ("as being") he were "truly touched and amazed" and what that action or composition involves is duly detailed: a humble tone, a distinct speech which is slow, but not so slow as to suggest a lack of fervency. All of this is quite accurately and openly characterized as the ability to "expresse ... outwardly." The parson dresses himself in the appropriate gestures and then "presents" himself, that is, makes a presentation or composition of himself. The qualifying, "yet not as himself alone" is exactly to the point. He is never himself alone; he is always in the act of composing himself, that is, of putting together or constructing the role he will then play.

In the next chapter, "The Parson Preaching," that role is called being holy, "the character of his Sermon is Holiness ... A Character that *Hermogenes* never dream'd of, and therefore he could give no precepts thereof" (p. 233; ch. 7). "Character" is the perfect word to capture what is going on here, since it means both distinctive mark or style and inward essence, refers at the same time to a representation and to the thing represented. The parson's sermon is marked (characterized) by holiness, but it is a holiness wholly made up of external marks, of signs. Hermogenes may be unable to present a list of precepts for producing the "holiness effect," but Herbert's parson displays no such inability: "first," he says, choose "texts of Devotion ... moving and ravishing texts"; then, he states that it is by "dipping and seasoning all our words and sentences in our hearts, before they come into our mouths, truly affecting and cordially expressing all that we say ... that the auditors may plainly perceive that every word is hart-deep" (p. 233; ch. 7). The effect produced is to be one of words coming directly from the heart but it is an effect that will follow upon a careful rehearsal of the appropriate cries and gestures. The result will be "truly affecting" in two senses: the desired effect will have been achieved – the audience will be affected – and the success will be the product of a true or superior exercise of the skill of "affecting," of putting on.

The same doubleness of reference is also present in the phrase "cordially expressing," which again offers a formula for simulating by outward signs (by expression) the interior ("cordial") reality. The words may *appear* to be "hart-deep" – the spontaneous and unprompted exclamation of an unfeigned piety – but in fact they will be taken from a stock inventory of pious-sounding phrases, an inventory whose contents the parson begins immediately to list: turn often, he advises, and make "many Apostrophes to God, as, Oh Lord blesse my people, and teach them this point; or, Oh my Master, on whose errand I come, let me hold my peace, and doe thou speak thy selfe." This is how the parson achieves not heart deepness but its appearance, by piling up layer on layer of pre-packaged *signs* of sincerity. On this point the prose is precise and unabashed: "Some such irradiations scatteringly in the sermon carry great holiness in them." We are then told that holiness is also "carried" by "frequent wishes of the people's good." Indeed "there is no greater sign of holiness" than such wishes and therefore one should take care that they be "woven into Sermons, which will make them appear exceeding reverend." The last instruction is often to urge "the presence, and majesty of God, by these, or such like speeches," examples of which promptly follow. And lest one mistake the point of this amazing sequence, it concludes with the general observation that "such discourses" – discourses artificially built up in the manner here described – "*shew* very Holy" (p. 234; ch. 7, my emphasis).

I am aware that the previous paragraph could be read as a severe criticism of Herbert, indeed as an accusation of hypocrisy. But in fact I intend no such criticism, and if hypocrisy is the appropriate term for what I have described, it is so in the root sense of the word – "playing a character on a stage." Herbert's parson is always play-acting, and because he is play-acting he is never being himself. In a technical sense one might say that he practices and counsels a massive insincerity, but in the context of what Rosemond Tuve long ago identified as Herbert's lifelong goal of self-immolation,[17] massive insincerity is the mark not of a failure but of an almost unthinkable achievement (just try it); for if the parson (and through him Herbert) does in fact manage to be wholly insincere, he realizes, or at least comes close to realizing, the desire to not be himself, to not be more, to not swell through store, to not have a story of his own. That, after all, is what insincerity is, to not be speaking from the heart, to have a disjunction between one's words and actions and one's innermost thoughts, indeed to have no innermost thoughts, but to be a succession of false appearances, to be all surface, superficial, without depth, thin, to be continually composed, confected, constructed, to feign. What Herbert sees is that, in relation to the mode of life for which the Christian yearns – a reunion with the will of God – sincerity, the claim of saying and doing what *you* mean, is a temptation, is the greatest temptation. And what he also sees and here exemplifies is that the way to defeat the temptation of sincerity is to be always in a posture of affectation, to have the character of having no character by being a number of characters (in the theatrical sense) seriatim, to be a hypocrite, to be always presenting (composing) oneself and therefore never being oneself, to be always other, because you are always dispersed.

It is an incredible project, especially in the context of the anti-representationalism that is so prominent in sixteenth- and seventeenth-century thought. In effect, Herbert is reversing the hierarchy of values that is constitutive of Platonic-Stoic-Christian thought as it is found in the works of authors otherwise so diverse as Spenser, Shakespeare, Jonson, Bacon and Milton. It is as if Jonson were to turn and celebrate (rather than vilify) Inigo Jones for being all show and no substance, for being indeed the "earl of show, for all thy work is show."[18] Jonson ends his vitriolic poem (one of many) by exclaiming that however many surfaces Jones's artistry can paint, however many effects he can create, the one thing he cannot create, either of others or of himself, is an "honest man."[19] An honest man would be a sincere man, a man whose center stood firm against the variable pressures of a protean world, a man whose inner point of reference was the measure of everything he saw and did, a man who took to heart Polonius's famous counsel, "to thine own self be true." He would be what R.A. Lanham (with not a little sarcasm) has named him, Serious Man, and his prototype would be the Socrates of the *Dialogues*, the man who dies rather than betray himself, the "Martyr-of-the-Central-Self ... utterly his own man."[20] Opposed to Serious Man in Lanham's two member taxonomy is Rhetorical Man, *Homo Rhetoricus*, for whom "dramatic motive" – that is, the motive to impersonate, to feign – "forms the groundwork of all 'respectable' motives";[21] that is, of all motives that are supposedly "heart deep."

In the history of Western thought Rhetorical Man has never had a good press while Serious Man has been invulnerable to attack since, as Lanham observes, to quarrel with him would be to quarrel with "a fundamental Western Ideality,"[22] an ideality whose watchwords are integrity and sincerity, values that undergird an essentialism which finds an expression in innumerable places from Sidney's "fool . . . look in thy heart and write" to Herbert's own Neoplatonic preference in "Jordan (1)" for a "true" over a "painted chair" (line 5). Of course, the dismissal of fine language in favor of the solid things of the world and heart is itself a rhetorical convention (witness in addition to Sidney's Astrophel, Shakespeare's Iago, Coriolanus, and Hotspur, Spenser's Archimago, Skelton's Colin Clout, the speaker of Donne's satires, and even Herbert himself in the third of his extant orations ["*non rhetoricor, Academici*"]),[23] and one could argue, as Lanham does, that Serious Man has always been Rhetorical Man's favorite role. Still, it seems to me that the Herbertian project differs significantly from those others with which it might be compared. The parson is not trying (vainly), as are the protagonists of so many other Renaissance poems and plays, to escape *from* rhetoricity, but to escape *into* rhetoricity, into surface, superficiality, into show; he is not engaged in an (impossible) attempt to be himself in a world of appearances, but in the (perhaps equally impossible) attempt to be nothing more than an appearance, to be nothing more, to be nothing.

Moreover, he sees it as his business to move others in the same (non)direction. To that end he makes surprise visits to his parishioners in the afternoons of weekdays, for then "he shall find his flock most naturally as they are, wallowing in the midst of their affaires: whereas on Sundays it is easie for them to compose themselves to order, which they put on as their holy-day cloathes, and come to Church in frame, but commonly the next day put off both" (p. 247; ch. 14). In a recent edition of the poetry "wallowing" is glossed as "engaged in, without the present negative connotations,"[24] but the editor is betrayed into an historical inaccuracy ("wallow" in its negative connotations is standard usage in the King James Bible) by the familiar Platonic prejudice in favor of the natural and the interior. In the editor's reading, the parson is critical of his parishioners for spiritually dressing up on Sundays, for putting on an act; but in fact the parson is critical of his parishioners for not dressing up on the other days, for not putting on an act, for falling back into being themselves – "naturally as they are." The strategy is the reverse of the usual one in which you stagger your visits in order to be sure that your flock is not putting on its best face; here the parson staggers his visits so that his flock will be unable to relax ("wallow") and will always be putting on its best face. He wants his parishioners to "compose themselves to order," to put on holiness, because only a put on – affected, confected – holiness will be free of what he will later in the tract term the "tincture" of the "private" (p. 287; ch. 37). It is in the private mode that they "wallow" and comport themselves "naturally," and not as they would if they knew they were always being watched, performing on stage, "in frame." The church as theater, as show, is not a metaphor the parson avoids; rather, he courts it in order to exaggerate the public space in which he wants his parishioners to operate, always afraid lest they be caught not playing a role.

TRACKING GOD'S WAYS

It is at this point that the dark underside of the Herbertian project comes into view. For it would seem that by extending his program of total theatricality – of never being off-stage and "naturally as he is" – to his parishioners, the parson produces a society that is regulated down to the last detail. To the extent that his strategy is successful, no one of his charges ever experiences an unguarded moment, but lives in fear of a visit whose prospect controls behavior even (especially) when it does not occur. The result is an authoritarian regime, and one might wonder how so much authority and control can emerge from a project of self-effacement. The answer lies in another one of the parson's self (or anti-self) descriptions: "the Countrey Parson . . . is a . . . tracker of Gods wayes" (p. 72). That is to say, he walks in the tracks of another and has no way of his own (he copies, exactly in the sense recommended in the last lines of "Jordan [II]"), a posture that seems to breathe humility until one takes in the whole of the sentence as it unfolds: "So the Countrey Parson, who is a diligent observer, and tracker of Gods wayes, sets up as many encouragements to goodnesse as he can . . . that he may, if not the best way, yet any way, make his Parish good" (p. 244; ch. 11). Being a tracker of God's ways does not mean that one performs no actions but that one performs actions like God's, which in turn means that, like God, one employs any means that comes to hand ("yet *any* way") in order to effect an end – bringing one's parishioners to goodness – that justifies those means.

A whiff of the unrestrained power this justification authorizes enters the prose with the last clause – "*make* his Parish good" – and the full extent of that power emerges as the parson's activities in relation to his flock are more completely described. The key to everything he does as a tracker of God's ways is that he stands "in Gods stead to his Parish," and therefore, "there is nothing done either wel or ill, whereof he is not the rewarder or punisher" (p. 254; ch. 20). And if one doubts the extent to which this impulse to social control is to be indulged, it is a doubt that does not survive another such description: "The Countrey Parson, where ever he is, keeps Gods watch; that is, there is nothing spoken or done in the

Company where he is, but comes under his Test and censure" (p. 252; ch. 18). (At this point, the same editor, again zealous to protect Herbert and his text from what they are obviously saying, glosses "censure" as "[e]valuation, without present negative connotation."[25])

Even this statement falls short of communicating the zeal with which the parson carries out his duties, for it suggests that his parishioners might escape notice when they are not in his company. However, as we learn in a chapter entitled "The Parson's Completeness," he so contrives it that they shall always be in his company by insisting that in his parish all offices of whatever kind shall be performed by him and by him alone: "The Countrey Parson desires to be all to his Parish, and not onely a Pastour, but a Lawyer also, and a Phisician. Therefore hee endures not that any of his Flock should go to Law; but in any controversie, that they should resort to him as their Judge" (p. 259; ch. 23). Even so, one might think that there would be times when his flock has need neither of judge nor lawyer, nor physician, nor pastor, and is therefore (quite literally) out of his sight, but it is at these times that the parson betakes himself to a hill from whose vantage point, we are told, he is able to survey his flock and "discover" its vices (p. 264; ch. 26). It is his particular skill to spy not the obvious vices of "Adultery, Murder, Hatred," etc. but those of a "dark, and creeping disposition," whose "natures are most stealing, and beginnings uncertaine" and whose detection requires the kind of vigilant "canvasing" (pp. 264–265; ch. 26) the parson so assiduously practices.

This particular aspect of the parson's performance is recounted in a chapter entitled "The Parson's Eye," and given the titles of surrounding and related chapters – "The Parson as Father," "The Parson in Sentinel," "The Parson in God's Stead," "The Parson Punishing," "The Parson's Surveys" – Herbert's idealized pastor begins to look like the engineer and operator of a system of surveillance that answers perfectly to the account of Bentham's Panopticon in Foucault's *Discipline and Punish*:

All that is needed, then, is to place a supervisor in a central tower . . . By the effect of backlighting, one can observe from the tower, standing out precisely against the light, the small captive shadows in the cells of the periphery. They are like so many cages, so many small theatres, in which each actor is . . . constantly visible. The panoptic mechanism arranges spatial unities that make it possible to see constantly and to recognize immediately . . . Full lighting and the eye of the supervisor capture better than darkness . . . Visibility is a trap.[26]

As Foucault points out, one justification of the Panopticon and other "Enlightenment" disciplinary spaces is that the power they exert is not the power of a single person (such as a sovereign) but of the impersonal face of society, and therefore it could be said that disciplinary techniques were not carried out in the name of anyone in particular.[27] It is exactly in these terms that Herbert defends his parson against the charge that in zealously discovering the faults of offenders in his parish he violates the biblical injunction to be charitable:

But this is easily answered: As the executioner is not uncharitable, that takes away the life of the condemned, except besides his office, he add a tincture of private malice in the joy, and haste of acting his part; so neither is he that defames him, whom the Law would have defamed, except he also do it out of rancur. (p. 287; ch. 37)

Here in a concise form is both a rehearsal of Herbert's theory of (non)personality and an analysis of the way in which that theory negotiates the passage from a dispersal of power and the loss of story to a reconcentration of power in a story that is at once seamless and totalitarian. Like the executioner, the parson is never himself, is never anything "besides his office"; he is always acting his part and thereby making no claim to have a story of his own; but this very condition of being void of story – of having no continuous being, no personal desires, no inner orientation, no tincture of the private – frees him to act as an agent of a larger story – the story of a bureaucracy or of a God – and thus to acquire a prepared-in-advance justification for anything he does. The result is a narrative that unites absolute contingency and absolute design. The design belongs to the parson, but it is experienced as contingency by his charges, who live with no certainty except the certainty that their own designs can be interrupted and unlinked at any moment. Because they never know when he is going to show up, they are unable to give themselves to the purposes of their "own affairs" and instead must await the eruption into those affairs of a purpose whose springs remain hidden. By providing his charges with the experience of continual anxiety, the parson fulfills one of his chief obligations, which is "to reduce [the members of his flock] to see Gods hand in all things, and to beleeve, that things are not set in such an inevitable order, but that God often changeth it according as he sees fit, either for reward or punishment" (p. 270; ch. 30).

This is an extraordinarily complex statement which repays analysis no less than a line in one of Herbert's poems. The order *is* in fact inevitable; it is the order of God's will, but it is shown in the frustration of other orders – the natural, the logical, the cultural – on which man is tempted to depend. In short, God disrupts the plots in which man attempts to insert himself and insists that he see himself as an unwilling actor in a plot that is forever escaping his understanding. God prevents man from making sense of his existence, except by the reference to the extra-rational category of "God's hand" (or what he "sees fit"), a category one invokes in feeble response to a universe of pure chance. If chance and randomness are the only thing you can count on, it becomes difficult, if not impossible, to wrest meaning and intelligibility from your experience. By removing predictability, God and his parson prevent their charges from making coherent sense of their lives and ready them to rely for sense on the will of their masters.

The result is a narrative of cosmic jealousy ("Thou shalt have no other gods before me") abetted by absolute power, and it is a narrative that Herbert rehearses with an almost unholy glee: "God delights to have men feel, and acknowledge, and reverence, his power, and therefore he often overturnes things, when they are thought past danger; that is his time of interposing" (p. 272; ch. 30). That is, it is God's practice and delight to look for those times when men have deluded themselves into thinking that events have now acquired an intelligible shape, and then he intervenes in an act which replaces shape and pattern with contingency:

As when a Merchant hath a ship come home after many a storme, which it hath escaped, he destroys it sometimes in the very Haven; or if the goods be housed, a fire hath broken forth, and suddenly consumed them ... So that if a farmer should depend upon God all the year, and being ready to put hand to sickle, shall then secure himself, and think all cock-sure; then God sends such weather, as lays the corn, and destroys it: or if he depend on God further, even till he imbarn his corn, and then think all sure; God sends a fire and consumeth all he hath. (pp. 270–271; ch. 30)

And God does these things not because he loves disorder and discontinuity for their own sake, but for the sake of their effect on those who might be tempted to a prideful self-confidence: "Now this he doth, that men should perpetuate, and not break off their acts of dependence, how faire soever the opportunities present themselves ... [one] ought not to break off, but to continue his dependance on God ... and indeed, to depend, and fear continually" (p. 271; ch. 30).

This description of God's intention and practice is, as we have seen, also a description of the parson's intention and practice; this, then, is what it means to be a tracker of God's ways and be "in his stead." The difference of course is that God's surveillance is not something for which he has to work; it comes along with his omnipresence, with his all-seeing eye. The parson on the contrary enjoys no such supernatural power and he must contrive to simulate God's easy surveillance with a complex system of social, political and juridical mechanisms in which the area of contingency is progressively reduced until every moment and every action bears the mark of a controlling design; the citizens who live in this system must "depend and fear continually," that is, they must never be allowed to feel that anything they do is unrelated to the pressure of a master plot of which they are not the authors. Rather than being void of story, this world is replete, indeed overflowing, with story, a story of dependence and manipulation that everyone is forced to enact.

OLD AND NEW PIETIES

A reading of *The Country Parson* so at odds with the traditional accounts of the tract raises more than a few questions. Why have so many missed the darkness and terror of Herbert's vision, and why *is* the vision so dark and terrible? How does one account for it? To the first question I would respond by pointing to the history of Herbert criticism, a history inaugurated by Izaak Walton's hagiographical life, and a history that to this very day cannot free itself from hagiography. To the second question – how does one account for the Herbert I have described? – there are a range of possible answers, no one of which is wholly satisfying. One might begin by linking the parson's efforts to monitor, and by monitoring, eliminate the inner life of his parishioners, to Herbert's response to Andrew Melville's attack on rites and ceremonies. Repeatedly mocking the puritan proclivity for undressing or "living without clothes," Herbert warns that a soul, "bare of sacred rites," has been rendered "bare to conquest / By Satan."[28] Nothing could be further from his religious temper than Milton's declaration (in answer to the question, "What, no decency in Gods worship?") that "the very act of prayer and thanksgiving with those free and unimpos'd expressions which from a sincere heart unbidden come into the outward gesture, is the greatest decency that can be imagined."[29] In Herbert's theology it is the "outward gesture" that makes good what a heart, naturally and totally foul, cannot, by itself, perform. Where Milton wishes to encourage spontaneity, Herbert wishes to extinguish it.

Still, this does not explain the parson's program of surveillance, his imposition of a control so total that he is jealous of any to whom his parishioners might turn for aid or counsel. Once again, however, there are historical materials that would seem to provide an explanatory context. In a culture obsessed by the mysterious workings of an all powerful and omnipresent deity, it is hardly surprising that men would think of God as someone by whom they are being continually disciplined. This is the argument, persuasively made, by Debora Shuger under the rubric of "absolutist theology." What she says of Donne could apply equally well to Herbert: "His preaching, and his king are all analogously related, all participants in absolutist structures of domination and submission."[30] Jonathan Dollimore makes the same point with the help of a passage from William Perkins's "A Discourse of Conscience":

The master of a prison is knowne by this to have care over his prisoners . . . and so Gods care to man is manifested in this, that when he created man and placed him in the world, he gave him conscience to be his keeper, to follow him alwaies at his heeles, and to dogge him . . . and to prie into his actions, and to beare witnesse of them all.[31]

The emphasis on conscience and an inner discipline is of course puritan, but one could turn to Thomas More's *Dialogue of Comfort Against Tribulation* for quotations that would externalize the discipline in ways Herbert's parson would recognize and approve.

God our chiefe gayler, as himselfe is inuisible, so vseth he in his punishments inuisible instrumentes, and therfore not of like fashion as the tother gaylers doo, but yet of like effect, and as paynfull in feeling as those. For he leyeth one of hys prisoners with an hote feuer, as euill at his ease in a warm bedde, as the tother gayler layeth his on the cold ground: he wringeth them by the browes with a meygreme: he collereth them by the neck with a quinsye [sore throat]: he bolteth them by the armes with a paulsy . . . he manacleth their handes with the gowt . . . he wringeth them by the legges with the crampe in their shinnes: he byndeth them to the bedde borde with the crycke in the backe, and layeth one there alonge, and as vnhable to ryse, as though he laye by fast the feete in the stockes.[32]

Statements like this one support Schoenfeldt's assertion that in Renaissance Europe there is a close connection between divine power and torture. He cites Luther's confident declaration that when princes punish, "It is not man, but God, who hangs, tortures, beheads, strangles."[33] In comparison to this, the discipline of the God of Herbert's parson, working as he does largely on grain and ships, seems almost tame.

Another possible explanation for the severity of the parson's regime is more theoretical and less historical. Jonathan Goldberg turns for illumination to Freud's linking of the notion of conscience with the pathology of paranoia: "Patients . . . complain that all their thoughts are known and their actions watched and over looked."[34] This, as Goldberg points out, is exactly the complaint of so many Herbert speakers, who always imagine themselves "in the position of subjection"; and as "the *object* of scrutiny."[35] Following Goldberg's lead, we could argue that the paranoid fantasy of perpetual surveillance is an inevitable consequence of Herbert's strong monotheism, and that since one response to that fantasy is to identify with the surveillant, the program of the country parson is merely a logical extension of that response. Here the moral would be precisely that of Herbert's poem "The Reprisall": if you can't beat him (and you certainly can't), join him; that is, join your will or your wing to his – and thereby gain for yourself – no longer *your* self alone – the power that is properly his; turn submission and lowliness into the exercise of power. This is precisely what is done in innumerable sermons composed by preachers on every conceivable side of every conceivable debate in which every conceivable action is justified by its having been performed at God's behest and in his name. Or one could, as many historicists have now begun to do, invoke those manuals of courtesy that instruct in precisely this art, in the myriad ways by which gestures of humility and deference can be the means of seizing and maintaining power. It would then be a simple matter to argue (as Schoenfeldt does) that as a practiced courtier and court rhetorician Herbert would have quite naturally conceived of his relationship with God in terms analogous if not equivalent to his relationship with James I. Again Shuger provides a gloss: "The theological corollary of royal absolutism is radical monotheism, the total concentration of power into a single figure."[36]

With so many explanatory paths in prospect, it would seem that the answer to my question – how are we to account for the dark and sinister aspect of Herbert's work? – is that it is overdetermined; we should have expected nothing else. It is, however, an answer I want to resist because by giving it we run the danger of making the Herbertian experience disappear into its possible sources and analogues. Instead, I would agree with Schoenfeldt when he insists that "Herbert's poems ... chillingly ... imagin[e] God as wielding various implements developed by western culture specifically for the imposition of pain."[37] It is the chill I want to emphasize, for even in an age that refuses the pieties of literary high humanism, the piety that has always characterized Herbert studies continues, albeit in a different form. At the beginning of this century we were still reading, or so we thought, a Herbert of simple, almost childlike piety. In the revisionist period that began with the studies of Rosemond Tuve and Joseph Summers, the piety was shown to be anything but simple, but piety nevertheless. And even in the most up-to-date discourses of the very newest Historicists, we are told of a Herbert who "attempts to break

through the surfaces of social experience to a nearly immediate communication from heart to heart," and who produces "a 'plain,' fully transparent
speech which makes impossible all artificiality."[38] The critic who writes
these words acknowledges the theatricality of the parson's performance,
but avers nevertheless that it is a performance whose aim is "to exclude the
theatrical by basing what is fabricated, the public image, on what is
essential, the holiness within."[39] A statement like this testifies to the desire
(apparently irresistible) of so many professional readers to transform their
favorite poets into exemplars of an inner integrity they also share. But this
will not do for the Herbert I have been describing, who sees that the way
to holiness is not to break through surfaces, but to multiply surfaces,
indeed to become a surface; not in order to have holiness within, but to
have nothing within, not to purify "inner states of mind and feeling,"[40]
but to achieve the absence of inner states and feeling.

"Achieve" of course is the wrong word; the requirement, as I noted at
the beginning of this chapter, is more severe: to not achieve, to not be
conscious of an achievement which would thereby – by consciousness of
it – be forfeit. That is why the most remarkable thing about *The Country
Parson* is its total lack of interest in the interiors of either its title figure or
his parishioners. In the poetry, the weather of the inner life is a continual
obsession, and as an obsession – with the status of the self, of a being that
would have duration – it constitutes a temptation. In *The Country Parson*
that temptation seems to have been mastered, and Herbert is able, in the
person of his parson, to give himself over completely to the externals of
saving ceremonies, to vestments that wear him. There are poems like that
too, notably "Aaron," a poem about dressing up, about putting on the
armor of God, and thereby becoming dead to the self, "Christ is my only
head / . . . / . . . striking me ev'n dead" (lines 16–18); not bringing new life
to me, but extinguishing me. As the armor goes on – and it just goes on;
we don't see him putting it on; we don't see him do anything – each piece
"replaces," rather than revivifying or refurbishing, what it covers, until,
in the manner of the transformation so brilliantly presented in the film
Robocop, there is something entirely new, an animated suit of clothing
where there was once a person. Of course, once liberated from person-
hood this animated automaton can then proceed (again, like the hero of
Robocop but with even less vestigial memory) to do absolutely terrible
things in the name of a higher power.

What remains startling (if not wholly original) in Herbert's work and
thought is this relationship between the drive toward self-abnegation and
the appropriation by the radically diminished self of everything that

self-abnegation would supposedly have relinquished. In "Josephs Coat," Herbert cites triumphantly, "I live to show his power" (line 13) and in that single half-line he displays the ambiguity that lends such a strength – such terrible beauty – to his work. He lives in order to be an illustration of God's power as it acts on him, to be a canvas for God's pencil, a showpiece of his irresistibility; and he also (or is it therefore?) lives in order to *show* that power to others by exercising it on their persons even as it has been exercised on his. If this is piety, it is difficult to say whether the appropriate response to it is admiration or fear, both of which are demanded by the God whose ways Herbert tracks.

NOTES

1 George Herbert, "A Dialogue Anthem," in *Works*, ed. F.E. Hutchinson (London, 1959), 1–4.
2 John Milton, *Paradise Lost*, in *Complete Poems and Major Prose*, ed. Merritt Y. Hughes (New York, 1957). Henceforth cited in this chapter as *PL*.
3 John Milton, "At a Solemn Music," in *Complete Poems and Major Prose*, 28. In making this point I do not mean to suggest that Eden is static or without dynamism. It is just that the dynamics – including the possibility of cognitive error and unhappy decisions – unfold within the security of an innocence that is theirs so long as they do not eat the apple. In Eden no action aside from the action of disobeying God's sole command is fatal or irreversible. In fallen life, fatality lurks around every corner.
4 Barbara Leah Harman, *Costly Monuments: Representations of the Self in George Herbert's Poetry* (Cambridge, MA and London, 1982), 166.
5 Ibid., 99, emphasis in original.
6 Ibid., 169, emphasis in original.
7 Richard Strier, *Love Known: Theology and Experience in George Herbert's Poetry* (Chicago and London, 1983), 252.
8 Joseph Blount Cheshire, ed., *A Priest to the Temple, or, the Country Parson . . . By George Herbert* (New York, 1908), 6.
9 W. Allen Powell, "The Nature of George Herbert's Audience as Revealed by Method and Tone in 'The Country Parson' and 'The Temple,'" *Proceedings of the Conference of College Teachers of English of Texas* 36 (1971), 36.
10 Cristina Malcolmson, "George Herbert's *Country Parson* and the Character of Social Identity," *Studies in Philology* 85 (1988), 246.
11 Ibid., 248.
12 Kristine Wolberg, "All Possible Art: George Herbert's *The Country Parson* and Courtesy," *John Donne Journal*, vol. 8, nos. 1 and 2 (1989), 168.
13 Michael C. Schoenfeldt, *Prayer and Power: George Herbert and Renaissance Courtship* (Chicago and London, 1991), 99.
14 Malcolmson, "George Herbert's *Country Parson*," 261.
15 Wolberg, "All Possible Art," 186.

16 Cheshire, ed., *A Priest to the Temple, or, the Country Parson*, 231; ch. 6.

17 Rosemond Tuve, *A Reading of George Herbert* (London, 1952), especially 189–190.

18 Ben Jonson, 'To Inigo, Marquis Would-Be a Corollary," in *The Oxford Authors: Ben Jonson*, ed. Ian Donaldson (Oxford and New York, 1976), 465.

19 Ibid.

20 Richard A. Lanham, *The Motives of Eloquence: Literary Rhetoric in the Renaissance* (New Haven, CT, 1985), 47.

21 Ibid., 14.

22 Ibid., 47.

23 Herbert, *Works*, 445.

24 George Herbert, *The Country Parson, The Temple*, ed. John N. Wall, Jr. (New York, 1984), 75.

25 Ibid., 79.

26 Michel Foucault, *Discipline and Punish* (New York, 1995), 200.

27 Ibid., 109.

28 George Herbert, *Latin Poetry*, trans. John Mark McCloskey and Paul R. Murphy (Athens, OH, 1965), 37, 39.

29 John Milton, "An Apology," in *Complete Prose Works* ed. Don M. Wolfe, vol. 1 (New Haven, CT, 1953), 941–942.

30 Debora K. Shuger, *Habits and Thoughts in the English Renaissance: Religion, Politics and the Dominant Culture* (Berkeley, CA, 1991), 209.

31 William Perkins, cited in Jonathan Dollimore, *Radical Tragedy: Religion, Ideology and Power in the Drama of Shakespeare and his Contemporaries*, 2nd edn. (Durham, NC, 1993), xlvii.

32 Sir Thomas More, *Utopia* with *The Dialogue of Comfort*, ed. Judge John O'Hagen (London, 1923), 323–324.

33 Schoenfeldt, *Prayer and Power*, 125.

34 "On Narcissism," cited in Jonathan Goldberg, *Voice Terminal Echo: Postmodernism and English Renaissance Texts* (New York, 1986), 108.

35 Ibid.

36 Shuger, *Habits and Thoughts*, 169.

37 Schoenfeldt, *Prayer and Power*, 117. I do not, however, follow Schoenfeldt's argument to all of its conclusions. I agree with Richard Strier that Herbert's poetry does not so much display or enact "self seeking courtliness" and "manipulation" as it makes ironic critical use of them (*Resistant Structures: Particularity, Radicalism and Renaissance Texts* [Berkeley, Los Angeles, London, 1995], 111–112). Strier is also correct, I think, when he observes that "Religion in general is something of a problem for New Historicism" (p. 73). On this point see my "Milton's Career and the Career of Theory," in *There's No Such Thing as Free Speech, and It's a Good Thing, Too* (New York, Oxford, 1994), 264–265.

38 Malcolmson, "George Herbert's *Country Parson*," 263.

39 Ibid., 262.

40 Ibid., 263.

CHAPTER 9

Authors–readers: Jonson's community of the same

INTRODUCTION

In the course of her incisive and powerful study of the rise of professionalism, Magali Sarfatti Larson identifies as one of the chief cognitive supports of the professional ethos something she calls the "ideology of merit" (213).[1] By this she means what is to us the very familiar notion (not to say conviction) that in modern corporate and academic life one rises by virtue of native ability and demonstrated competence rather than by the accidents of birth and fortune. Larson labels this notion "ideological" first because it is elaborated in the service of certain well-defined interests (largely those of the corporate bourgeoisie), and second because it masks what actually happens when the professional sets out to climb the ladder of advancement. What the professional tells himself (because he has been told it by others) is that as an individual, he is "essentially the proprietor of his own person and capacities, for which he owes nothing to society" (222), but in fact, as Larson points out, he owes everything to society, including the self whose independence supposedly enables and underwrites his achievements. That is to say, it is only with reference to the articulation and hierarchies of a professional bureaucracy that a sense of the self and its worth – its merit – emerges and becomes measurable. The ladder of advancement is not only a structural fact; it is a fact that tells the person who occupies a place on it who he is and what he has accomplished. By providing goals and aspirations and alternative courses of action, the ladder also provides the very "means of self-assertion" (199). "Career," Larson declares, "is a pattern of organization of the self" (229); or to put it another (less aphoristic) way, the self of the professional is constituted and legitimized by the very structures – social and institutional – from which it is supposedly aloof.

In Larson's analysis, professionalism and its contradictions constitute a departure from an earlier aristocratic model in which preferment is a

function of a "traditional social hierarchy" (90), and rewards are distrib-
uted on the basis of "social privileges" that pre-exist "the entry into
practice." She has in mind, of course, the system or network of patronage
that has recently become the object of so much scholarly attention, and
while she is surely right to contrast that network – where access and
mobility are largely determined by class – to the vertical passage offered
by the mechanisms of education and training, the two worlds of modern
bureaucracy and ancient privilege are alike in at least one respect: they
present their inhabitants with the problem of maintaining a sense of
individual worth within the confines of a totalizing structure. In the
Renaissance as well as in the twentieth century, that problem is known
by the word "merit." As Robert Harding has recently observed, theorists
of patronage were as concerned as their modern counterparts that preferment be based, insofar as it was possible, on considerations of merit and
virtue. To be sure, considerations of birth were themselves part of the
"merit calculus" – "it is to be presumed," says one treatise, "that the son of
a good father will bear himself heir of his virtues" – and merit, as Harding
points out, "was conceived more in terms of innate talents rather than
talents acquired by training and education," but still in all, it is clear from
the evidence that the distinction between "true desert" and merely political and social preferment was as much in force (albeit in a somewhat
different form) as it is today.[2]

The fact that it was in force has an obvious psychological consequence:
everyone wants to believe that his rewards have been earned rather than
bestowed, and conversely, everyone wants to believe that his ill fortune
is a comment not on his abilities, but on the perversity of a corrupt and
blinkered system. In a modern bureaucracy it is harder to believe the
second, since the system advertises itself as one that responds only to
competence and genuine achievement rather than to the accidents of birth,
or national or geographic origin. In the world of Renaissance patronage it
is harder to believe the first, since every recognition or reward comes
tagged with the name of someone who could have very well withheld it
and to whom one is obligated in ways that cannot be ignored.

This is especially true of the court poet whose productions almost
always bear on their face the signs of subservience – dedications, occasional
celebrations, flatteries, petitions, expressions of gratitude, recordings of
debt. How can someone whose work seems indistinguishable from the
network of patronage maintain a belief in its independence and therefore
in the independence of his own worth and virtue? I propose in this essay to
ask that question by taking up the case of Ben Jonson, a poet whose every

title would seem to mark him as a man dependent not only for his sustenance but for his very identity on the favor and notice of his social superiors. In what follows I will proceed somewhat indirectly, moving from a revisionary account of Jonson's poetic strategies to an analysis of the relationship between those strategies and his effort to assert his freedom and dignity in the face of everything that would seem to preclude them.

I.

Although Ben Jonson's poetry has been characterized as urbane and polished, much of it is marked by a deliberate and labored awkwardness. This is especially true of the beginning of a Jonson poem, where one often finds a meditation on the difficulty of beginning, a meditation that will typically take the form of a succession of false starts after which the poem stumbles upon its subject, having in the meantime consumed up to a third of its length in a search for its own direction. Thus, for example, the poem in praise of Shakespeare spends its first sixteen lines exploring the kinds of praise it will *not* offer before Jonson declares at line 17, "I therefore will begin," and even then what follows is a list of the poets to whom Shakespeare will *not* be compared.[3] In the "Epistle to Katherine, Lady Aubigny" (*The Forest*, no. 13) Jonson goes on for twenty lines about the dangers one courts by praising before he draws himself up to announce: "I, madame, am become your praiser" (21). The opening of the "Epistle to Master John Selden" (*Underwood*, no. 14) is more abrupt: "I know to whom I write," but although he knows, it is another twenty-nine lines before he hazards a direct address and says to Selden, "Stand forth my object." In the Cary-Morison ode (*Underwood*, no. 70) the halt and start of the verse is imitated by a character – the "brave infant of Saguntum" – who draws back from entering the world and therefore never manages to enter the poem, although he seems at first to be its addressee. And in what is perhaps the most complicated instance of the pattern, "An Elegy on the Lady Jane Paulet" (*Underwood*, no. 83), Jonson melodramatically portrays himself as unable to recognize the ghost of the Lady, who then identifies herself and immediately vanishes from the poem, leaving the poet with the task of writing an inscription for her tomb, a task he attempts in several aborted ways before resolving to leave off heraldry and "give her soul a name" (22), a resolution that is immediately repudiated by a declaration of poetic inability – "I durst not aim at that" (25) – so that as we reach line 30 of the poem we are being told that its subject cannot possibly be described.

What I would like to suggest in this essay is that Jonson's habit of beginning awkwardly is not simply a mannerism but is intimately related to the project of his poetry, and indeed represents a questioning of that project, since the issue always seems to be whether or not the poem can do what it sets out to do. The issue is also whether or not the reader can do what he is asked to, for quite often the interrupted or delayed beginning of a poem is part of a double strategy of invitation and exclusion in which the reader is first invited to enter the poem, and then met, even as he lifts his foot above the threshold, with a rehearsal of the qualifications for entry, qualifications which reverse the usual relationship between the poet and a judging audience. Here the salient example is "An Epistle Answering To One That Asked to Be Sealed of the Tribe of Ben" (*Underwood*, no. 47), where the reader must stand with his foot poised for seventy-eight lines. But a more manageable though equally instructive example is a small, hitherto unremarked-upon poem in the *Ungathered Verse*.[4]

In Authorem

> Thou, that wouldst finde the habit of true passion,
>   And see a minde attir'd in perfect straines;
> Not wearing moodes, as gallants doe a fashion,
>   In these pide times, only to shewe their braines,
>
> Looke here on *Bretons* worke, the master print:
>   Where, such perfections to the life doe rise.
> If they seeme wry, to such as looke asquint,
>   The fault's not in the object, but their eyes.
>
> For, as one comming with a laterall viewe,
>   Unto a cunning piece wrought perspective,
> Wants facultie to make a censure true:
>   So with this Authors Readers will it thrive:
>
> Which being eyed directly, I divine,
> His proofe, their praise, will meete, as in this line.
>   Ben: Jonson.

The tension that finally structures this poem at every level surfaces in the very first line in the word "habit," which means both "characteristic form" and "outward apparel." The tension lies in the claims implicitly made by the two meanings. The claim of one is to be presenting the thing itself while the claim of the other is limited to the presentation of a surface, and since that surface is a covering there is a suggestion (borne out by the examples of use listed in the *OED*) that what covers also hides and conceals. The uneasy relationship between the two meanings is brought out by the phrase "true passion." Can we truly see true passion if what we see is its habit? The question is not answered but posed again in line 2. Can a mind perfectly seen also be "attir'd"? Is the perfection we are asked to admire the perfection of the mind or of the dress that adorns it and therefore stands between it and our line of vision? The ambiguity of "habit" reappears in "straines," which, in addition to being an obvious reference to Breton's verse, carries the secondary meaning of pedigree or lineage. Is the perfect strain a perfect verbal rendering, i.e., a representation, or is it a perfect progeny, the direct offspring of the truth and therefore a piece of the truth itself?

As one proceeds through the first stanza, these questions are not insistent, in part because the poem's syntax has not yet stabilized. This syntactical hesitation is, as we shall see, typical of Jonson's poetry and allows him to keep alive options that will later converge in a single but complex sense. Thus, for example, it is unclear whether lines 3 and 4 are in apposition to "minde," and therefore descriptive of what the reader can expect to find, or in apposition to "Thou" (1.1) and therefore descriptive of the reader, who is required to do the finding. What is clear is that the description is negative, characterizing something or someone that does not show itself in modes or colors or even wit ("braines"). It is therefore with a particular sense of challenge that the second stanza issues its imperative: "Look here!" Look where, one might ask, or at what, since we know that it cannot be at variegated surfaces or eye-catching fashions. The only instruction we receive is to look at "such perfections," but these perfections, whatever they are, have not been given any palpable or visible form. Almost as if to forestall a complaint that we have been assigned an insufficiently explicit task, Jonson delivers a pronouncement on those who find themselves unable to perform it: "If they seeme wry, to such as looke asquint, / The fault's not in the object, but their eyes."

It is at this point that the relationship between the object (so carefully unspecified) and the reader's eyes becomes the poem's focus and its real subject. In the third stanza, the requirements for right vision are forthrightly presented in a simile that is as complicating as it is illuminating. Perspective is a device by which one produces in art the same visual effects that are produced without artifice in nature. It is the manipulation of surface in order to produce the illusion of depth; it is the practice of deception in order to disclose the real, and it therefore, as Ernest Gilman has observed, "bestows a double role" on the artist "as truth-teller and liar, and on the viewer as either ideal perceiver or dupe."[5] The paradox of perspective – its "cunning" is designed to neutralize the deficiencies of its own medium – is the paradox already hinted at in the doubleness of "habit," "straines," and "shewe." Is what is shown a revelation or is it an interposition – a "*mere shewe*" – that puts true revelation at even a further remove? Does Breton's work give its reader a sight of "true passion" or does it stand between that sight and his deceived eye? Are the "perfections" that seemingly "rise to the life" (always the tainted claim of illusionistic art) the perfections of appearance only? Such questions are not answered but given a particularly pointed form by the simile's argument, which contrasts the distortion that attends a "laterall" or sideways view with the view of a spectator who is correctly positioned. But that position has itself been forced upon him by the laws of perspective and by the manipulative strategy of the artist who deploys them. From within those laws and that strategy, the observer's judgment may indeed be "true" (11), but is it true to what really is, or true only to the constructed reality imposed on him by artifice?

In imitation of Jonson, I have deliberately withheld the context (or perspective) in which these questions receive an answer, the context of the court masque, a perspectival form at whose center is the figure of the monarch, at once audience and subject. In the theater presided over by Jonson and Inigo Jones, the king's chair occupies the only point in the hall from which the perspective is true. He is therefore not only the chief observer; he is what is being observed both by the masquers who direct their actions at him and by the other spectators, who must strive to see the presentation from his position if they are to "make a censure true." Moreover, since the masque is itself a celebration of the king's virtue, what he watches is himself, and insofar as his courtiers, in their efforts to align their visions with his, reproduce the relationship courtiers always have to a monarch, they are also at once the observers of an action and the performers of what they observe. One can no longer say then that the spectators are taken in or deceived by a contrived illusion, for they are themselves the cause of what they see, and in order to make a "censure true" they need only recognize themselves. There is no distance between them and a spectacle or representation of which they are the informing idea. The relationship between viewer and presentation is not one of subjection and control, but of identity; they are, in essence, the same, and because they are the same the court saw in the masque "not an imitation of itself, but its true self."[6]

It is here in the notion of an observer who is both indistinguishable from what he sees and its cause that the ethical and epistemological dilemmas of representation are resolved or at least bypassed, and it is that notion which informs the concluding lines of stanza 3: "So with this Authors Readers will it thrive." Of course, this line bears a perfectly reasonable sense as the conclusion to the simile's argument: the readers of Breton's work will judge it correctly to the extent that their line of vision is direct rather than oblique. But in the context of the masque experience, to which the entire simile has reference, a truly direct vision is the consequence of having recognized oneself and therefore of having become the reader of one's own actions – having become, in short, an author-reader. The composite noun which appears exactly in the center of Jonson's line is an answer (plainly there for all who have the eyes to see) to all the questions the poem implicitly raises. Insofar as the problem of the poem has been to find a position from which a reader of Breton's work can correctly judge it ("make a censure true"), that problem is solved by the assumption of an author-reader – that is, of a reader whose mind is attired with the same perfections as the mind informing the book. Judgment for such a reader will not even be an issue, since the act of judging implies a distance or a gap that has already been bridged by the identity, the sameness, of the censuring mind and its object. In this felicitous epistemology, perception is not mediated or "asquint" because it is *self*-perception; there is no obstruction between the eye and its object because there is literally nothing (no thing) between them. The dilemma of representation – its inability to be transparent, to refrain from clothing or covering – is no longer felt because representation is bypassed in favor of the instantaneous recognition, in another and in the work of another, of what one already is.

To solve the poem's problem in this way, however, is only to make the poem itself a problem, along with Breton's work. What exactly is their status? If what the fit reader would see in Breton's work is already in his mind, while others simply "want facultie," what is there left for the work to do? What *could* it do? And insofar as these questions apply to Breton, so do they apply equally to Jonson, who is as much "this author" as anyone else, and is certainly *this* author in relation to *this* poem. Isn't its work as superfluous as the work it purports to praise? Isn't its reader, its author-reader, directed to look at something he already is? All of these questions are rendered urgent by the first word of the concluding couplet, "Which," a word that is itself a question: "Which?" To what does it refer? The only possible candidate in the third stanza is the "cunning piece wrought perspective" of line 10, but it can hardly be that which is to be "eyed directly," since the noun-phrase is part of a simile, of an indirect or lateral approach, and is therefore by definition at a remove from direct perception. No matter how far back one goes in the poem, a satisfactory referent for "which" will not be found; *which* is just the point. The pronoun that stands in for nothing present or available refers to the perfection the poem cannot name because any name or habit serves only to obscure it. "Which" is a sign within the poem of what it cannot do, and a sign also of what is required of its reader as well as of the reader of Breton's work, to eye directly, that is, without any intervening medium, to find in himself what no poem or habit can represent. A reader who can so "eye" will not take from the poem, but give to it the center that will always escape its representational grasp, and the true act of communication which then follows is described (but not captured) in the sonnet's amazing final line: "His proofe, their praise, will meete, as in this line."

"His proofe, their praise" completes the work of "Authors Readers" by bonding the two agents together in a reciprocal and mutually defining relationship. His proof, in the sense of "that which makes good" his effort, is their praise; i.e., by praising him they give evidence of his work's merit. But that praise is also *their* proof, that is, by providing his proof, they prove themselves capable of recognizing his merit and thereby attest to its residence within themselves: "His proofe, *their* praise." But of course this immediately turns around to become once again the matter of his praise. By fashioning a book that calls for a praise that reflects on the praisers, Breton "proves out" in the sense of producing good results, and therefore earns still another round of praise; their proof, *his* praise. This self-replenishing circuit of proof and praise, praise and proof is reflected in still another meaning of proof, "a coin or medal usually struck as the test of a die, one of a limited number" (*OED*). It is in this sense that Breton's work is a "master print," a die that strikes off coins in its own image, something that at once tests and is tested (attested) by the absolute sameness of its progeny; it is an object that confers value and has its value conferred on it by the activities of those it makes. Of course this is equally true of Jonson's poem, which is the progeny of Breton's work, a piece of praise that is both Jonson's and Breton's proof, and a die that potentially extends the circuit to those of its readers who can receive its stamp and so become pieces of producing (proving) currency in their turn.

All of these meanings are concentrated in the problematic assertion that the meeting of proof and praise occurs *in this line.* The problem is that on one level, the level on which the poem finally never performs, nothing meets in this line. To be sure, the words "praise" and "proofe" meet, but they are not filled in or elaborated in any way that would validate the claim of the line to contain the essences for which they stand. But on another

level, the level on which the poem acts out an anti-representational epistemology, the absence at the center of the line is what makes the assertion
good, provides its proof; for the line in which "praise" and "proofe" meet
is not the physical (external) line of print and paper but (1) the line of
vision established by the instantaneous self-recognition of eyes similarly
clear, eyes that communicate directly and without mediation, and (2) the
genealogical line that is continually being extended whenever another
author-reader is moved to write or praise (they are one and the same)
and so give proof of his membership in the community of the clear-
sighted. The members of that community eye directly because they have
been "eyed" directly, that is, given eyes, by the inner vision that makes
them one. They see the same perfection not because some external form
compels them to recognize it, but because it *in*forms their perception so
that it is impossible for them to see anything else. They see themselves;
they see the same. In that sense they have "eyes divine" and they can even
announce themselves, as Jonson does, with the indirection characteristic of
this poem, as "I divine."

It is a remarkable little poem, but it is also, I think, altogether typical
and points us to a recharacterization of Jonson's poetry in which some
of the more familiar terms of description will be called into question. First
of all, it will hardly do to label Jonson a poet of the plain style if his poems
continually proclaim their inability to describe or "catch" their objects.
That inability is not only proclaimed; it is discoursed upon at length
in the very poems that announce it. The poet dares not aim at the soul
of Lady Jane Paulet because "it is too near of kin to heaven ... to be
described" (29–30). The mind of Lady Venetia Digby cannot be captured
by the usual metaphors "The sun, a sea, or soundless pit" (*Underwood*,
no. 84. iv, 12). These, Jonson explains, "are like a mind, not it" (13). "No,"
he continues, "to express a mind to sense / Would ask a heaven's intelligence; / Since nothing can report that flame / But what's of kin to whence
it came" (13–16). In some poems Jonson seems to claim just that status for
his art, as when he declares in the "Epistle to Katherine, Lady Aubigny,"
"My mirror is more subtle, clear, refined, / And takes and gives the
beauties of the mind" (43–44). But as it turns out what he means is that
his poem is a mirror in the sense of being blank, empty of positive
assertions, filled with lists of what Lady Aubigny is not, of the compan-
ions she does not have, of the masks she does not wear, of the paths she
does not take, of the spectacles and shows from which she turns. The
poem does not so much occupy, but clears its ground, so that when
Jonson says of it that it is a glass in which Lady Aubigny can look and see

herself (29), his claim is true because there is nothing in it or on it – no account, no description, no representation – to prevent it from functioning as a reflecting surface. She will see nothing in it but her own "form," which she shall find "still the same" (23).

Jonson's poems of praise (and this means most of his poems) are all like that; they present the objects of praise to themselves; they say in effect, "Sir or Madam So and So, meet Sir or Madam So and So, whom, of course, you already know." Once this is said, the poem is to all intents and purposes over, although the result paradoxically is that it often has a great deal of difficulty getting started since it is, in effect, all dressed up with nowhere to go. Epigram 102 says as much in its first two lines: "I do but name thee Pembroke, and I find / It is an epigram on all mankind." Epigram 43, "To Robert, Earl of Salisbury," is even more explicit: "What need hast thou of me, or of my muse / Whose actions so themselves do celebrate." In Epigram 76, the process is reversed; the poet spends some sixteen lines imagining a proper object of his praise only to dismiss in line 17 what he has written as something merely "feigned" before declaring in line 18, "My Muse bad Bedford write, and that was she."[7] Of course, if he had hearkened to his muse in the beginning and had written the name Bedford, there would have been no need to write the poem, a crisis that is avoided by making that realization the poem's conclusion. Given an epistemology that renders it at once superfluous and presumptuous (it is "like a mind, not it"), a Jonson poem always has the problem of finding something to say, a problem that is solved characteristically when it becomes itself the subject of the poem, which is then enabled at once to have a mode of being (to get written) and to remain empty of representation.

Representation is the line of work that Jonson's poems are almost never in, except when their intention is to discredit, and indeed it is a discreditable fact about any object that it is available for representation, for that availability measures the degree to which it is not "kin to heaven" and therefore can be described. The clearest statement of this esthetic of negative availability is Epigram 115, "On The Townes Honest Man,"[8] who is not named, because as Jonson explains, "But, this is one / Suffers no name but a description" (3–4); that is, he is the exact opposite of those (like Pembroke and Lady Bedford) who can be named but not described, because description can only "catch" surfaces and coverings, and is itself a covering. The point, of course, is that the town's honest man is all surface; he has no stable moral identity and therefore there is nothing *in* him to which a name could be consistently attached. He is a creature of momentary desires, whims, interests and movements, and therefore his non-essence is perfectly captured by the ever-changing surface and moment to moment adjustments of verse. The very incapacity of Jonson's poetry even to approach the objects of its praise makes it the perfect medium for the objects of its opprobrium. The chameleon-like actions of the town's honest man (usually thought to be Inigo Jones) are chronicled with a particularity and directness one never encounters in the poems addressed to Jonson's patrons and heroes. When he says at the end of the poem "Described, its thus," he has earned the claim, and when he asks "Defined would you it have" and answers, "The Townes Honest Man's her errant'st knave" (34–35), the pun on "errant'st," at once greatest and most erring, tells us why a definition of the usual kind will not be forthcoming. By definition, a definition fixes an essence, but if an entity is always in motion, is always erring, it has no center to be identified and it cannot be defined; it cannot receive a name.[9]

What we have then in Jonson's esthetic are two kinds of poetry: one that can take advantage of the full resources of language in all its representational power, although what it represents is evil, and another which must defeat and cancel out the power of representation, because the state it would celebrate is one of epistemological immediacy and ontological self-sufficiency. What one wants is not something "like," but "it," and therefore what one doesn't want is a poem. Depending on how it is read, the sixth stanza of *Underwood*, no. 84. iv ("The Mind") is descriptive of both kinds of poetry:

> I call you muse, now make it true:
>   Henceforth may every line be you;
> That all may say that see the frame,
>   This is no picture, but the same. (21–24)

If this stanza were to appear in Epigram 115, its every line would be "you" in quite a literal sense, since the "you" in question would have not one identity but the succession of "identities" that fill every line. Every line can also be a reference to the art of painting (the dismissal of which is the subject of *Underwood*, no. 84. iv), and in that sense too every stroke of the artist's brush in Epigram 115 fully captures whatever momentary form the town's honest man has taken. Anyone who looks at this picture – that is, at this portrait of movement and instability – will see the same, that is, will see perfectly represented the endless self-fashioning that makes up the life of the "errant'st knave." The same stanza reads quite differently, however, when we relate it to the "mind" of Lady Digby, the drawing of which Jonson claims to be able to "perform alone" (3), without the aid of the painter. That boast does not survive the third stanza and the realization (which I have already quoted) that "nothing can report that flame / But what's of kin to whence it came" (15–16). Of course, that would be no report at all, since to report is to convey something to another, whereas in this transaction (if that is the word) what is of kin simply recognizes itself, recognizes, that is, the same. At this point, the poem is running the familiar Jonsonian danger of asserting itself out of business, and, in what amounts to a rescue mission, the poet moves to save it by turning it over to its subject/object: "Sweet mind, then speak yourself" (17). This injunction or invitation or plea can be read in several ways: "Sweet mind, speak in place of me," a reading that preserves the poem's claim to communicate, although with a borrowed voice, or (2): "Sweet mind, speak yourself," in the tautological sense of declaring yourself as opposed to the mediating sense of speaking *about* yourself, which shades into (3): "Sweet mind, speak without mediation, without aid, without voice, without poem, but simply by being."

It is these latter two readings that finally rule as the mind that is bid to "say" remains just out of reach of the verse and of the reader's apprehension. Indeed, the poem anticipates its own repeated failure when it asks to know "by what brave way / Our sense you do with knowledge fill / And yet remain our wonder still" (18–20). How can something that is the cause of all knowledge be itself unknown, remain presentationally silent, be our wonder *still* (always, unmoving, quiet)? The question is not answered but given a succession of experiential lives, as every attempt to make the mind speak, to give it a habit as it were, collapses under the weight of its own inadequacy. Richard Peterson describes these lines as "an evocatively tactile and mobile representation of Lady Digby's mind,"[10] but if anything is represented it is the failure and impiety of representation, and if the verse is mobile, it is because whenever it seeks to rest, it finds that its object has once again escaped. (Again, compare "On The Townes Honest Man," where the escaping or dissolving of a nonobject is what the poem accurately and repeatedly mimes.)

Our possession of that object is at its firmest (although most abstract) at line 55, when it is described as "polisht, perfect, round, and even," but even that hermetic and closed form is presented as a thing of the past that "slid moulded off from heaven" (56). The sliding continues in the next stanza as the mind is embodied in a succession of forms that are always in the act of disintegrating, a cloud, oil (but as it pours forth), showers, drops of balm, in every case a substance that is passing into a state more rarefied than the one in which it is being "presented." In line 63, the verse toys with us by promising a moment in which the mind "stays," but it stays to become a "nest of odorous spice"; that is, it doesn't stay at all. Neither does it rest, despite the teasing appearance of that word at the beginning of line 65, where it is immediately glossed by the phrase "like spirits," and, moreover, "like spirits left behind." Even this fleeting image is itself left behind as it is expanded to include the alternatives of "bank or field of flowers," flowers which are said to be begotten by a "wind" (67) that enters the poem as an image of the ever-receding mind: "In action, winged as the wind" (64). In the impossible but typically Jonsonian logic of the poem, the mind as wind begets itself.

The mind finally comes to rest inside the person of Lady Digby, where it was before this self-extending and self-defeating search for representation began. "In thee ... let it rest" (68) is the poem's final admission of defeat; "it" will remain enclosed; it will not come out; it will not be brought out; it will not be represented. Instead, it will remain in communion with itself, with what it possesses and informs. When Jonson says, "yet know with what thou art possesst" (70), the circuit of knowledge has been narrowed to the space between Lady Digby and her mind, which is no space at all; there is literally no room for anything else because she entertains only ("but") such a mind. The exclusivity of this fellowship is not broached but made more apparent when it welcomes another member, "God thy Guest" ("But such a mind, mak'st God thy guest"), who is at once guest and host, possessor and possessed. The circle of this trinity closes out everything, and especially the poem of which one can now truly say, "This is no picture, but the same." If every line is Lady Digby it is only because every line has emptied itself out in the impossible effort to capture her, leaving her and her guest and those of kin to whence they came in a state of perfect self-recognition, with nothing and no one (including the would-be observer-reader) between them.

One could say then that the poem displays what George Herbert would call a "double motion." It enacts the defeat of representation by never quite being able to present its object, and it more or less "chases" that object to the portals of its proper home, where, as in the last scene of *The Pilgrim's Progress*, one catches the barest glimpse of a kind of community that is open only to those who are already members of it. That community can no more be described or "caught" than can the minds of those who populate it. Just as the mind of Lady Digby or of her unnamed counterpart in the poem "To the World" can only be characterized in terms of the actions it shuns and the obligations it does not recognize, so can the society in which such minds "really" live be characterized only in terms of what *cannot* hold it together or constitute its order, the structures of power, wealth, preferment, influence, everything in short that Jonson refers to as "Nets," "Toys," "baits," "trifles, traps and snares," "gyves," "chains," "engins," "Gins" ("To the World, A Farewell," 8, 12, 18, 24, 30, 34, and 36). These, he says in "An Epistle to Master Arthur Squib," "are poor ties, depend on those false ends. / Tis virtue alone, or nothing that knits friends" (11–12). The ends in question are both the purposes or motives of those who allow themselves to be defined by society's values and the ends or rhymes (poor ties) of poems that issue from and support those same false values. In either case the true knitting is accomplished by "nothing," that is by *no thing* that is visible or measurable, but by a virtue that escapes, because it is a substance apart from, either the lines of influence in the world or the lines of description in a poem. The true poem and the true community are alike in that neither can be equated with the outward forms (of rhymes, honors, rank) that apparently tie them together.

In effect, then, Jonson is continually asserting the unreality both of what fills his poems – titles, offices, estates – and of the society in which those surfaces are the false measures of worth. It would seem therefore that he is no more a social poet than he is (except in a very special sense) a plain-style poet, and for the same reason. The plain style, as Wesley Trimpi and others have taught us, is particularly suited to the accurate representation of what men actually do in response to the pressures of everyday life.[11] However, Jonson's interest is in what some men and women, including himself, actually *are* in a realm of being wholly removed from the everyday, even though it happens to occupy the same temporal space. The very appropriateness of the plain style to one kind of society renders it entirely inappropriate to the society that Jonson so pointedly declines to represent, even as he invites us to join it.

Of course, as we have seen, that invitation is not an invitation at all, but a test, for it functions less as a means of expanding the community than as a device for closing the door in the face of those who are not already "sealed." As such a device, the poetry performs an action precisely analogous to the granting of favor and preferment by the wealthy and the powerful to those who petition them. It names who is in and who is out, and awards not knighthoods, or offices or commissions or pensions or lands, but membership in the tribe of Ben. In a way, then, it is a social poetry, but only in the sense that it sets up, by refusing to describe, a society that is in direct competition with the society whose details fill its lines; by appointing himself the gatekeeper of that society, Jonson manages (at least in his poetry) the considerable feat of asserting and demonstrating his independence of the "poor ties" that supposedly constrain and define him. In short, Jonson establishes in these poems an *alternate* world of patronage and declares it (by an act of poetic fiat) more real than the world in which he is apparently embedded. He invokes the distinctions that structure (or at least appear to structure) his material existence – distinctions of place, birth, wealth, power – but then he effaces them by drawing everyone he names into a community of virtue in which everyone is, by definition, the same as everyone else. He calls his heroes and heroines by their proper titles – Lady, Sir, Lord, Knight – but then he enrolls them in his list under the title they all indifferently share.

That is why, despite the signs of specificity that are everywhere in the poetry, everyone in it is finally interchangeable. The only true relationship between members of a Jonson community is one of identity, and no matter how many persons seem to crowd into a poem, the effect of the argument is always to reduce them to one, to the same. The first five lines of Epigram 91, "To Sir Horace Vere," is almost a parody of the technique:

> Which of thy names I take, not only bears
> A Roman sound, but Roman virtue wears:
> Illustrious Vere, or Horace, fit to be
> Sung by a Horace, or a muse as free;
> Which thou art to thyself . . .. (1–5)

Here, the community is formed by dividing its one member into two, and then declaring (in a declaration that would hardly have seemed necessary before the poem began) that the two are the same. When the newly reunited Horace Vere is declared fit to be sung by another Horace or even by a muse of different name but like spirit ("as free"), it would seem that the population of the community is expanding. However, it immediately contracts when the "muse as free" is identified (a telling word) as "thou thyself," and the absolute closedness and self-sufficiency of the community is reconfirmed. One is hardly surprised to find that the rest of the poem is concerned with what Jonson, as now superfluous muse, will *not* do. "I leave thy acts," he says, explaining that if he were to "prosecute" in detail Vere's every accomplishment he would seem guilty of flattery, and if he were to celebrate some and omit others he would seem guilty of envy. It is a nice rationale for furthering the project of this poem, which is to get written and yet say nothing at all. Jonson *does* announce that he will say something about Vere's "Humanitie" and

"Pietie," but he says only that they are "rare" (16) and "lesse mark'd" (14), which they certainly are in this poem if by "mark'd" one means set down or described. The poem ends without having taken one step from the circle formed by the two names (really one) in its title, "To Sir Horace Vere."

In an influential essay, Thomas Greene has called our attention to the prominence in Jonson's poetry of the notion of the "gathered self" which is always to itself "the same" (Epigram 98, 1.10), a self whose ends and beginnings "perfect in a circle alwayes meet" (Epigram 128, 1.8), a self which presents such a closed face to the world that it is invulnerable to invasion and remains always "untouch'd," a self which may appear to travel and undergo changes in location and situation, but in fact never moves at all. What I am suggesting is that as objects and as discourses Jonson's poems are themselves gathered and closed in exactly these ways: rather than embracing society, they repel it; rather than presenting a positive ethos in a plain style, they labor to present nothing at all and to remain entirely opaque. Greene asserts that "the concept of an inner moral equilibrium . . . informs . . . Jonson's verse";[12] but it would be more accurate to say that the concept of an inner moral equilibrium *escapes* Jonson's verse, which is always citing the concept as its cause but never quite managing to display or define it. It remains "inner" in a stronger sense than Greene's argument suggests; it remains *locked* in, forever inaccessible to any public inspection or validation. In its determination never to reveal what moves it, Jonson's poetry repeatedly enacts the teasing career of the brave infant of Saguntum, always only "half got out" before it hastily returns and makes of itself its own urn, so that we are left to say of it, "How summed a circle didst thou leave mankind / Of deepest lore, could we the centre find" (*Underwood*, no. 70, 9–10).

2.

I am aware that this description of Jonson's poetics will strike some as being too like Edmund Wilson's "notorious account" of Jonson as an anal-erotic, a hoarder who withholds from others the treasures he collects and remains consistently "aloof, not yielding himself to intimate fellowship."[13] Wilson goes on to link Jonson's deficiencies of personality to his "difficulties as an artist," and he sees those difficulties reflected in characteristic artistic failures, in the absence of development or of "any sense of movement," in the lack of variety despite the appearance of multiplicity, in a tendency to everywhere reproduce his own personality

("Jonson merely splits himself up"), in a disastrous restriction of range and sympathy that contrasts so markedly with the expansiveness of Shakespeare. What I am proposing here is a view in which observations not unlike Wilson's (although to be sure in a different vocabulary) lead to an explanation not of Jonson's "glaring defects," but of the power of his poetry, a power that depends, paradoxically, on the determined reticence of that poetry, on its unwillingness to open itself to inspection, on its often-proclaimed inability to specify or describe the values that inform it, on its tendency to issue invitations (to look, to understand, to be sealed) that have the effect not of bringing readers into the community but of keeping them out.

Obviously, the question is how does one justify a poetry so described, a poetry that is committed to not asserting, to not communicating, to not being about anything? Curiously enough, the answer lies right on the surface of the question. Poetry that so withholds itself and closes its face to anything outside its circle puts pressure on those who read it to demonstrate, in the very act of reading, that they are already in. Rather than acting as an exhortation to virtuous activity (in a manner consistent with the didacticism of many centuries) these poems provide their intended readers, who are also their addressees, with an occasion for recognizing that whatever informs these poems – and it is never, can never, be specified – informs them too. At the same time that they restrict access to the community, the poems also – and by the same act – *generate* the community; generate it not by creating its members (who are already what they are), but by providing a relay or network by means of which they can make contact with and identify one another. That is why generation in the world of Jonson's poetry occurs not by sex but by reading, by the reading of like by like, and it is essentially a male phenomenon in which the organ of begetting is the eye.

This chaste sexuality is the subject of a remarkable series of poems that begins with Epigram 62, "To Fine Lady Would-Be." Lady Would-Be's crime is that she divorces the sexual act from true fruitfulness; rather than giving forth life, she prevents life from issuing, and remains deliberately sterile; the only writing she inspires is an epitaph for the children she did not have: "Write then on thy womb; / Of the not born, yet buried, here's the tomb" (11–12). In a certain way, then, Lady Would-Be's womb is an enclosure similar to the enclosure formed by the Jonsonian community, but there is a crucial difference between the two, and that difference emerges in the two poems that follow.

Epigram 63, "To Robert, Earl of Salisbury," begins as if it were surveying the landscape in search of a certain class of persons:

> Who can consider they right courses run,
>   With what thy virtue on the time hath won,
> And not thy fortune, who can clearly see
>   The judgment of the king so shine in thee;
> And that thou seek'st reward of thy each act
>   Not from the public voice, but private fact;
> Who can behold all envy so declined
>   By constant suffering of thy equal mind? (1–8)

Taken by themselves these lines have a double structure. They ask a question – who is discerning enough to judge you, Salisbury, by inner rather than outer criteria? – and in the course of asking it, they perform precisely the judgment they seek and thereby identify the poet as one of those "who can." The interdependence (indeed, the identity) of the virtue that at once informs Salisbury's "each act" and Jonson's act of praise is nicely captured by the phrase: "And not thy fortune," which participates in two constructions. As a co-subject of the verb "won" it is part of the characterization of Salisbury: "it is your virtue not your fortune that has earned you your honors." But as the delayed object of "consider," it further specifies the quality of judgment that is required by Salisbury's presence in the world: "who is it that is able to consider thy virtue and not thy fortune"?

All this is complicated enough, but at line 9 the poem takes a turn that completely changes our understanding of what it is doing, or, to be more precise, is not doing: "And can to these be silent, Salisbury?" The poem is not, as it first seemed, an inquiry into the identity and whereabouts of persons of judgment; rather, the existence and constituency of these persons is assumed, and the poem is revealed to be asking a question about their behavior: "who is it that would be capable of recognizing your virtue, Salisbury, and yet remain silent?" But, of course, this question is no more *seriously* entertained than the question it displaces. It is a rhetorical question whose directed answer is "no one": "No one could discern you for what you truly are, Salisbury, and not respond with praise." But if that is the answer to the poem's "real" question, the poem itself has lost its point, twice: for not only have the persons of judgment already been identified, but they have already and necessarily (they *cannot* remain silent) given the response for which the poem supposedly calls. The entire performance has been circular, moving from the title – "To Robert, Earl of Salisbury" – through nine circuitous and misleading lines back to the title, to the name "Salisbury" (9), which now sounds as an invocation and as the only assertion the poem is willing to make.

And yet, although the poem fails as communication (it imparts no information) and is superfluous as an exhortation (Salisbury has already been given his due), it succeeds and has significance as *testimony*, as evidence that Jonson is no more able to remain silent than those whose praise he praises, and will therefore escape the curse of the closing couplet:

> Cursed be his muse that could lie dumb or hid
> To so true worth, though thou thyself forbid. (11–12)

It is here that the contrast with the preceding poem becomes unmistakable. Jonson's womb, unlike Lady Would-Be's, will not be the tomb of the unborn, but will give birth, spontaneously and involuntarily, to acts of recognition and witness. The poem itself is just such an act – one of the "early fruits / of Love" brought forth by the sight of "noblest Cecil," whose virtues, Jonson reports in Epigram 64 ("To the Same") have "laboured in my thought" (15) – and as such it renders the curse as unnecessary and (in a sense) pointless as the lines that precede it. Those who are silent in the face of Salisbury's example are already cursed by their inability to recognize and therefore to claim a share in his virtue; and those who have that ability have already displayed it by producing the exclamations for which the poem calls and of which it is a signal instance.

Nor is that the end of it. Just as Salisbury, simply as a fact in the world, engenders in the poet a love that bears immediate fruit in these lines of praise, so do these lines engender in readers of like mind and temper (readers who need only hear the name "Salisbury") the very same fruit. Not only is procreation in the Jonsonian community spontaneous, it is also contagious, one act of recognition giving birth to another, and then to another, and so on in a self-extending sequence that is reported in the poem: "who can clearly see / The judgment of the king so shine in thee" (3–4). The knowing observer sees in Salisbury's good fortune the acumen of the king, an acumen he must himself share in order to be able to commend it; as one of those observers, Jonson produces this praise (which is his "proof" in all of the senses we have previously seen) and *his* judgment is then approved by those readers who, by responding affirmatively to the poem, testify to their place in the community whose members it at once names and (in the manner of a litmus test) seeks out. The line of "readership" (Salisbury is read by the king who is read by the discerning who are read by Jonson who is read by the discerning as he reads or rereads Salisbury) is also a line of generation in which merit, rather than being "sepulchured alive" (Epigram 64) as it is in Lady Would-Be's womb, is reproduced and given new life every time it is recognized.

That recognition can only be given by those who are themselves meritorious, who are able to praise Salisbury because they are the same. It is therefore no casual gesture that Jonson performs when he entitles the second of the Salisbury epigrams: "To The Same." On one level, of course, the title merely refers the reader to the subject of the preceding poem, but on another it is a compliment doubly paid: first to Salisbury, who remains the same no matter what external changes have been brought about by fortune's reward, "the public voice," or "envy," and second to Jonson, who remains able to discern what is truly praiseworthy in Salisbury. A constancy that persists independently of the accidents of fortune can only be espied by one whose vision remains unaffected by those same accidents. Thus the poet too must remain the same if he is to be able to see sameness amidst the worldly marks of difference and indeed it is the business of the poem (which could well be titled "To the Same From the Same") to declare and display just that ability.

The poem is ostensibly written to celebrate Salisbury's "accession of the Treasurership," but in the first eight lines Jonson labors to detach Salisbury's worth from the "public" fact of that or any other honor and at the same time to detach the worth of his praise from the same apparent occasion. Rather than being the evidence of Salisbury's virtue, his new office is seen almost as a threat to that virtue, insofar as one might mistake the man for the title and thereby mistake the reason for the poet's praise. That is why he must begin with the curious phrase (surely unique as a poetic beginning), "Not glad."

> Not glad, like those that have new hopes or suits
>   With thy new place, bring I these early fruits
> Of love, and what the golden age did hold
>   A treasure, art: contemned in the age of gold:
> Not glad as those that old dependents be
>   To see the father's rites new laid on thee; (1–6)

Jonson must clear himself of the suspicion, even before it can have been raised, that he is prompted to write by something so ephemeral as a change in outward state, the suspicion that his vision may be affected by anything one might, in the ordinary run of things, see; by "hopes" or "suits" or "place" or "gold" or "rites"; and since he is not moved by any of these things, he is able to claim that his poem (which, typically, has managed for nearly half its length to avoid assertion) is neither flattery nor self-display: ". . . nor to show a fit / Of flattery to thy titles nor of wit" (7–8). Not admiring "show" (surface, false glitter, theatricality), his performance cannot itself be characterized as a show, and does not itself show (in the sense of reveal) anything, but remains closed to those for whom its value – and the value of its subject – is not already self-evident.

At line 9 Jonson finally admits to being gladdened by something:

> But I am glad to see that time survive
>   Where merit is not sepulchured alive,
> Where good men's virtues them to honours bring,
>   And not to dangers; when so wise a king
> Contends to have worth enjoy, from his regard,
>   As her own conscience, still the same reward. (9–14)

Again the contrast with Epigram 62, "To Fine Lady Would-Be," is unmistakable. What gladdens Jonson is the fertility of a community that by repeatedly recognizing its own adds to the merit it declines to bury. The rewards that accrue to Salisbury and to others like him are less significant as instances of personal gain than as the general and shared gain of men who honor themselves by honoring others, as Jonson does by giving involuntary voice to this and the previous poem. Not only is virtue its own reward (Salisbury does not need his title and office), but it rewards those who acknowledge it by marking them as virtuous too. What makes the king's choice of Salisbury praiseworthy is that he does no more (or less) than provide an external sign of what "worth" has already earned. "His regard" is the same as hers, and he reaps the immediate benefit of being known as worthy himself, as "the same."

The force of a virtue that endlessly reproduces itself is so great that it takes over the poem, which is now seen to have exceeded the intention of its putative maker:

> These noblest Cecil, laboured in my thought,
>   Wherein what wonder see, thy name hath wrought:
> That whilst I meant but thine to gratulate,
>   I've sung the greater fortunes of our state. (15–18)

In a sense, then, the poem is taken away from Jonson, but what he gets back is greater than what he loses, not only a place in the community but the honor of being the means of extending it. That honor, and the process by which it is conferred, is even more fully described and reported in *Underwood*, no. 78, "An Epigram to My Muse the Lady Digby on Her Husband, Sir Kenelm Digby." At that poem's conclusion, Jonson imagines what will happen when Lady Digby brings his lines of praise (in which, he predicts, she will "read" her husband because she already knows him in the way that like knows like) to Sir Kenelm. He will read them and receive their praise by praising them in turn, and then will give them to the "knowing Weston" (28) – knowing his own as he is himself known – who will himself show them to others, who will show them to others in an endless and finally all-encompassing chain:

> ... Then, what copies shall be had,
>   What transcripts begged; how cried up and how glad
> Wilt thou be, muse, when this shall them befall!
>   Being sent to one, they will be read by all; (29–32)

They will be read by all because they read all, that is, they test the response of all who encounter them, a response that always takes the form of adding to the gladness they bear. That is why being sent to one they are sent to all; not only because one, if he is the right one, will involuntarily extend the gift, the gladness; but because the extension is from one to others, who are his copies as he is theirs, who are so much the same that there is finally no distinction between the transcripts and the original. (This is a kind of intertextuality, but one in which each text, be it poem or person, is a copy pulled from a master plate of bodiless virtue.)

If the members of Jonson's community are (in a very strong sense) the same, it is not surprising to find a sameness in the poems addressed to them, poems which are often, except for the finally superfluous name, interchangeable. Thus Epigram 67 continues the sequence begun in Epigram 63, although the subject is not now Salisbury but Suffolk. Again, the poet's first concern is to clear himself, in advance, of any suggestion that he writes for the wrong reasons. Although "Most think all praises flatteries" (2), his praise is drawn from him involuntarily by the compelling perspicuity of Suffolk's virtues. In this poem, therefore, Suffolk will be "raised" (4), that is elevated, by truth; however, that truth, in the form of Jonson's lines, has in turn been "raised," in the sense of being produced or nurtured, by the very thing it celebrates. In a manner altogether typical of Jonson, line 4 – "As to be raised by her is only fame" – refers simultaneously to the poem's subject and to the poem itself, which are now indistinguishable.

Having thus fixed the meaning and origin of his praise before he offers it, Jonson can then begin. But as it is so often the case in his poetry, the beginning, even though it is delayed, is a false one:

> Stand, high then, Howard, high in eyes of men,
>   High in thy blood, thy place. (5–6)

The practiced (and knowing) reader of Jonson will recognize these as the marks of an inferior recognition, and he will not be surprised to find them immediately set aside in favor of a recognition more telling:

> ... but highest then
> When, in men's wishes, so thy virtues wrought
> As all thy honours were by them first sought,
> And thou designed to be the same thou art,
> Before thou wert it, in each good man's heart. (6–10)

The sense of this is double. It means, first, that the power of Howard's virtue is most in evidence when those who recognize it are moved to wish for him the public honors he has not yet received, and it also means that those who recognize it are moved to imitate what they recognize. The next two lines are even more complicated. In one syntax they are a continuation of the primary sense: "you were thus (by virtue of the wishes men have for you) marked out for your present state even before you obtained it; you were what you now are (the same) before you became it." But in another syntax, "designed" is an active verb and refers to Suffolk's design or intention to remain what he is ("to be the same thou art") no matter what external changes (for good or ill) befall him. In still a third syntax, "designed" is once again passive and refers to the fashioning or designing of Suffolk by God, who foresaw that he would always be what he is, either before the king raised him or before he took his place in each good man's heart. The point is that it is unnecessary to untangle these senses, since in a world where all good men are informed by the same spirit the designs of one are necessarily the design of every other and of the informing spirit itself. That spirit is named explicitly in the final couplet, which also recapitulates the genealogical line that makes up the community of virtue: "Which, by no less confirmed than thy king's choice / Proves that is God's which is the people's voice" (11–12). "Proves" – not in the sense of providing independent corroboration, but in the circular sense both reported and instanced by this poem. The king's choice confirms the people's choice which confirms Suffolk's actions which confirms the unforced truth of Jonson's praise which confirms and extends the founding gesture of God's having recognized Suffolk as his own, that is, as the same.

That recognition does not occur in time, that is, at any particular time, but has always occurred, and therefore its extension into other acts of recognition (by the king, by each good man, by the poet) is assured, and is not contingent on temporal circumstances. Events in the community of the virtuous are pseudo-events. They never mark the entrance into the

world of anything new, but simply offer an occasion for the re-marking of
what has always been, of the same, and the poems that report these
"events" imitate their structure by exhibiting a circularity that subverts
their apparently linear and discursive form. The point can be illustrated
by still another poem titled: "To the Same," Epigram 86. In the first
line of that poem, Jonson characterizes himself as someone who lacks a
certain knowledge: "When I would know thee, Goodyeare, my thought
looks . . . ." The implication is that there are moments when the knowledge of Goodyeare has escaped him and he must seek it in the world;
however, the search ends in the very next line, where it is revealed to have
been unnecessary: "Upon thy well-made choice of books and friends . . . ."
For Jonson, to look upon Goodyeare's choice of friends is to look upon
himself, since the preceding poem (in relation to which this is "To the
Same") is a record of their friendship. That poem is or will be one of
Goodyeare's books, so that when he is praised in the next line for "making
thy friends books, and thy books friends" (4), the circle of reference is
entirely closed: Jonson is both friend and book and is therefore (in a way
paradoxical but inevitable given the structure of the Jonsonian universe)
the double cause of the knowledge from which he claims, in line 1, to be
separated. Thus when he declares in lines 5 and 6, "Now I must give thy
life and deed the voice / Attending such a study, such a choice," he sets
himself a task he has already performed merely by having been the object
of "such a choice" and the producer of at least one book (this book) that
Goodyeare studies. Insofar as Goodyeare lives and can be read in the
books and friends he chooses, he has been given voice by Jonson's every
act and gesture. The present act of voicing this poem (which, characteristically, says nothing at all about Goodyeare) cannot therefore be the *singular*
act suggested by the temporal urgency that seems to inform: "Now I must."
Jonson can do nothing *but* give voice to Goodyeare's life so long as he
breathes and writes. It is this involuntary sense of "must" that is finally
intended here, as once again a Jonson poem defaults on its announced
project – giving knowledge of Goodyeare – because that project has already
been completed before the poem is written and by means (the recognition
of like by like) of which the poem is an extension. If the way to know
Goodyeare is to know those who are known (acknowledged to be friends)
by him, then the way to know Goodyeare – and the only way – is to know
yourself as one who is so known, as one who is the same, and that is a
knowledge you can never be without (the pun is intended) because it is
continuous with being and antedates every attempt to specify it. That is
why the key verb in the final line is in the past tense – "It was a knowledge

that *begat* that love." The knowledge that begat and still begets Jonson's love of Goodyeare (in still another backward reference to the willful infertility of Lady Would-Be) is a knowledge of what he himself is and of what is like him because it likes him, and it is also the knowledge that begat this poem, which is therefore produced by what it supposedly seeks. "Rare poems ask rare friends," declares Jonson in "To Lucy, Countess of Bedford, with Mr. Donne's Satires"; and by "ask" he means not "request" but "reach out to." Rare poems only give themselves, yield themselves up to rare readers, to readers who are already repositories of what is asked for. Only those few readers will "ask and read / And like" (12–13), and they will like because they are like, because they are kin to whence the poem came. What they ask for is what they already have, and what they find is what they already are, which is also what they will read (i.e., understand). Such readers (authors-readers) are themselves read – revealed in their true character – by that very ability to ask and like. It is a transaction of perfect if closed reciprocity in which to give something – a poem, a praise, a liking, a reading – is at the same moment to be getting it back.

3.

This reciprocity, at once endlessly self-replenishing and defiantly excluding, is the essence not only of the transaction between Jonson's poetry and the community of its readers, but of the friendship that binds that community together and provides its true – that is, nonspecifiable – ties. Not surprisingly, although friendship is the constant subject of this poetry, it is a subject that is more invoked than described. Like Jonson's other master values, it is present largely as what cannot be presented or re-presented; it is at once known in advance and what cannot (in the usual discursive sense) be known. Although the question of record in a Jonson poem will often be, "What is friendship?" the answer can only be, "If you have to ask, you couldn't possibly know."

Consider as an example the opening lines of a poem we have already met, "An Epistle to Master Arthur Squib":

> What I am not, and what I fain would be,
>   Whilst I inform myself, I would teach thee,
> My gentle Arthur, that it might be said
>   One lesson we have both learned and well read. (1–4)

In these first four lines the poem repeatedly enacts the closing of its own circle. The first enactment occurs immediately with the negative promise of knowledge that will be withheld ("What I am not"). In the second half of line 1, however, there seems to be an opening outward to the possibility of future revelation ("what I fain would be"), but that possibility is shut down when the indirect object of the verb "inform" is not the reader but "myself." It is revived again by the promise in the phrase: "I would teach thee," but that promise is withdrawn when the referent of the pronoun "thee" is pointedly restricted to "My gentle Arthur." The second half of line 3 brings still another promise, of something that "might be said," but it too is disappointed by line 4, which identifies what will be said with a lesson that both Jonson and Squib have already learned and therefore need not learn again.

More starkly than any other poem we have examined, the epistle to Squib displays the determined reticence of an art that refuses to submit itself to scrutiny and judgment. Both the action it performs and the actions it reports look inward toward the already constituted community of observers and readers. Jonson writes the poem only in order to be (apart from Squib, from whom he is indistinguishable) its only reader. He will "inform himself" in two senses: he will inform no one but himself, and he will put himself into a form (of a poem that avoids explicit assertion) that only he and Squib can read because they already possess (and are possessed by) the truth it will not tell; he will spin himself out, and then "turn" his own "threads" (21) so that he might know, in still another and self-confirming way, what he already is. Meanwhile the reader will learn only what he is not: "I neither am, nor art thou, one of those" (5). The list that follows is an inventory of the motives that do *not* animate Jonson and Squib. Neither of them caters mechanically and servilely to the moods of the other (they do not "hearken to a jack's pulse"). They do not flatter one another in the hope of cadging a meal or a drink (their friendship is not the "issue of the tavern or the spit"). The ties that bind them are not economic (theirs is not a "kindred from the purse"). "These are poor ties, depend on those false ends" (11). One might think that false ends are selfish (self-serving) ends, but when the character of a true friend is finally specified, it turns out to be selfishness in a pure form: ". . . look if he be / Friend to himself that would be friend to thee. / For that is first required, a man be his own" (21–23). Of course, this is proverbial (one thinks of Polonius as well as of Seneca and Cicero), but the proverb has a special force in the context of the poem's insistence on characterizing friendship in asocial terms (a characterization it extends by being itself asocial), as the fruit not of obligations incurred or of deficiencies supplied but of self-sufficient beings whose only claim on one another is that in their independence of all external supports they are the same. He who understands this can then "rest" (25); that is, he need do nothing either to earn or reward friendship. He need simply remain what he already is, and with this currency – which is nothing more or less than his entire being – he will have bought "a richer purchase than of land" (26).

Richard Peterson has noted that in this and other poems, friendship is described in commercial terms – as coin, as a venture, as a harvest-yielding crop – and yet at the same time it is opposed to actions performed in the hope of a literal profit.[14] The counterpoint between two systems of economics, one at work in the greater world and the other peculiar to the internal and abstract world of the tribe of Ben, is more than a leitmotif in the poetry. It defines with a particular clarity the paradox of a community that is at once expansive and self-enclosed, and it provides Jonson with still another way of declaring unreal the dependence that apparently constrains and defines him. Here, a key poem is *Underwood*, no. 13, "An Epistle to Sir Edward Sackville, now Earl of Dorset." It is a poem addressed by a borrower to a lender – that is, by a beneficiary to a patron – yet it is not a poem of gratitude or supplication, and there is no hint as it develops that the speaker conceives of himself as the subordinate or unequal party in an exchange. Instead, he turns the usual relationship between donor and recipient around by making the acceptance rather than the granting of the favor the crucial act of judgment. Jonson acknowledges that his humble fortune puts him in need of even the "smallest courtesies" (16), but insists that "I make / Yet choice from whom I take them, and would shame / To have such do me good I durst not name" (17–18). The "noblest" benefit of a gift, he tells us, is more the "memory from whom / Than what he hath received" (21–22). The nobility of the memory attaches to both parties. The recipient is noble because he thinks more on the character of the giver than on the size of his gift; the giver is noble because he displays that character both in his choice of beneficiary and in the manner of his giving. Thus Sackville proves himself a worthy bestower by responding to Jonson's petition before it is made; he does not wait for the poet's "prayers" but moves to "prevent" (11) them by acting as soon as he perceives the need. Indeed, so immediate is his action – it is "done," says Jonson, "as soon as meant" (12) – that it completely short-circuits any sense of sequence. It is as if Jonson never asked for anything at all but was simply the object of a gesture so spontaneous that it seemed to have no cause, no *occasional* stimulus, except for the recognition by one noble nature of another.

That recognition is, as always in Jonson, bidirectional and instantaneous, and leaves no room – no temporal space – for the usual (and invidious) distinctions between creditor and debtor, petitioner and petitioned, client and patron. The entire transaction, not really a transaction at all, is summed up in a quintessential Jonsonian couplet:

> For benefits are owed with the same mind,
> As they are done, and such returns they find. (5–6)

This couplet has two literal readings. The first is literal in the context of the usual understanding of the relationship between borrower and lender: one's attitude toward a debt incurred is a function of the manner ("mind") with which the loan has been proffered. But in the context of Jonson's world, the phrase "same mind" has an even more literal meaning and refers to the identity of the two parties. Since Jonson and Sackville are alike manifestations of the virtue that informs them, any benefit one confers on the other is a benefit conferred on himself. In short, benefits are not owed at all, since they are repaid in the very moment when they are bestowed. The return that the giver "finds" is found immediately, in the "credit" that accrues to him for having given proof of his nature by responding "freely" (13–14) – without having been "forced" (24) and with no thought of gain – to one whose nature is the same.

The dynamics of this exchange trace out what every society has vainly sought, an economy that generates its own expansion and is infinitely self-replenishing, an economy in which *everyone gains.* Jonson gains by having his necessities "succored" (8) even before he names them. Sackville gains by having his gift accepted by someone who is concerned not with the wealth but with the character of his patron. His acceptance is praise and brings honor to the creditor, who is thus instantly reimbursed. (In debts as in dinners, "It is the fair acceptance [that] creates / The entertainment perfect.")[15] Jonson in his turn gains by receiving credit for having chosen the "noblest" of donors, and that credit returns immediately to Sackville ("such returns they find"), who is doubly crowned, first by having been chosen, and second (although at the very same moment) by having provided his brother with an opportunity to display and "prove" his judgment. Together, by their reciprocal and mutually validating actions, the two men exemplify the poem's recipe for the perfect – that is, debt-free – relationship between borrower and lender:[16] "Gifts and thanks should have one cheerful face / So each that is done and ta'en becomes a brace" (39–40). "Becomes" is a word whose temporal implications should not be insisted on. Since Jonson and Sackville are already "one

cheerful face" – are already acting with the "same mind" – their giving
and taking are simultaneous and interchangeable. The true message of the
couplet is, as is so often the case in this poetry, tautological: they are a
brace because they are a brace.

This perfect economy, in which loss is impossible because benefits are
continually and effortlessly multiplying, is elaborated against the background of the more usual conditions of monetary exchange. When Jonson
says that "I who freely know / This good from you as freely will it owe"
(13–14), he means that he owes it so freely that he is under no obligation
to repay it. Indeed, by freely accepting it, he has already repaid it in the
currency of friendship, a currency whose soundness is independent of the
more literal repayment that may or may not occur. That independence
is the subject of *Underwood*, no. 17, "Epistle to a Friend." The occasion is
Jonson's failure to repay a debt on the appointed day, and the argument is
that his default is in fact a favor, since it provides his creditor with even more
opportunities to affirm his "noble nature" and by so doing to enjoy even
greater profits than would have been his had the poet been more punctilious:

> They are not, sir, worst owers, that do pay
>   Debts when they can; good men may break their day
> And yet the noble nature never grudge;
>   'Tis then a crime, when the usurer is judge,
> And he is not in friendship. Nothing there
>   Is done for gain. (1–6)

When good men break their day, they will do so as good men, that is,
with an unconcern that bespeaks their understanding of what is truly
valuable in any transaction, and the creditor will match that understanding by never grudging, by not looking "unto the forfeit" (12), by acting
with a generosity that reaps a moral harvest "richer" (17) than the return
he forgoes. The relationship between this "no-fault" transaction and
the stricter accounting of another system of economics is mirrored in the
double sense of line 4: "'Tis then a crime, when the usurer is judge." The
usurer, judging only by surfaces and inessentials, will see in the poet's
default only a crime, and it will be *his* crime – and his loss – that he can see
nothing else, that he fails to see the "nothing" or no thing that "knits
friends." Because he is not "in friendship" he can claim no share of
friendship's freely given and immediately reciprocal rewards. He does
everything for gain and thereby cuts himself off from the gains that come
unsought to those who, by investing their capital in "trust" (14), add to
their store in the very act of expending it.

In this and other poems one cannot say whether economics is a metaphor for friendship or friendship a metaphor for economics. The usual terms of tenor and vehicle do not apply, for in their relationship the two systems display the characteristics we have found so often in Jonson's universe. They are mutually convertible, interchangeable, finally indistinguishable; they are the same, and because they are the same, they don't say anything about one another; their equivalence is another means by which the lines of communication in Jonson's world are kept entirely internal. In both, what is hazarded is judgment, and in both the investment is its own (and simultaneous) yield, a yield that is shared by the other party with no diminishing of its quantity. Of course, the very same account can be given (and has already been given) of the dynamics of praise. Here again, judgment is the action and the commodity, and its conferring and receiving redound to the honor and credit of both praiser and praised, who pass back and forth between them an ever self-augmenting store. And, finally, making a fourth to this family of equivalences, is the writing of poetry, an act which, as Jonson never tires of telling us, carries all the risks and rewards of lending, borrowing, praising, and "friending." All of these interchangeable activities are the multiple yet single subject of *Underwood*, no. 14, "An Epistle to Master John Selden," a poem that will allow us to bring together the various themes we have pursued in this essay.

The poem opens, in the usual fashion, by declaring itself unnecessary:

> I know to whom I write. Here I am sure
> Though I am short, I cannot be obscure (1–2)

He knows to whom he writes because he writes to someone exactly like himself. That is why he cannot be obscure. Obscurity is a function of discourse; it occurs when language imperfectly captures an intention which is therefore not "readable" by a receiver or hearer. Obscurity then is a danger or risk attendant on distance, a consequence of the unhappy fact that the speaker (or writer) and hearer are different. But of course they are not. Jonson and Selden are the same, and because they are the same their intentions are shared, already known to one another, and need not be communicated. Conversely, if they were not the same, if they were not mutually constituting members of a self-identifying community, no quantity of words would be sufficient to produce an understanding that was not already in place. More words are like more money; they cannot purchase something that is finally independent of them.

The occasion of the poem (which will not be short despite its superfluousness) is a quantity of words that Selden has produced in the form of a book. He has sent the book to Jonson for approval, and the poet responds by reflecting analytically on the act and its significance:

> Your book, my Selden, I have read and much
> Was trusted that you thought my judgment such
> To ask it; though in most of works it be
> A penance, where a man may not be free. (5–8)

The interchangeability of mutually validating actions is mirrored in the surprise that awaits the reader at the beginning of line 6. In line 5, it is Jonson who is acting, and it is natural to expect that "much" is *his* intensifier, to be followed by an active verb like "admired" or "approved." But instead, the verb is passive and Selden is its agent. The two have changed places, or, more precisely, they now share (or mutually occupy) a place, the place of judgment. Judgment is what Selden asks for when he sends Jonson the book, but the fact of his sending it is a judgment on Jonson, on his trustworthiness ("much / Was trusted"), and the fact of *that* judgment is a judgment on Selden, on his willingness to submit his work to someone who will evaluate it independently of any consideration of affection or gain. What Selden seeks – a just verdict, a discerning eye – he himself exercises in the very manner of his seeking. He already has what he asks for, and he gives it to his friend in the asking, who can then give it back again by discharging his "office" (9) with no sense that it is a penance, a burden weighted by implicit but powerful pressures. The transaction is like the poem. It is itself already informed by the good it would name, and it is therefore at once superfluous, since everyone (who counts) is already in possession of the sought-for commodity, and profitable, since every expenditure of judgment, if it is true, adds to its own store by redounding to the credit both of the judger and the judged.

Indeed, the distinction between judge and judged will not hold because the latter is only getting back what was his in the first place. Whatever praise Selden receives will have been produced not by Jonson but by the self-declaring force of his character and his accomplishments. In a strict sense, then, Jonson is not the author of the poem, but an involuntary witness to the presence of virtue in the world, and he says as much at the beginning of the last section, when he cries: "I yield, I yield, the matter of your praise / Flows in upon me, and I cannot raise / A bank against it" (61–63). The praise Selden then receives is self-conferred and the poem quite literally and quite typically becomes what it always was, a presentation by its addressee to himself: "Thus enjoy thine own."

Also typically, the poem now (at line 67) begins: "I first salute thee." But the salute refuses to be limited to Selden. The communication of virtue is, as we have seen in other poems, contagious; its benefits are conferred in multiple and multiplying directions and only increase each time they are divided. The image of a river overflowing its banks precisely captures the quality of a force that is self-replenishing and self-extending, and at that very moment it extends itself to Edward Hayward, the "chamber-fellow" (72) to whom Selden has dedicated his book. In the lines that follow, Hayward and Selden act out the same sequence (not really a sequence) of gifts reciprocally given and taken that marks the relationship between Selden and Jonson. Selden gives Hayward the honor of a dedication and receives the honor back immediately, proving himself to be one who prefers to some "great name" (69) an obscure person who "knows to do / It [the book] true respects" (72–73). He can do it "true respects" because his reading is animated by the very same spirit that moves Selden to write:

> . . . he can approve
> And estimate thy pains, as having wrought
> In the same mines of knowledge. (73–75)

Hayward, in short, approves and estimates what he already knows; he approves himself and thus receives from Selden still another gift which is like the first (the dedication itself) immediately, and with profit, returned.

It is returned simultaneously to Jonson, who, by approving and estimating the pains of both Selden and Hayward, shows himself worthy of their fellowship and finds, without seeking it, a like portion of the praise he bestows. The riches of an economy that knows only surplus accrue to him without effort and he exclaims in an excess of joy at the rewards he cannot help but reap:

> . . . O how I do count
> Among my comings-in, and see it mount,
> The gain of your two friendships! Hayward and
> Selden: two names that so much understand;
> On whom I could take up, and ne'er abuse
> The credit. (79–84)

He cannot abuse the credit because the line of credit is endless. To draw on it is to replenish it because what you draw on is a reservoir (of friendship) that is augmented by everyone who comes to drink from it. What Jonson gains from the friendship of Hayward and Selden he more than supplies by adding himself to their circle, and as a member of that circle he immediately gains again (and gives again) what he has given to it. He is at once a part of what Hayward and Selden understand – that is, support – and an understander or supporter himself. That shared understanding is so total and so instantaneous, so independent of language or any other discursive form, that it need not be communicated: "But here's no time, nor place, my wealth to tell, / You both are modest: so am I. Farewell" (85–86). These closing lines are disingenuous, for not only would the telling of his wealth be an act of vulgar self-display, it would be at once unnecessary and impossible: impossible because to tell his wealth, in the sense either of tallying it or reporting it, is to increase it. The counting (or recognizing) of gain is itself a gain and therefore always outruns the attempt to measure it. And would be unnecessary, for those to whom it could be told are themselves what would be told (are pieces of virtue's currency) and therefore already know what they are, while on the other hand, those who do not themselves constitute the wealth could never be told it. The modesty claimed in the last line is a thin mask for the familiar face of exclusion. Jonson reaches out (as he does in so many poems) to those with whom he is already sealed, and as he says to them a superfluous "farewell" – superfluous because they fare well simply by being what they are – he says to the rest of us a farewell that has the unmistakable sound of a closing door.

4.

What that door closes on is a society that refuses to display itself and defines itself as the very opposite of that which *shows*. One might say then that everything important that happens in that society (and therefore in Jonson's poetry) happens offstage. And once one says that, the way is open to classifying the poetry as anticourtly, for as Frank Whigham has recently observed, "the ideal courtier is *never* offstage," but must continually "shew himselfe" in order to find an identity in the response and recognition of an audience.[17] So self-consciously rhetorical is courtly life that moral categories themselves are realized as various performative styles. The transcendental suffers a "demotion" (636) and "public opinion takes precedence over one's own moral perception" (635). Even one's sense of his own worth is gained in the theater of courtly conversation. "The jugement which wee have to know our selves is not ours, but wee borrow it of others," writes Stefano Guazzo, indicating the extent to which virtue is equated with reputation and is "radically dependent on the eye and voice of the audience" (637).

It hardly need be said that on every point Jonson is opposed to this vision of a theatrical life. He declares himself secure in a self-knowledge that has nothing to do with reputation. He thinks of himself as one of those who "though opinion stamp them not, are gold" ("An Epistle Answering to One That Asked to be Sealed of the Tribe of Ben," 1.4). Indeed, so far is he from courting public recognition that he flees it, and is reluctant even to venture out in speech, lest by "showing so weak an act to vulgar eyes," he "put conscience and my right to compromise" (7–8). As always, the motion is one of withdrawal (in imitation of the infant of Saguntum) into the fortress of the centered self. It is in order to maintain the security of that fortress, he tells us in *Timber or Discoveries*, "that there was a wall, or parapet of teeth set in our mouth ... that the rashness of talking should not only be retarded by the guard and watch of our heart; but be fenced in and defended by certain strengths placed in the mouth itself."[18] If, as Heinrich Plett remarks, the courtier lives only as a social being and is in "private 'retreat' ... a cipher," it is only in private retreat that the Jonsonian self truly lives.[19]

And yet, it would finally be reductive and even wrong to assimilate Jonson's poetry to the category of anticourt satire. Of course there are a few poems – "To the World, A Farewell," "To Sir Robert Wroth," "An Epistle to a Friend, to Persuade Him to the Wars," "On Court-Worm," "To Censorious Courtling," "On Court-Parrot," "To Courtling" – that are obviously satirical, but by and large the body of the poetry lacks something essential to satire, the intention to indict or to reform. The verse is not projected outward into a world it would shape, but inward into a world it would protect. The message is never "go out and remedy these evils," but rather, "keep yourself *safe* from these evils": "Well, with mine own frail pitcher, what to do / I have decreed; keep it from waves and press, / Lest it be jostled, cracked, made nought, or less" ("An Epistle Answering ...," 55–57). There is a lesson here, to be sure, but it is not exhortative in the usual sense because it is so negative and defensive. In the end, the poetry does not ask us to do anything or even to learn anything. One can say of it finally what can be said of almost no other verse in the period: it is not designed to be *persuasive*. It does not attempt to move its audience, but to push it away, and if the response of three centuries is any measure, it has achieved a strange success.

We end then with a question of motive. Why would anyone write a poetry that does not persuade or teach or assert or present or represent or define or describe or incite? This question is the answer to the question with which we began: how can a poet operating in the world of patronage assert and maintain a claim of independence? As we have seen, Jonson responds to this challenge by writing a poetry which declares unreal the network of dependencies and obligations that to all appearances directs and regulates his every action. It is an extraordinary project, much grander in its way than any Sidney could have imagined when he spoke of poets who deliver a golden world, for it involves a quite brazen act of denial in the midst of what seems irrefutable evidence. There is every visible sign that Jonson is constrained by all the ties ("These are poor ties, depend on ... false ends") that he proceeds to reject. He writes in gratitude or in petition to patrons. He writes on the occasion of the birthday of a king or prince. He writes to courtiers and to booksellers. He writes to creditors. And yet in all of these cases he manages, by a willful act of assertion, to reverse his subordinate position and declare himself the center of a court and society more powerful and more durable than any that may seem to contain him. It is a classic instance of a familiar psychological strategy. The outsider who must rely on others for favor and recognition imagines himself as the proprietor and arbiter of an internal kingdom whose laws he promulgates and whose entrance he zealously guards, admitting only those he would "call mine"[20] to an elect fellowship. It would be easy to dismiss this strategy as wishful thinking and easier still to see it as a piece of self-deception practiced by a man who is unwilling to deal directly with his own envy and aggression and instead displaces them onto an excoriated and exiled other. But for the present I am content to marvel at the controlled power of a poetry that manages to convince itself – and on occasion manages almost to convince us – that to owe money is already to have repaid it, that to ask a favor is to have granted one, that to praise kings is to exercise majesty, and that in the very posture of supplication and dependence one can nevertheless be perfectly free.

NOTES

1 M.S. Larson, *The Rise of Professionalism* (Berkeley and Los Angeles, 1977). Citations appear in the text.
2 Robert Harding, "Corruption and the Moral Boundaries of Patronage in the Renaissance," in *Patronage in the Renaissance*, ed. Guy Fitch Lytle and Stephen Orgel (Princeton, 1981), 54–56.
3 For perceptive observations on Jonson's use of negative constructions, see Richard C. Newton, "Ben./Jonson: The Poet in the Poems," in *Two Renaissance Mythmakers: Christopher Marlowe and Ben Jonson* (Baltimore and

London, 1977), 165–195. Unless otherwise noted, all citations are to *Ben Jonson's Poems*, ed. Ian Donaldson (London, Oxford and New York, 1975).

4 Here, the text I am using is *The Complete Poetry of Ben Jonson*, ed. William B. Hunter, Jr. (New York, 1963).

5 E. Gilman, *The Curious Perspective* (New Haven, 1978), 38.

6 Stephen Orgel and Roy Strong, *Inigo Jones: The Theatre of the Stuart Court* (London and Berkeley, 1973), 2.

7 On this and related points, see Harris Friedberg's excellent essay, "Ben Jonson's Poetry: Pastoral, Georgic, Epigram," *English Literary Renaissance*, 4 (1974), 115–116.

8 Here I am again using William B. Hunter, Jr.'s text.

9 For the relationship between Jonson's antitheatricality and his ideal of the "unmoved personality," see Jonas Barish, "Jonson and the Loathed Stage," in *A Celebration of Ben Jonson*, ed. William Blissett, Julian Patrick, and R.W. Van Fossen (Toronto and Buffalo, 1972), 38, 45, 50. As Barish rightly observes, "worth, in the Jonsonian universe, as in that of his Stoic guides, is virtually defined as an inner and hence an invisible quality" (45). On the relationship between names and the moral status of both the named and the namer see Martin Elsky, "Words, Things, and Names: Jonson's Poetry and Philosophical Grammar," in *Classic and Cavalier: Essays on Jonson and the Sons of Ben*, ed. Ted-Larry Pebworth and Claude Summers (Pittsburgh, 1983).

10 Richard Peterson, *Imitation and Praise in the Poems of Ben Jonson* (New Haven and London, 1981), 85.

11 Wesley Trimpi, *Ben Jonson's Poetry: A Study of the Plain Style* (Stanford, 1962), 9, 41.

12 Thomas Greene, "Ben Jonson and the Centered Self," *Studies in English Literature*, 10 (1970), 329.

13 Edmund Wilson, "Morose Ben Jonson," in *The Triple Thinkers* (New York, 1948), 220, 219. In an attempt to defend Jonson against Wilson's charges, his admirers have in large part succeeded only in producing the poet of smooth urbanity that appears in most of our accounts. For an exception see the stimulating essay by Arthur Marotti, "All About Jonson's Poetry," *ELH*, 39 (1972), 208–237.

14 Peterson, *Imitation and Praise*, 227.

15 *Inviting a Friend to Supper*, ll. 7–8.

16 The relationship is exemplified in still another way by the fact that much of the poem is "borrowed" from Seneca's *De Beneficiis*. Jonson's relationship to his sources precisely parallels his relationship with his creditors; he honors both by taking from them and he is honored in turn by the wisdom of his choice.

17 Frank Whigham, "Interpretation at Court: Courtesy and the Performer–Audience Dialectic," *New Literary History*, XIV (Spring, 1983), 634.

18 *Ben Jonson: The Complete Poems*, ed. George Parfitt (Baltimore, 1975), 384–385.

19 Heinrich F. Plett, "Aesthetic Constituents in the Courtly Culture of Renaissance England," *New Literary History*, vol. xiv (Spring, 1983), 613.

20 "An Epistle Answering …," l. 74. See, for a discerning discussion of the difficulty of being a laureate poet within a system of courtly patronage, pp. 165–179 of Richard Helgerson's *Self-Crowned Laureates: Spenser, Jonson, Milton, and the Literary System* (Berkeley and Los Angeles, 1983).

CHAPTER 10

Marvell and the art of disappearance

Murray Krieger ends his recent book, *The Institution of Theory*, by pleading guilty to the charge that, even after all these years, he is still an "apologist for poetry."[1] These days being an apologist for poetry means resisting the various historicisms – old, new, cultural, material – whose expansive arguments are made at the expense of the aesthetic, a category (and area) that either disappears in the analysis of "discursive systems" or is identified (and stigmatized) as the location of a status-quo politics anxious to idealize its own agendas. Krieger's strategy is to claim for poetry what our new theorists claim for history and politics: the capacity to complicate and, by complicating, disperse the power of ideological formations. Rather than being in need of demystification, the literary text instructs us in the art – and, far in advance of deconstruction, performs the work – of undoing unities and opening up apparent closures: "totalization is that which the discourse of ideology imposes, and it is that from which, potentially, the counter ideological discourse of the literary text can liberate us" (73). Literature, in short, is "counter theoretical" (87) – where by "theoretical" Krieger means "ideological" – and "in these ideological days, it is the pressure to resist, as well as the role of literature in supplying it, that is sorely needed" (75).

In essence, this is an up-to-date version of Sidney's *Apology* (itself a Renaissance refurbishing of Horace), but with a difference. While both Sidney and Krieger find a special job for literature to do – one beyond the capacities of either history or philosophy – in Sidney's argument that job is hortatory in a positive sense. The reader who, in one of Sidney's memorable examples, comes upon the image of Aeneas carrying old Anchises on his back will be moved to wish himself such a person and therefore be more inclined to act in that same way when the opportunity presents itself. (The moment and the lesson are the essence of humanism.) In Krieger's argument, in contrast, readers are moved by poetry to *refrain* from action, at least of the precipitously ideological kind, and to tarry for a while in the realm of "leisure" or "ideological freedom" that "the poetic fiction" provides (65). Whereas Sidney sees poetry as sharing with history and philosophy a political task, but performing it more effectively, Krieger sees poetry as working against the political projects to which history and philosophy are often attached and instantiating instead a political project of its own, the project of resistance.

It is easy to see why this particular apology for poetry is attractive: given the high value we now place on political commitment, and the suspicion (voiced on all sides) of detachment and disengagement, it is satisfying to find a way of investing disengagement with a political effectivity. Nevertheless, there is another apology for poetry, more radical (although as old as the hills), that one occasionally spies just below the surface of Krieger's argument, especially in those pages where he revisits (nostalgically, I think) the discourse of the New Criticism, rooted in the Kantian ideal of "the transcendence of all our private desires" (60), and in the conception of the work of art as a unique and self-enclosed construct (63), "a self sealing form" so internally complete and totalizing that "it exclude[s] everything else" (71). This stronger version of aestheticism has become suspect because it seeks no compromise with human concerns and indeed pushes them away, and that is why Krieger, as attuned as he is to the critical and cultural currents of the present moment, pushes it away. Nevertheless (although it is presumptuous of me to say so), that stronger aestheticism is really what he wants and I am going to nudge him in its direction by revisiting a poet who wants it too.

That poet is Andrew Marvell, and what makes him a very emblem of the issues Krieger raises is the fact that he is at once the most public and social of men – a tutor to Fairfax's daughter and Cromwell's ward, Latin Secretary of the Council of State, a member of parliament for twenty years – and the least knowable. "I am naturally inclined to keep my thoughts private," Marvell writes in a letter in 1675, and the same sentiment ends a poem ("Mourning") that begins as a meditation on meaning and the possibility of specifying it:

> I yet my silent judgment keep,
> Disputing not what they believe:
> But sure as oft as women weep,
> It is to be supposed they grieve.[2]

The question of record is: "What does it mean when women weep?" The closest the poem comes to providing an answer is the word "sure." But what the speaker is sure of is that one may suppose that women's weeping signifies grief; that is, one is sure of a supposition, but the truth (or falsehood) of what is supposed remains hidden. Neither the poem nor the speaker will yield it up, and therefore they don't yield themselves up either. The result is not what Krieger describes as the hallmark of poetry under the New Criticism – every meaning "confronted by its self-contradiction" (63) – but something more stringent and parsimonious, a shrinking away from meaning altogether. "Mourning" does not give us multiple meanings or many judgments, but rather no meanings and a withholding of judgment. Both poem and speaker "keep" to themselves, neither venturing out nor letting anything (or anyone) in.

This is the action (if that is the word) Marvell's poetry attempts (surely the wrong word) to perform, the action of withholding, of keeping to itself, and what is withheld is meaning, the imputation of a significance that originates with the agent who would bestow it. At the most general level this agent is man:

> Luxurious man, to bring his vice in use,
> Did after him the world seduce. ("The Mower against Gardens," 1–2)

"After him" means (I am aware of the irony) both "in the wake of" and "in the image of." By seeing, and thus organizing, the world as the categories of his consciousness enable and command him to do, man makes what is primary secondary and what is secondary – the acts of perception and prediction – primary. If, as William James famously declares, "the trail of the human serpent is over everything,"[3] it is the smell and slime of that trail from which Marvell recoils in disgust. Man cannot keep his hands, and what is worse, his mind, off of things. His vice is consciousness itself, that appropriative motion which insists on itself as a point of reference in relation to which everything else is then defined. Like Wallace Stevens's jar, human consciousness takes dominion everywhere.[4]

In "The Garden" (23–24), Marvell identifies this prideful taking of dominion with the act of naming, for as John Carey observes, naming, especially of natural objects – which of course are not "objects" in their own eyes – "destroys the unnamed innocence of the thing itself." Things named, Carey continues, "have been interfered with by language."[5] Moreover, man's interference is involuntary; in the very act of seeing, the coordinates of his own perception frame and mark out the relative – not essential – shape and place of all that comes within his view. In "The Mower against Gardens," man encloses: "He first enclosed within the gardens square / A dead and standing pool of air" (5–6). He alters:

"With strange perfumes he did the roses taint, / And flowers themselves were taught paint" (11). He adds: "And a more luscious earth for them did knead" (7). "Gardens square" is a double interference; there are no gardens in nature; the squaring of what was not there before is a flaunting and redoubling of an original outrage. The flowers that are taught to paint themselves are no longer themselves; they wear the garment of the landscape artist. The earth that is enriched by human cultivation becomes more than – and therefore different from – what it is; by being kneaded it is given more than it, in and of itself, needs. Giving more is what man inevitably does; that is why he is called "luxurious," that is, excessive, *self-indulgent*, superfluous, above and beyond what is necessary. He simply cannot allow anything to be itself; he cannot leave anything alone.

To be left alone, to not be interfered with, to not be appropriated, is the desire of all Marvellian actors, and it is the frustration of that desire about which they endlessly complain. Two such complainers speak all the lines in "A Dialogue Between the Soul and Body," and despite the apparently agonistic form of the poem, the goal of each is not to triumph, but to decouple. Each desires to be sufficiently distinguished from the other so that a line between them can be cleanly drawn. "Each complains," as Donald Friedman says, "that it has been made what it is by the other and . . . imagines a state of being in which it would be freely and independently itself."[6] The language of tyranny and enslavement that characterizes both speakers does not indicate a desire to be master, but a desire, stronger than Greta Garbo's, to be alone ("Two paradises 'twere in one / To live in Paradise alone" ["The Garden," 63–64]). The soul's complaint is not simply that it feels grief, but that the grief is "another's" (22).

Indeed, the point is even deeper than that – since grief itself can only be experienced in relation to loss, deprivation, or disappointment, it is the product of *relationships*, of entanglements; were one to live entirely within oneself, with no motion outward and no intrusions into the space of one's being, grief would not be a possibility. Nor would any of the other emotions be possible, as we see from the equivalent statement by the soul:

> Joy's cheerful madness does perplex
> Or sorrow's other madness vex;
> Which knowledge forces me to know,
> And memory will not forgo. (37–40)

The vexations of sorrow and joy depend on memory, and memory is a function of time, of the disabling ability to recall in the present what has happened to one in the past. Memory is necessary to action (if you don't

know where you've been, how will you know where to go next?), and in
many if not most accounts of being, memory is honored; but action,
engagement with the world of others, is precisely what the body and soul,
in their different but related ways, wish to avoid. Indeed, each also wishes
to avoid knowledge, for as the verse quite explicitly says, "knowledge
forces" (39). That is, knowledge is a commerce on a two-way street: one
either knows *about* another or one is known *by* another, and in either
case knowledge cannot be experienced independently; you can only "do"
it in the company of someone else, who is either its object or its agent.
Knowledge requires extension, both horizontally to others and vertically
in relation to a past that strains toward a future. Knowledge, memory,
grief, joy, sorrow are all attributes of the life lived in time, of an existence
that is not accidentally but essentially temporal (available to narration and
known only in narration), and therefore not in and of itself essential at all.

In short, and as I have already said, consciousness itself – the realm
of consecutive and reflective thought – is the chief obstacle to the
desired state of being in these poems. The point is made clearly in "The
Coronet," a poem in which the speaker's efforts to lay a pure offering
at his savior's feet fail, and fail precisely because they are made, because *as*
efforts they originate at a distance from the object of desire and thus
apprehend (a word not innocent) that object from a perspective not its
own. In "Eyes and Tears," Marvell speaks of the "self deluding sight" that
"In a false angle takes each height" (5–6), and we are meant to realize,
first, that any angle is a false angle in that it cannot be true to the non-
angle from which the object knows itself, and, second, that sight is always
self-deluding since what it delivers is the view from some angle. That is
why the exertions of the speaker in "The Coronet" are, quite literally, self-
defeating; whatever their direction, they will come bearing "wreaths of
fame and interest" (16); that is, they will merely reproduce the condition
of distance – of nonidentity – that makes them necessary in the first
place. The difficulty is summed up in lines that declare the futility, and
indeed sinfulness, of summing up:

> And now when I have summed up all my store
> Thinking (so I myself deceive)
> So rich a chaplet thence to weave ... (9–11)

Taken in isolation, line 10 says it all: simply by thinking, by assuming a
stance of reflection (in relation to a past that now configures both the
present and the hope of a future), the agent deceives himself as to the
possibility of achieving his goal, deceives himself into thinking that,

by thinking, he will be able to annihilate the distance thought inevitably declares and extends. Any summing up, any adding up of sums, any putting of things together, any gathering of store, any of the gestures that are the content of consciousness, only further embeds one in the angled, and, because angled, false life of temporality, of deferral, of non-coincidence with the essence of being. The alternative is literally inconceivable and is largely represented (another gesture signifying defeat) in the poem by words and phrases that would in other discourses carry a positive value, but here are merely different versions of the same debilitating abilities: to "seek" (4), to "gather" (6), to "weave" (11), to "find" (13), to "twin[e]" (14), to "fold" (15), to "frame" (22), to "set with skill" (24), to "ch[oose] out with care" (24), and even to "care." Opposed to these inevitable shapes of conscious effort are the negative actions attributed to Christ: *un*tying and *dis*entangling ("Either his slippery knots at once untie; / And disentangle all his winding snare" [20–21]). One must, that is, be tied to nothing, entangled only in one's own snare and no one else's, set off in one's own frame, neither measuring nor measured by the frame of some other.

But how would one do that, or, rather, how would one so completely undo entanglements as to achieve this incredible independence? This is the problem that vexes many of Marvell's speakers, among them the Nymph who voices her famous and famously enigmatic complaint. What she is complaining about is, first, change, and then (and ultimately) the corruption that attends relationality: "The wanton troopers riding by / Have shot my fawn and it will die" ("The Nymph Complaining for the Death of Her Fawn," 1–2). The action is abrupt and intrusive; it comes in sideways ("riding by"), as if the characters from another poem have for a moment burst into this one and left behind something to decipher. Why did they do it? "Thou ne'er didst alive / Them any harm" (4–5). What does it mean? "I'm sure I never wished them ill" (7). These questions are barely registered (let alone answered) before there is another abrupt intrusion, this one produced by the Nymph herself who, without pre-amble, says "Inconstant Sylvio" (25). It is Sylvio who had given her the fawn, but who then, after having "beguiled" her (33), left it behind as a gift marked by his duplicity. Even before the troopers came riding by, he came riding by and in a somewhat longer space of time performed as they would, with motives she can only wonder at. All she is sure of is what he *said* – "I know what he said, I'm sure I do" (30) – but in the light of his betrayal she cannot be sure of what he meant. Indeed, the trouble is that he meant anything at all, that she was required to read him, that there was a gap between what he presented (in both his person and his gift) and what he was. (His is the double mind of which the Mower complains ["The Mower against Gardens," 9] even as he displays it.) That is what the world of meaning is, a realm where nothing is coincident with itself but requires for its completion, for its self-realization (which is therefore not a *self*-realization at all), the frame of something other, of some prior history or future goal. In the world of meaning, nothing can be taken at face value because the value of the face always resides elsewhere. (Everything is a sign.)

In the interval between her two encounters with meaning, which are also encounters with deferral, the Nymph turns to the fawn with whom, she reports, "I set myself to play" (37). "Setting oneself" is the language of plan and design, but the design here is to have none, and rather to play, a word that appears prominently in Marvell's poetry, where it almost always means non-purposeful activity, activity that is not the product of motives or strategies, activity that is merely consecutive, discontinuous activity in the sense that each of its moments is a hostage neither to the past nor the future. It is therefore, as the Nymph immediately says, "solitary," not bound to anything but itself, and "idle" (40), that is, innocent of teleology.

That innocence, however, is precarious, and the Nymph knows as much, for even before the wanton troopers have appeared she is worrying that the fawn itself might change:

> Had it lived long, I do not know
> Whether it too might have done so
> As Sylvio did. (47–49)

That is, in time the fawn too might acquire motives, and present a surface that could not be trusted, a surface that would have to be read in long-range (past and future) terms rather than simply received and experienced. Moreover, insofar as she finds herself imagining a world populated by agents who think strategically, who mean, the Nymph herself is becoming such an agent, someone who cannot take anything for what it is, but must always be looking for hidden reasons and, therefore, harboring such reasons herself. Even when she speculates on the long-term effects of the fawn's diet – "its chief delight was still / On roses thus itself to fill" (87–88) – the result she imagines is emblematic of her fears: "Had it lived long, it would have been / Lilies without, roses within" (91–92). That is, not through and through the same, but self-divided, double, duplicitous. Perhaps, then, the fact that the fawn did not live long should be considered a blessing rather than a cause for complaint, for it is only when the fawn grows up, and with it the Nymph, that the idle idyll they now share will be disrupted in ways even more upsetting than the disruption performed by the wanton troopers; perhaps the "short time" (52) when Nymph and fawn enjoyed a love in "play" would give way to the red and white carnal love to which her half-conscious blushes already point. It is significant that the fawn is ungendered, referred to only as "it," an equivocation designed to hold back the time when its "pure virgin limbs" (89) may not be so pure or so virgin.

In her desire (abetted, ironically, by the action of the wanton troopers) to arrest the moment of self-contained and inconsequential play, the Nymph is one with the male speakers of Marvell's two pedophilic poems, "Young Love" and "The Picture of Little T. C. in a Prospect of Flowers." In these poems, an unselfconscious being, that is, a being whose sense of herself is not borrowed from another or from an awareness of what she once was and will someday be, is observed in play by an older man who can observe and reflect on but cannot experience (because he can reflect on) her "simplicity": "See with what simplicity / This Nymph begins her golden days!" ("The Picture," 1–2). Seeing the simplicity, being able to recognize it, is to be unable to live it, for it is recognized as something the observer lacks, and lack – desire to be something other than one is, indeed knowledge that there is something else to be – is the antithesis of the simple state. True (that is, authentic) simplicity is wholly self-sufficient, complete in and of itself, neither signified nor signifying. It is therefore a condition continually threatened, as in these poems, by the future imagined for the young girl by her voyeuristic admirer. Some day, he speculates, she may assume a role in some "high cause" (9), that is, in some epic story, and he can only hope to extend the time "Ere" her "conquering eyes … have tried their force to wound, / Ere, with their glancing wheels, they drive / In triumph over hearts that strive" (18–21). "Force," "wound," "wheels," "drive," "triumph," "strive" – this is the vocabulary of forward movement, of time that does not provide endless spaces for directionless play but exerts its pressures in ways that inevitably produce alteration; this is the vocabulary of design, and of agents, who, in the course of the unfolding of design, become other than they were, either because they have striven and thus defined themselves by ends not yet in view, or because they have been conquered and become defined by the ends of those who have triumphed.

It is design and an existence defined only in relation to design, in relation to something you are now not, in relation to relation, that the Nymph complaining wants to avoid, and she takes her cue from moments in which the fawn cannot be seen:

> Among the beds of lilies, I
> Have sought it oft, where it should lie;
> Yet could not till it self would rise,

> Find it, although before mine eyes.
> For in the flaxen lilies' shade,
> It like a bank of lilies laid. (77–82)

In order to be seen – captured in another's perspective – the fawn must rise in such a way as to receive definition from a surrounding background; in short, it must appear, where appearance is understood as being set off by something external to it. It follows, then, that in order to escape being defined by another, one must dis-appear, find a mode of being that is not available to the appropriation of sight, and that is what the fawn does when it merges with the bank of lilies so completely that it cannot be picked out. The effect is noted precisely by the Nymph: it is before (in front of, ahead of) her eyes, but not within their sphere of appropriation; the fawn has escaped into a realm where what it is depends on nothing but its own frame of reference.

It is this achievement that the Nymph attempts to match when she resolves to "bespeak thy grave and die" (111). Notice that the claim is not to speak about the fawn's grave, but to speak it, to express it so perfectly that there is no distance between the expression and the thing expressed, so perfectly that expression is no longer expression – a sign of nonidentity – but tautology. On its face, the Nymph's way of making good on her claim is curious: she will have a statue of herself weeping "cut in marble" (112). What could be more an instance of representation and therefore of the distance she wishes to erase than the cutting of a statue? From idea, to medium, to engraver, to tool, to message – with each stage in the process, the condition of mediation, of non-coincidence with the origin, with the thing itself, would seem to be more firmly established. But then the Nymph declares the case to be exactly the reverse:

> . . . but there
> Th' engraver sure his art may spare,
> For I so truly thee bemoan,
> That I shall weep though I be stone,
> Until my tears, still dropping, wear
> My breast, themselves engraving there. (113–118)

The key phrase is "themselves engraving," which means both being at once their own medium and message (a state literally inconceivable) and putting themselves into the grave, i.e., entombing themselves. The relationship between the two is precise: if there could be a mode of representation that scorned the aid of anything external to the thing represented, the result would be the dis-appearance of that thing, since it could only be seen from its own perspective; from any other perspective, from another angle, from angle in general, the thing would be unavailable, would not be present, would be dead, would be *engraved.* The moral is bleak: true life requires representational death; tears that engrave themselves (in both senses) are their own signs and therefore do not signify, they do not point to anything and nothing else points to – is a sign of – them; they are not known by any alien agent; they are not seen, no angle – by definition false – delivers them; they have escaped from the world of meaning.

Or at least that is the desire. As the poem ends the Nymph adds a component to her sculptural tableau: the fawn too will be carved, "of purest alabaster made" (120); but that is just the trouble: it will be "made," fashioned by another and therefore not itself, and it is with this admission, an admission of failure, that the poem comes to its unhappy conclusion:

> For I would have thine image be
> White as I can, though not as thee. (121–122)

That is, although I would like to have thine image be no image at all, have it *be* thee rather than *as* (not quite up to, at a distance from) thee, the best that I, or any other self-conscious agent, can achieve is a whiteness that is still too much on this side of visibility. The project of dis-appearing will always fall short of success if only because the effort itself shows. To be sure, the Nymph is enigmatic – if she never figures out what the actions of either the troopers or Sylvio mean, generations of critics have never managed to figure out what she means – but as an enigma she is still known, if imperfectly.

In Marvell's corpus, the desire not to be represented, not to be known, not to be forced by an angle into appearance, is fully realized only by a non-animate agent, "On a Drop of Dew." The poem of this title begins with a simple, but ultimately unfollowable, direction, "See":

> See how the orient dew . . .

The image seems firm enough until the first word of the second line: "Shed from the bosom of the morn," "Shed" names an action that is already past, and consequently when we look for the object to which the imperative directs us, it has already fled our apprehension, escaped our grasp. I intend this last literally, for seeing is itself a relational activity in which the object is seen – placed, fixed, captured – within the viewer's perspective and not its own. This drop of dew simply does not want to be seen and it repeatedly moves away from the line of vision that would take it in, that would enclose it, and instead it "Round in itself encloses / And in its little globe's extent / Frames as it can its native element" (6–8). This is as precise as it is impossible; a frame is by definition separate from that which it holds in place, but this drop of dew is held in place – is given definition, shape and identity – by itself, and is its own enclosure; it escapes capture by others by capturing or encasing itself, and the way it does this unthinkable thing – and it is important that it be unthinkable since to be able to think about it is to have framed and enclosed it – is the subject of the next few lines:

> How it the purple flow'r does slight,
> Scare touching where it lies,
> But gazing back upon the skies,
> Shines with a mournful light,
> Like its own tear . . .
> Restless it rolls and insecure,
> Trembling lest it grow impure. (9–13, 15–16)

Each of these lines describes the same motion: a withdrawing, a retreating, a resisting of contact; the drop never quite touches anything, instead it hangs there, suspended in midair, "like its own tear." This description or nondescription is particularly precise and teasing. Tears are framed by faces, but this tear is framed – is seen against – the background of the drop of dew which it also is. "Like" is finally a joke and is at the same time the victim of the joke (like its own tear, like its own joke); even syntax is defeated by this object that refuses to be apprehended by anything but itself.

That refusal takes the physical form of continual oscillation: "Restless it rolls and insecure." In any other context this might be a complaint, but the state of insecurity – of not being tied down to anything – is what the drop of dew desires, and restlessness does not name a deprivation but a triumph; were it at rest, it would be available for sighting, one could get a fix on it, but as long as it trembles, no sight line can establish a defining relation with it, and therefore the purity of its self-definition remains uncompromised. Later, in the second half of the poem, when the drop of dew has been analogized to the human soul, its movement is described in two remarkable, and remarkably antimimetic, lines:

> In how coy a figure wound,
> Every way it turns away. (27–28)

"Figure" is a mocking word on two levels. First it names that condition of perceptual clarity – of standing in outline against a background – that the drop repeatedly refuses; but figure also means figure of speech, a class of verbal actions characterized by every rhetorician as a deviation or turning away from direct or literal speech; but of course "coy" means just that, a turning away, a withdrawing, a delay, and therefore a "coy" figure is a withdrawing or a retreating in retreat or a delayed delaying, an indirection that turns away. The next line is a gloss on this inconceivable motion: "Every way it turns away." In what we might call "normal" turning away, one withdraws in relation to some points of reference – lines of sight – but grows nearer in relation to others; but this (non-)figure somehow, and we cannot know how, never turns toward anything; whichever way it turns, it maintains and increases its distance from anything that is not itself. This is not coyness of the usual kind, a strategy of delay and deferral designed to make the inevitable coming together even more sweet. This is coyness that is essential, one might even say defining, except that definition – in both the physical and conceptual senses – is what it perpetually flees.

What it flees to is its own dissolution, the state in which the effort it must so strenuously exert, the effort not to be touched, not to be framed, to disappear, is finally unnecessary:

> Such did the manna's sacred dew distill,
> White and entire, though congealed and chill,
> Congealed on earth: but does, dissolving, run
> Into the glories of th' almighty sun. (37–40)

The reference is to Exodus 16:11–22, and it seems straightforward enough until one notices that while the syntax makes the dew the property of the manna, it is the dew that distills and what it distills – leaves behind, as a purified entity – is the manna: "And when the dew that lay was gone up, behold . . . there lay a small round thing . . . on the ground" (Exodus 16:14). The manna is thus in the impossible but familiar Marvellian position of distilling itself, emerging not from any prior, governing entity, but from its own property. Moreover, although it emerges, it does not thereby surrender possession of itself to alien eyes and angles, for as we are told in Exodus, the children of Israel see "a small round thing" and call it manna because "they wist not what it was"; that is, they give it a name indicating their inability to categorize it, a name signifying that it has not been named, captured, framed by something other than its native element (which remains unknown). In the last two lines of the poem, the drop returns to that element, disappearing before our eyes, as the Nymph's fawn disappears before hers and as the manna of Exodus disappears even as the Israelites "see" it.

It does this in two steps. First, it congeals (39); that is, becomes more concentratedly what it is, adheres to its own particles, turns inward and away from the world; but that is its posture only "on earth," where it is threatened by the danger of alien appropriation. Once in its native element, it quite literally relaxes and gives itself to its proper home; there, one can assume, it is seen by "natives," by those just like it, seen, in effect, by itself. But what we see is its dissolution, its loss of definition; what we see, quite literally and almost in slow motion, is its dis-appearance; not, however, disappearance into nonbeing, but into a mode of being that escapes apprehension in the two fully relevant senses of that word: being grasped mentally, and being taken into custody, into prison. (As Donald Friedman has finely said, "all of our attempts to capture meaning in form are rendered inappropriate by the 'Glories of th' Almighty sun.'")[7]

One cannot, however, generalize from the drop's escape; after all, it was required to maintain its radically evasive behavior only for a few short hours before rescue arrived with the morn. For all human agents, including poets, the requirement is severer; one must contrive somehow to live many days and years and yet remain aloof from entanglements, from relationships that compromise the purity of self-reference, from relationship itself. One must, in short, contrive to *not* come into focus, to resist the efforts of any agent or discourse to get a fix on you, lest that fix become you by becoming the angle from which you are forced into appearance.

I have already observed that the impossibility of this project – this project of not being implicated in project – is Marvell's great subject, and it is a subject whose uneasy and contradictory imperative informs the greatest of his poems, "Upon Appleton House," a poem consistently at war with its own temporality, with its tendency, inevitable given the structure of language, to mean. "Upon Appleton House" is a poem critics are forever attempting to unify, but unity, rather than being what the poem desires, is the enemy of its non-aspiration, its aspiration not to mean, not to point to anything beside itself, not to go anywhere. Within its frame (far from sober, despite the claim of the first line), the enemy is most powerfully present in the person of the subtle nun who is distinguished by her skill at narrative. It is with this skill that she seeks to envelop the "Virgin Thwaites," who oft

> . . . spent the summer suns
> Discoursing with the subtle nuns,
> Whence in these words one to her weav'd
> (As 'twere by chance) thoughts long conceived. (94–97)

The parenthesis tells the story (of too much story): what is wrong with the nun's discourse is precisely that chance or randomness is merely pretended; apparently spontaneous speech is in fact the product of a premeditation that takes the form of a verbal net, of something woven in order to entrap. The point is made even more explicitly when the nun's speech is finished. First, the narrator at once describes its effect and renders unmistakable its sexual nature by observing that "the nun's smooth tongue has sucked her in" (200); and then Fairfax points the moral (as if it needed pointing) by characterizing the Nun's performance as a cheat (204), as an enchantment, as an imprisoning (206, 208), as something fraudulent (214), and as an art that operates to "alter all" (215). This last is the crucial charge because it specifies the danger inherent in all art. Alteration, in the sense of conferring on something a shape and meaning not properly its own, is the inevitable effect of framing, of positioning an object so that it can only be seen from an angle and not directly.

That is what the nun does when she draws the young Thwaites into a point of view in relation to which her alternatives are already restricted, and indeed it is what is done by any consecutive discourse, that is, by any discourse in which the identity of a moment is a function of what has gone before and what is yet to come. In consecutive discourse, one's person and actions are shaped by a story being told by another (be it the nun or fate or simply time), and it is within the perspective of that other that one lives and moves and has one's being. But if this is what is wrong with the nun's performance, it is difficult to see what the alternative might be, for even if the virgin Thwaites were to escape from the nun's story she would presumably escape into someone else's story, a story no less angled and no less pressuring; and indeed this is exactly what happens when young Fairfax takes the cloister by force and makes his way to where the "bright and holy Thwaites / weeping at the alter waits" (263–264). The passivity of her posture tells us what she waits for: to see who will win the struggle and thereby gain the right to embed her either in a new or in a continuing narrative, the right to make her into a subject. Even as the poem relates Fairfax's triumph it condemns him as no less an agent of design and premeditation than those he defeats.

But one must ask again, is there an alternative mode of action either for the perceiver or the perceived? Is it possible to move about in the world without being a hostage to some purposeful vision in relation to which one's actions and the actions of others are always and already meditated, never being simply what they are? "Upon Appleton House" is, like many of Marvell's other poems, an attempt to answer that question, and one part of his answer resides in the contrast he would draw between his performance and the nun's. Just before he reproduces the nun's extraordinary close-woven discourse, he gives us a self-description of his own: "While with slow eyes we these survey, / And on each pleasant footstep stay" (81–82). Slow eyes are eyes not hurrying in their movement in response to some teleological pressure; slow eyes do not feel at their back time's winged chariot. Similarly, pleasant footsteps are footsteps taken at no behest other than their own; they have no relation either to a previous step or to future steps which may or may not be taken; one can stay on them as long or as little as one likes, and thus they are the very antithesis of the steps – one leading to another – that define a good plot. Pleasant steps are, or wish to be, haphazard. Haphazardness is the poem's goal, and it is that goal (or un-goal) to which the nun's discourse is an affront. That is, her action should not be seen (as it often is) as an interruption of the story of the house of Fairfax, but as an interruption by story, and therefore by meaning, of the mode of slow eyes and pleasant footsteps. The desire of the poem, and of the poet, is not to arrive at the intersection of destiny and choice, but to defer and avoid both.

The career of deferral in "Upon Appleton House" deserves a fuller account than I can give here, although I can say that such an account would begin by rejecting as ironically intended the poem's opening claim to be a sober frame, and go on to observe (as Rosalie Colie and others have before me) the many ways in which sobriety is forestalled and frames are so rapidly and relentlessly multiplied that they never come into focus and therefore fail to provide the focus that would be necessary for sustained perception. Such an account would continue by remarking on the extraordinary self-description of a poet who at least claims to have escaped the demands of his medium, who has been able, or so he says, to hit "chance's better wit" (better, that is, than narration), who languishes "with ease" (593), who securely plays (607), whose side is "lazy" (643), whose foot is sliding (645), whose discourse strives to be like the self-reflecting river a succession of "wanton harmless folds" (633). All these, as I have said, are constitutive of the poet's chief claim, the claim to have fully disengaged, to have withdrawn from all the entanglements that would compromise self-definition and self-sufficiency. In stanza 76 he declares the process of withdrawal successful:

> How safe, methinks and strong behind
> These trees have I encamped my mind
> Where beauty aiming at the heart,
> Bends in some trees its useless dart,

And where the world no certain shot
Can make, or me it toucheth not.
But I on it securely play,
And gall its horsemen all the day. (801–808)

Only in "The Garden" do we find a more concentrated formulation of the Marvellian desire to not be touched, to be out of the line of any sight, to be so continually out of focus that no dart or beauty's eye will have a chance of hitting what would be its mark; the desire to play securely, that is, without care, without concern that this moment of play be responsive to the moments before it or anxious in relation to the moments that will succeed it. But even before these lines are spoken, Marvell has acknowledged the shadow that hangs over them, the shadow of reflective consciousness. He is, after all, *reporting* on this supposedly achieved state, viewing it from a reflective distance, "methinking" about it rather than simply living it. He is, as he himself announces, an "easy philosopher" (561), where "easy" is at once a claim to have escaped philosophy's requirement – the requirement to be not loose like the drop but rigorous, consecutive, deductive, hypotactic – and a rueful admission that the escape cannot be made so easily, that it is not so easy to be truly easy, that as a philosopher of ease he is still too much the philosopher, too much aware of his ease to be truly inhabiting it (wearing it as his frame and native element), working too hard at being easy.

He ceases the work the moment the real thing arrives: "The young Maria walks tonight" (651). The important word is "young": not yet a philosopher trying to think herself back into ease, she is like Little T. C. and the Nymph before the time of either Sylvio or the wanton troopers, unselfconsciously one with herself, complete and entire, like the drop. Without even trying (because she is not trying), Maria is in the impregnable position the poet so bravely (and suspiciously) claims:

> Blest Nymph! That couldst so soon prevent
> Those trains by youth against thee meant:
> Tears (wat'ry shot that pierce the mind)
> And sighs (Love's cannon charged with wind);
> True praise (that breaks through all defence);
> And feigned complying innocence,
> But knowing where this ambush lay,
> She 'scaped the safe, but roughest way. (713–720)

The catalog of things she escapes is comprehensive: not only the plots and designs ("trains") that men mean (i.e., intend), but meaning itself, the necessity in a world of stratagem of looking behind or above or below phenomena for the significance they do not bear on the surface. Hers is a mind that resists piercing – penetration, violation – by anything, even by true praise, which in the guise of simply mirroring essence makes a claim to have caught it, to have mastered it, to have become its frame. True praise, like feigned innocence, always comes professing its lack of motive, the absence of design, of train; but true innocence responds as Maria does, by *not* responding, by not even registering the "complying" (falsely accommodating) assault.

The poem could end here, but it doesn't. Instead, a detail in the description of Maria's happy state foretells its doom. In her, we are told, self-sufficiency is so perfectly achieved that "goodness doth itself entail / On females if there want a male" (727–728). Her goodness is self-generating and requires mixture with no other in order to produce its offspring, that is, itself. (It is its own tear.) But the deadly word "if" – "if there want a male" – reaches back to the previous line and releases the full and ominous meaning of "entail" – the act of imposing on persons or property an implacable succession of possession and ownership. Something entailed is never itself, for in relation to a sequence it did not originate it always belongs to another, to a story it did not write but cannot evade. That is what happens to Maria:

> Hence she with graces more divine
> Supplies beyond her sex the line,
> And like a sprig of mistletoe,
> On the Fairfacian Oak doth grow;
> Whence for some universal good,
> The priest shall cut the sacred bud;
> While her glad Parents most rejoice
> And make their Destiny their Choice ... (737–744)

The closed society of self-sufficient females lasts barely a stanza before the male who had been almost casually banished returns to supply what Maria cannot: a line, a lineage, a history, a story, whose driving force will take her out of herself – "beyond her sex" – and assign her a role she does not choose. The choice is made in the name of "some universal good" (can we miss the sarcasm here?), some grand epic narrative that first authorizes the ceremonial violation of her unfeigned innocence ("The priest shall cut the sacred bud"), and then calls the violation "Destiny." John Rogers is one of the few to note that these lines "represent an unsettling divergence from a complex of values the poem has established."[8] The values are those of pleasant steps, unhurried time, deferral, ease, all of which are suddenly dislodged by what Rogers correctly terms the "violent action" of the priest who cuts in destiny's name.[9] The destiny in question is most pointedly not hers – she does not even appear in the couplet that announces it – but belongs first to the parents who precede her and then to the male heir she is now obliged to produce. No longer the figure to whom everything in nature resonates, Maria is reduced to being a function – a mere relay – in a narrative to whose inexorable progress she has been sacrificed. It may not be the nun's smooth tongue, but something, surely, has sucked her in.

Like the Nymph, Little T. C., the infant of "Young Love," the unfortunate lover, the solitary wanderer in Eden, the bodiless soul, and the soulless body, Maria is not allowed to remain in the unselfconscious realm of play and leisure where her linguistic virtuosity has full play (all the languages are hers) but is not employed (709) in any purposive direction. She speaks "heaven's dialect" (712), a dialect whose meanings, as Marshall Grossman notes, remain "*in-potentia*," just hanging there, like the world arrested and hushed (681) for that moment before the "inevitable and necessary splash back into temporality and narrative."[10] The splash back into temporality, meaning and appropriation is the fate that awaits every human figure in the Marvellian corpus, with the single and unlikely exception of the addressee of his most famous poem, the coy mistress. She is an unlikely exception because the poem is so palpably designed to emplot her, to suck her in. Unique among Marvell's poems, "To His Coy Mistress" is from first to last an argument, and as an argument its goal is to absorb its object – the hearer – into its own structure so that her every action and thought would be conferred and determined by another.

The poem opens by rejecting the unpatterned and slow perambulating of pleasant steps that trace out Marvell's nonprogress in "Upon Appleton House." Here, there will be no leisure to "think which way / To walk, and pass our long love's day" (3–4), for each moment is informed by the urgency of a waiting end whose backward pressure turns everything into a beginning or a middle. In its driving insistency, its refusal to let events and persons appear in any terms other than the terms of its own project, the poem is the very embodiment of narrative desire, of the desire to possess, to assimilate, to control. In its mode it is indistinguishable from the speech of the subtle nun, with the difference only that it is more successful, for it so encloses the mistress within its toils that she is never heard from; she is simply the space the narrative appropriates, transforming her before she ever appears into the voiceless occasion of its unfolding.

And yet, from another perspective, a perspective from which the poem excludes us – or is it a perspective that excludes the poem? – the case might be said to be quite different. It is the perspective of the only attribute the poem grants the lady, both in its title and in its second line: she is coy, that is, withdrawing, retreating, turning away. And if coyness is her essence, the only quality predicated of her, then is not her essence fully and autogenously realized in her absence from the poem? Is not the narrative's triumph in silencing her really her triumph, for after all, from the beginning to the end, we know nothing about her, we have no line on her, she has escaped our grasp; she has disappeared: she has won.

It might seem an unlikely reading of Marvell that finds the triumphant moments in his poetry shared by (that oddest of couples) the coy mistress and a drop of dew. But in fact, the present essay participates in a strain of criticism at least as old as Jonathan Goldberg's brilliant explication of "The Nymph Complaining," which has borne fruit (sometimes of an oppositional kind) in the work of Marshall Grossman, Barbara Estrin, and Joan Hartwig. Goldberg poses the basic question, the question with which Marvell (in my account) is obsessed: "How can . . . voice preserve itself, its purity, and avoid the contaminating eddies of repetition in which it would cease to own it-self?" How, that is, can one "speak of one's own . . . and of nothing else?"[11] And his answer is, string out the story (28), avoid reference, "avoid loss by playing" in a "ritualized and endless sequence" (31) that is "endlessly disjunctive" (33); perform, over and over again "the refusal of going beyond" (which I have described as the refusal of meaning), so that one produces what would seem to be impossible, a text that is "not *really* 'about' something else" (37). In a slightly different vocabulary, Hartwig explores those moments in the poetry where (again impossibly) a cause is its own effect and an effect its own cause "without an intermediate step of transformed substance," "without requiring an intermediary function such as reason to grasp a cause to produce the effect."[12] The immediacy and self-referentiality is such, she notes, that "there is no need to have the mind interfere in the process with thinking" (73), and the result is a surface radically opaque, one that "seems to resist, and often to deny, that there is any level beneath it" (85). In another fine essay, Estrin finds the complaining nymph to be just such an opaque surface, and willfully so. In her utter indifference "to setting anything in the earthly realm aright," she responds to the male world that would appropriate her by creating "enclaves of self-enabling silence" complete with an audience (the fawn) wholly internal to her private meditations: "She has one lover and one reader, the deer's incorporation of her message, eliminating any need to record it."[13] "Firm in her withdrawal" (106), the nymph "plans her silence, substituting deprivation for violation and rendering herself fundamentally inviolable" (118). "Like the dissolving Manna in 'On a Drop of Dew,'" she finds "a resolution in dissolution and evaporating into the heavens from which future readers, reduced to wanton soldiers, are excluded" (119–120).

Of course, future readers, especially professional ones, will not take exclusion lying down, and they will labor heroically, as have many under the aegis of historicisms old and new, to reconnect Marvell and his poetry to the world from which they so resolutely turn away. Just what those labors have yielded might be inferred from a discussion that concludes the volume in which Hartwig's and Estrin's essays appear. The discussants are John Klause, Ann Baynes Coiro and Michael Schoenfeldt, each of whom has an investment in historical/political criticism and each of whom acknowledges a measure of failure. Klause notes the many recent classifications of Marvell as a Puritan libertarian, as a loyalist, as a trimmer, as a classical republican, as a moderate chiliast, but concludes that "a man so baffling as Marvell" may present "something humbling to grand interpretative aspirations" and constitute a rebuke to those who eagerly seek "the historical poet."[14] "Perhaps," Ann Coiro begins her contribution, "Marvell's poetry achieves nothing" (238), and is itself a prime instance of what he most values, "graven, permanent words" (240), that is, words which, because they are indecipherable, keep everything to themselves. As "physical inscriptions" rather than efforts at communication, the poems are "inevitably enigmatic because they remain hard and dead when we try to read them" (240). Not only does Marvell "elude us," she concludes, but he "seems to have intended to do so." We may "look upon" his poems, "but we cannot fully understand . . . The grave is indeed a fine and private place" (243). Schoenfeldt picks up Coiro's note on the half beat: "I have long admired Marvell's poetry but have also found it to elude the very terms in which I try to convey my admiration" (243). He conjectures that the impenetrability to which everyone attests may be "a defensive response to the immense pressures placed upon behavior and speech in an age of political turmoil" (244), but this effort to be politically correct by being political is little more than a gesture (what age has not been an age of political turmoil?), and rings with less conviction than his conclusion: "Marvell's lyrics . . . are difficult to stabilize because they purposefully exclude the interiority they purport to exhibit" (247).

So ends a discussion entitled "The Achievement of Andrew Marvell," itself the end piece of a volume whose first sentence finds the editors (both historically minded critics) declaring: "Andrew Marvell remains the most enigmatic of minor seventeenth-century literary figures" (1). (That is to say, he remains irredeemably literary.) I cannot help thinking that Marvell would be pleased by these reports of the collective failure to "sound" him, and I hope that being reminded of this failure (often spectacularly performed) will give some pleasure, of a decidedly aesthetic kind, to Murray Krieger on this occasion.

NOTES

1 Murray Krieger, *The Institution of Theory* (Baltimore: Johns Hopkins University Press, 1994), 92.
2 Andrew Marvell, "Mourning," lines 33–36. All references are to *Andrew Marvell: The Complete Poems*, ed. Elizabeth Story Donno (London and New York: Penguin, 1972).
3 William James, "What Pragmatism Means," in *Pragmatism: A Contemporary Reader*, ed. Russell B. Goodman (New York: Free Press, 1995), 60.
4 See, on this point, Donald Friedman's "Andrew Marvell," in *The Cambridge Companion to English Poetry: Donne to Marvell*, ed. Thomas N. Corns (Cambridge: Cambridge University Press, 1993), 283: "The Mower who inveighs against gardens speaks for a purist vision of a nature untainted by human intention; for him man is 'Luxurious,' and gardens a sign of his limitlessly arrogant drive to reform nature in his own image."
5 John Carey, "Reversals Transposed: An Aspect of Marvell's Imagination," in *Approaches to Marvell*, ed. C.A. Patrides (London: Routledge and Kegan Paul, 1978), 136.
6 Friedman, "Andrew Marvell," 291.
7 Donald Friedman, "Sight and Insight in Marvell's Poetry," in Patrides, *Approaches to Marvell*, 320.
8 John Rogers, "Marvell's Pastoral Historiography," in *On the Celebrated and Neglected Poems of Andrew Marvell*, ed. Claude J. Summers and Ted-Larry Pebworth (Columbia: University of Missouri Press, 1992), 220.
9 Ibid., 221.
10 Marshall Grossman, "Allegory, Irony, and the Rebus," in *The Muses Common-Weale*, ed. Claude J. Summers and Ted-Larry Pebworth (Columbia: University of Missouri Press, 1988), 202, 203.
11 Jonathan Goldberg, *Voice Terminal Echo: Postmodernism and English Renaissance Texts* (New York: Methuen, 1986), 26.
12 Joan Hartwig, "Tears as a Way of Seeing," in Summers and Pebworth, *Celebrated and Neglected Poems*, 80, 73.
13 Barbara Estrin, "The Nymph and the Revenge of Silence," in Summers and Pebworth, *Celebrated and Neglected Poems*, 102, 104, 103.
14 John Klause, Ann Baynes Coiro and Michael Schoenfeldt, "The Achievement of Andrew Marvell," in Summers and Pebworth, *Celebrated and Neglected Poems*, 238, 237.

CHAPTER II

Masculine persuasive force: Donne and verbal power

"MY FEIGNED PAGE"

For a very long time I was unable to teach Donne's poetry. I never had anything good to say about the poems, and would always find myself rereading with approval C.S. Lewis's now fifty-year-old judgment on Donne as the "saddest" and "most uncomfortable of our poets," whose verse "exercises the same dreadful fascination that we feel in the grip of the worst kind of bore – the hot eyed, unescapable kind."[1] Indeed my own response to the poetry was even more negative than Lewis's: I found it sick, and thought that I must be missing the point so readily seen by others. I now believe that to *be* the point: Donne is sick and his poetry is sick; but he and it are sick in ways that are interestingly related to the contemporary critical scene. In short, the pleasures of diagnosis have replaced the pleasure I was unable to derive from the verse.

Let's get the diagnosis out of the way immediately: Donne is bulimic, someone who gorges himself to a point beyond satiety, and then sticks his finger down his throat and throws up. The object of his desire and of his abhorrence is not food, but words, and more specifically, the power words can exert. Whatever else Donne's poems are, they are preeminently occasions on which this power can be exercised; they report on its exercise and stage it again in the reporting, and when one asks about a moment in the poetry, "Why is it thus?" the answer will always be: "In order further to secure the control and domination the poet and his surrogates continually seek." This is, I think, what Judith Herz is getting at in a recent fine essay when she remarks that "Donne ... will say anything if the poem seems to need it,"[2] an observation I would amend by insisting that the need to be satisfied is not the poem's but the poet's, and that it is the need first to create a world and then endlessly to manipulate those who are made to inhabit it.

In more than a few of the poems, Donne not only performs in this way
but provides a theoretical explanation of his performance. Such a poem is
the elegy usually entitled "The Anagram," a variation on the topos of the
praise of ugliness. What Donne adds to the tradition is an account of what
makes it possible, the capacity of words to make connection with one
another rather than with some external referent that constrains them to
accuracy. Four lines teach the lesson and exemplify it:

> She's fair as any, if all be like her,
> And if none be, then she is singular.
> All love is wonder; if we justly do
> Account her wonderful, why not lovely too?
> (23–26)[3]

That is, if your mistress is indistinguishable from the indifferent mass of
women, then say "she's fair as any," and if she is distinguished by the
oddness of her features, then say, "she is singular," i.e., a rarity. In either
case you will be telling the truth, not as it exists in some realm independent of your verbal dexterity, but as it has been established in the context
created by that dexterity. This is even truer (if I can use that word) of the
second couplet in which we are first invited to assent to an unexception-
able assertion ("All love is wonder") and then told that by assenting we
have assented also to the infinite conclusions that might be reached
by playing with the two words and their cognates. It is as if the couplet
operated not to form a proposition, but simply to establish an equivalence
between two sounds that can then be related in any way that serves the
interpreter's purpose. If love equals wonder, the so-called argument goes,
the condition of being full of wonder should equal the condition of being
full of love, but since loveful is not a proper word, let's make it lovely.

The obvious objection to this self-propelling logic of schematic figures
is that it knows no constraints and is wholly unstable; meaning can be
pulled out of a suffix or out of thin air, and the linear constraints of syntax
and consecutive sense are simply overwhelmed. But Donne forestalls the
objection by putting it into the poem, not however, *as* an objection but as
a rationale for the interpretive fecundity of his "method": "If we might
put letters but one way, / In the lean dearth of words, what could we say?"
(17–18). The answer is that we could say only one thing at a time, and that
the one thing we could say would be formed in relation to some prior
and independent referent. By refusing to be confined by the lean dearth
of words, Donne becomes able to say anything or many things as he
combines and recombines words and letters into whatever figurative, and

momentarily real, pattern he desires. As Thomas Docherty has recently observed, in this poem "anything we choose to call a stable essence is always already on its way to becoming something else."[4] The result is an experience in which the reader is always a step behind the gymnastic contortions of the poet's rhetorical logic, straining to understand a point that has already been abandoned, striving to maintain a focus on a scene whose configurations refuse to stand still.

The case is even worse (or better) with another of the elegies, "The Comparison"; for if the lesson of "The Anagram" is that the "lean dearth of words" is to be avoided, the lesson of this poem is that the lean dearth of words – the sequential fixing of meaning – can't be achieved. Structurally, the "plot" of the poem couldn't be simpler: the poet's mistress is compared feature by feature to the mistress of his rival and declared to be superior; but this simplest of plots soon becomes radically unstable because the reader is often in doubt as to which pole of the comparison he presently inhabits. The trouble begins immediately, in the first line: "As the sweet sweat of roses in a still"; the key words in this line could go in either direction; in classical and Italian epic the sweat of nymphs and goddesses is routinely and without irony regarded as sweet, but in other poems, such as Skelton's "Elynour Rummyng" (the scene of which not incidentally is a still), sweat is fetid and redolent of moral and physical decay. The matter isn't helped very much by the second line, "As that which from chafed musk cat's pores doth trill" (solemnly glossed by Helen Gardner and other editors), and it is only with the third line – "As the almighty balm of th' early east" – that the reader is sure of the verse's direction and knows that the subject of these lines is the object of praise. This stability lasts for several lines and into the first of the poem's turns, a turn that is carefully marked for unmistakable difference: "Rank sweaty froth thy mistress' brow defiles" (7). In what follows, the poet warms to his task, as "menstruous boils" give way to "scum" and then to "parboiled shoes" and "warts" and "weals" as vehicles of an extended negative comparison.

It would seem that the comparison is being extended further in the couplet that begins "Round as the world's her head," and ends with a reference to "the fatal ball which fell on Ide" (15–16). True, the circle is often invoked as a symbol of perfection in several philosophical, astronomical and symbolic contexts, but there is something more than a little grotesque in the image of a hugely spherical head, and it is hardly flattering to be linked with the apple of discord that led to Paris's disastrous choice, a choice that reenacts the scene of original sin of which the poem immediately reminds us by adding the forbidden apple to the items of which "her head" is a simulacrum: "Or that whereof God had such jealousy, / As for the ravishing thereof we die" (17–18). It is only with the next line – "Thy head is like a rough-hewn statue of jet" – that we realize, after the fact, that the affective direction of the verse has already changed, and then we only know because the lines we are now reading are *relatively* less attractive than the lines we have just read: "Where marks for eyes, nose, mouth, are yet scarce set; / Like the first Chaos, or flat seeming face" (20–21). In place of the absolute scale promised by the initial act of comparison, we have a sliding or analog scale in which the same quantity bears different values depending on its place in the sequence of the reading experience.

When the flat-seeming face of line 21 is identified as belonging to Cynthia (22), everything begins to shift again. On the one hand Cynthia, in her role as controller of tides and bringer-in of storms, is a proper figure to bring up the rear of a list that includes Chaos; but on the other hand, Cynthia is also the figure of female chastity. Like everything and every-one else in the poem, she participates in both of the directions that are supposedly being distinguished, and her multivalence reaches out to infect Persephone, who arrives in the next line: "Like Proserpine's white beauty-keeping chest." The question is just whom is Proserpine supposed to be "like." The structure of the syntax links her strongly to Chaos ("Like the first Chaos"), but the whiteness of her beauty associates her just as strongly with pale Cynthia in her more positive aspects. The doubt is removed in line 24 with the adjective "fair," but needless to say it will be reintroduced at later moments when we again discover that we have been in the wrong relation of judgment to a woman who keeps changing into her opposite.

It is an amazing performance, a high-wire act complete with twists, flips, double reverses, and above all, triumphs, triumphs at the expense of the two women who become indistinguishably monstrous when the poet makes it impossible for us to tell the difference between them ("the language of vilification contaminates that of praise"),[5] and triumphs, of course, at our expense, as we are pushed and pulled and finally mocked by the incapacity he makes us repeatedly feel. But it is a triumph that has its cost, as the last half-line of the poem makes clear:

> . . . comparisons are odious.
> (54)

This is a moment of revulsion, not from the women for whose features he is, after all, responsible, but from the act by which he makes of them (and us) whatever he wills. Comparisons are odious because they are too easy. Given the requisite verbal skill, it is impossible for them *not* to succeed, and their success carries with it a lesson that turns back on itself, the lesson of a plasticity in nature so pervasive that it renders victory meaningless. What pleasure can be taken in the exercise of a skill if it meets no resistance? And what security attends an achievement that can be undone or redone in a moment, either by the verbal artificer himself, or by the very next person who comes along?

It is a lesson that has just been learned by the speaker of *Elegy 7*, a complaint-of-Pygmalion poem in which the first-person voice discovers to his distress that the woman he has fashioned has detached herself from him and is now free to go either her own way or the way of another. He begins by recalling her as she was before they met, and remembers her exclusively in terms of the languages she did not then understand: "thou didst not understand / The mystic language of the eye nor hand / . . . I had not taught thee then, the alphabet / Of flowers, how they devisefully being set / . . . might with speechless secrecy, / Deliver errands mutely" (3–4, 9–12). The point is not only that these were languages unknown to her, but that independently of them she was herself not known because she was as yet unformed. What she now understands now understands – in the sense of supporting or providing a foundation for – her; she is the sum of the signifying systems whose coded meanings and gestures now fill her consciousness and that is why her previous state is characterized as the *absence* of signification: "ill arrayed / In broken proverbs, and torn sentences" (18–19). "Arrayed" means both "clothed" and "set into order": by being clothed in *his* words she attains an order where before there was only linguistic – and therefore substantive – chaos, *broken* proverbs, *torn* sentences. Quite literally, his words give her life: "Thy graces and good words my creatures be: / I planted knowledge and life's tree in thee" (25–26).

The horror is that after having in-formed her, he finds that she is no less malleable than she was when she was nothing but verbal bits and pieces waiting for someone who might make her into something intelligible. The two stages of creation – from incoherent fragments into sequenced discourse – are finally not so different from one another if the configuration achieved in the second stage is only temporary, if once having been planted, knowledge and sense can be *sup*planted by another gardener who brings new knowledge and an alternative sense. The poet cries out in dismay: "Must I alas / Frame and enamel plate, and drink in glass? / Chafe wax for others' seals?" (27–29). In short, must others now "write" you, inscribe you, as I have done? Cannot the work of signification be frozen once it has been accomplished? What the speaker here discovers, three hundred and seventy-five years before Derrida writes "Signature Event Context," is the "essential drift" of language, the capacity of any signifier to "break with every given context, engendering an infinity of new contexts in a manner which is absolutely illimitable."[6] Once an intelligible sign has been produced, one can always "recognize other possibilities in it by inscribing it or *grafting* it onto other chains." "No context can ... enclose it," a truth the speaker of *Elegy 7* now ruefully acknowledges as the poem ends: "Must I ... / ... break a colt's force, / And leave him then, being made a ready horse?" This final line and a half could not be more precise: the shaping power he exerted before the poem began is given its precise name – force – but, once given, the name declares its own problematic; he who lives by force is precariously at the mercy of force wielded by others, by strangers. The grafting of signifiers – and, remember, that is all she is, a chain of signifiers – onto other chains cannot be stopped, and it cannot be stopped because there is nothing to stop it, no extralinguistic resistance to its inscribing power, a power the speaker once again displays when he un-creates what he has made by de-gendering it. He leaves his rival not with a "her" but a "him," a ready-made horse in place of the previously ready-made woman. It is as if he were attempting to forestall the reinscription of his creation by performing it himself and thus removing from the world the graces his words have placed there. It is a particularly nasty instance of someone saying, "If I can't have her, no one will," with a decided emphasis on the will.

It should be obvious by now that in these poems the act of writing is gendered in ways that have been made familiar to us by recent feminist criticism. The male author, like God, stands erect before the blank page of a female passivity and covers that page with whatever meanings he chooses to inscribe. This is how the speaker of the elegies *always* imagines himself, as a center of stability and control in a world where everyone else is plastic and malleable. But this self-dramatization of an independent authority can be sustained only if the speaker is himself untouched by the force he exerts on others. Were that force to turn back and claim him for its own by revealing itself to be the very source of *his* identity (which would then be no longer his), he would be indistinguishable from those he manipulates and scorns; he would be like a woman and become the object rather than the origin of his own performance, worked on, ploughed, appropriated, violated. (This is in fact the posture Donne will assume in many of the *Holy Sonnets.*) The suspicion that this may indeed be his situation is continually surfacing in these poems, as when in "The Comparison" the despised mistress is said to be "like the first Chaos," an image that seems to place the poet in the preferred position of shaping creator, the bringer of order; but he cannot occupy that position unless Chaos – the feminine principle – precedes him and provides him with the occasion of *self*-assertion. Chaos is thus *first* in a sense infinitely less comfortable than the one he allows himself to recognize;[7] for it is necessary both to the emergence of his being – such as it is – and to the illusion of his mastery, a mastery that is never more fragile than at those moments when it is most loudly proclaimed.

That proclamation and its fragility are the double subject of *Elegy 3*, "Change." This poem is built on a supposed contrast between the speaker and a woman whose constancy he doubts even though the firmness of her love has been "sealed" by "hand and faith, and good works too" (1). The key word is "sealed" because it names his desire, that things be settled once and for all in a way that precludes change and variation. He is prepared to do his part and agrees even to interpret her occasional lapses as proof of her fidelity ("though thou fall back, that apostasy / Confirm thy love" [3–4]), but he finds nevertheless that he fears her, and for a reason we have already met in *Elegy 7*:

> Women are like the arts, forced unto none,
> Open to all searchers, unprized, if unknown.
> If I have caught a bird, and let him fly,
> Another fowler using these means, as I,
> May catch the same bird; and, as these things be,
> Women are made for men, not him, nor me.
> (5–10)

The fear is not of one woman, or even of women in general, but of the condition that women seem particularly to embody: the condition of being open to interpretation, and therefore to change. Like poems and paintings, women are always receiving the seal of some new appropriative interpretive gesture and so refuse to remain "sealed" in the comforting sense of line 2. But even this is not the true fear; it is rather a displacement of it onto a convenient other. As Wilbur Sanders observes, the poem is "shot through with incompatible worries and aggressions."[8] The aggression is, as so often is the case, against women, but the worry is about his own identity, which he here shores up by defining himself as the fixed pole in relation to which women stray and wander: "if a man be / Chained to a galley, yet the galley is free; / Who hath a plough-land, casts all his seed corn there / And yet allows his ground more corn should bear" (15–18).

"Chained" reaches back to "sealed" and indicates that there is at least one person whose word is his bond; that person then casts himself in the role of the honest plowman (another figure of the masculine inscriber), thereby incorporating himself into the tradition of Piers Plowman and other plain-speaking heroes.

At this point, the images and their attendant arguments are coming so quickly and forcefully that we may forget to ask an obvious question: at whom are they directed? The original audience is the lady herself addressed in complaint, but she has long since been left behind. Arthur Marotti thinks that the poet now turns to his fellow libertines,[9] but the more likely addressee is the poet himself. That is, the poem at this point becomes an attempt at *self*-persuasion, but by falling into this mode the poet courts the very danger he sees in his defining other, the danger of change; for if his effort of self-persuasion is successful he will no longer believe what he professed to believe at the beginning of the poem; he will no longer be in the same place and he will no longer be the same person. In fact, the change is already occurring in the ambivalence of words like "chained" and "bound," which suggest both a desired stability and an uncomfortable confinement. The speaker's own vocabulary is surreptitiously preparing the ground for the moment when he will do an about-face. But when that moment comes, that is, when he changes, he attributes the change to the pressure exerted by the woman, who now returns in order once again to provide the necessary vehicle of displacement. He asks of her, "canst thou love [liberty] *and* me" (my emphasis), a question that answers itself. Of course she cannot. There remains only one alternative: given the rule that love depends on likeness between the lovers ("Likeness glues love"), he decides that if their love is to survive he must become as she, although even as he reaches this conclusion he rebels against it: "Likeness glues love: then if so thou do, / To make us like and love, must I change too? / More than thy hate, I hate it" (23–25). Here the speaker portrays as a crisis yet to be confronted an alteration he is already undergoing, and as he moves inexorably in the direction of the feared Other, he proliferates personal pronouns, as if his failing sense of identity could be restored by language, the very medium that refuses to leave him a space. "I-hate-it" is a textbook example of an utterance that insists on the independence of the subject from the forces (the "it") that threaten it, and that subject makes one last-ditch attempt to keep itself from being swept away: "rather let me / Allow *her* change, than change as oft as she, / And so not teach, but force my opinion" (25–27; emphasis added). Helen Gardner comments that "'force' would seem to be used in the sense in which we 'force' a text of Scripture, making it bear a sense beyond its own."[10] The speaker wants to bear his *own* sense, wants to be inscribed by convictions to which his will has assented; he doesn't want to be someone else's text. What he fails to see is that the condition of being his own text, of persuading himself, is no different from the condition he fears; for insofar as he is the object-audience of his own arguments, he is quite literally talking himself into something, into something *other* than he was.

That is precisely what happens at the end of the poem when he makes a perfect revolution from the stance of the opening lines to conclude: "change is the nursery / Of music, joy, life and eternity" (35–36). Critics complain that this conclusion seems inauthentic, that the "work seems to come apart intellectually and emotionally,"[11] but the complaint assumes the survival of a first-person voice of whom unity and integrity might be predicated. But that voice has been the casualty of its own poem, undone by the gymnastic virtuosity that impels both it and the poem forward. All that remains is what Sanders calls "the serene beatitude of these lines," a beatitude that might mark an achieved coherence in a poem like Spenser's *Mutabilitie Cantos*, whose conclusion it resembles, but here marks only the dislodgement of the centered self by the fragmentary, ecphrastic discourse it presumed to control.[12] As Docherty puts it, there remains "no identifiable 'Donne', no identifiable or self-identical source or authority . . . Donne is that which is always the Other [to] himself."[13]

The continual reproduction of a self that can never be the same, that can never be "its own" is at once reported and repeatedly performed in the last of the elegies I shall consider, *Elegy 16*, "On His Mistress." The poem is an address to a woman who has offered to accompany the speaker on a journey disguised as his page, and commentary has foundered on the biographical speculation that the woman in question may have been Donne's wife. But the fact of the dramatic occasion is not revealed until line 15, and before that line the poem is focused neither on the woman nor on her proposed stratagem but on itself and on the other verbal actions that have preceded it.

> By our first strange and fatal interview,
> By all desires which thereof did ensue,
> By our long starving hopes, by that remorse
> Which my words' masculine persuasive force
> Begot in thee, and by the memory
> Of hurts, which spies and rivals threaten'd me,

> I calmly beg: but by thy fathers wrath,
> By all pains, which want and divorcement hath,
> I conjure thee...
>
> (1–9)

This long syntactic unit is an extended oath, but while oaths typically invoke some extraverbal power or abstraction, this oath invokes previous oaths. Even when the verse names emotions that would seem to be prior to words, they turn out to have been produced by words: desires that proceed from interviews (exchanges of talk), hurts that flow from threats, pains fathered by the expressions of wrath. The lines call up a familiar Ovidian world of plots, dangers, crises, but the principal actors in that world are not the speaker or his mistress or her father, but the various speech acts in relation to which they have roles to play and meanings to declare. A phrase like "fathers wrath" names a conventional linguistic practice, not a person, and when the speaker swears by it, indeed *conjures* by it, he acknowledges the extent to which the energy he displays is borrowed from a storehouse of verbal formulas that belong to no one and precede everyone.

Yet even as that acknowledgment is made, the speaker resists it by claiming that the power that is working in this scene has its source in him, or, more precisely, in the "masculine persuasive force" by means of which he produces (begets) his mistress's character. The three words that make up this phrase are mutually defining and redundant. The masculinity he asserts is inseparable from his ability to persuade – that is, to control – and "force" is just a name for the exercise of that control, an exercise that validates his independence and thereby confirms his masculinity. But even as the power of masculine persuasive force is asserted, the line itself assigns that power to the *words* – "my words' masculine persuasive force" – which thereby reserve for themselves everything the speaker would mark as his own, including his own identity. In the guise of telling a story about a man, a woman and a proposed journey, the poem stages a struggle between its own medium and the first-person voice that presumes to control it. That struggle is enacted again in the next line and a half when the speaker declares that his words are subordinate to the inner reality of which they are the mere expressions: "all the oaths which I / And thou have sworn to seal joint constancy" (9–10). The assertion is that the constancy is a feature of his character and is prior to the oaths that serve only as its outward sign; however, no sooner has that assertion been made than it is flatly contradicted by the (speech) action of the next line: "Here I unswear, and overswear them thus." "Overswear" means "swear over," both in the sense of "again" and in the sense of *re*inscribing, of writing over what has been written previously. Not only does this overswearing undermine the constancy that has just been claimed, it also renders empty the personal pronoun that stood as the sign of the claimant. A consciousness that can rewrite its own grounds in the twinkling of an eye is not a consciousness at all, but a succession of refigurings no different finally from the refigurings it boasts to have produced in others.

The speaker, however, cannot let that difference disappear lest he disappear with it, and in the lines that follow he attempts to reaffirm it by insisting that his mistress remain firmly identifiable. In response to her suggestion that she accompany him disguised as a page, he says, "Be my true mistress still, not my feigned page," but given his earlier claim to have begotten her, to have fashioned her through the power of his words, the plea is incoherent. What he asks from her – stability of identity – he has already taken away. She cannot be the wax tablet on which he inscribes his will – indeed his "feigned page" – and yet be the fixed pole in relation to which other fixities, including his will, can be defined. He can't have it both ways.

Nevertheless he presses on and tries again: "Dissemble nothing, not a boy, nor change / Thy body's habit, nor mind's" (27–28). Again the plea is undercut by everything that precedes it. How can she be herself, if the self she presents is made up of the words he would put in her mouth? How can something characterized as a "habit" – a style, or form, inherently changeable – be asked to maintain its essence? These questions answer themselves, but they also point to the speaker's desperation and to the fear that stands behind it, fear not for her safety or person, but for himself; for he knows that unless her body and mind have an integrity that repels assaults, his own integrity is disastrously compromised. Masculine authority can be asserted only in relation to a firmly defined opposite; were the opposition to blur in either direction, the fixity of *both* poles would be immediately compromised. In order for him to be a man she must be unmistakably and essentially a woman.[14] When he says, "Be yourself," a command that follows ludicrously upon his injunction that she "feed on this flattery," he is really saying, "Be yourself because if you are not, I cannot be *my*self, and I can no longer claim to be exerting masculine persuasive force." That is why the truly threatening prospect is the prospect of her metamorphosing into a boy, for if that were to happen, he would either have to assume the role of a woman, or, what is worse, betray his masculinity by entering with her/him into an unnatural relationship. So threatening is this prospect that he cannot confront it directly but instead displaces it onto an imagined scenario in which she is pursued throughout Europe by a succession of indiscriminate seducers: "Men of France, changeable chameleons, / . . . Will quickly know thee, and know thee; and alas / Th' indifferent Italian, as we pass / . . . well content to think thee page, / Will hunt thee with such lust, and hideous rage, / As Lot's fair guests were vexed" (33–41). The ploy is obvious: it will not be he, but the French and Italians, the traditional figures in England of everything transitory and variable, who will force her; it is they who are changeable, purveyors of mere fashion, devisers of theatrical scenes (this accusation in the midst of a scene he is even now devising); it is they, not he, who blur distinctions and threaten even the boundaries of gender in their (and how precise this is) "indifferent lust." It is they, not he, who by giving reign to that lust lose their own identities even as they seek to corrupt hers. But of course the ploy will not work; the activities he projects onto them are too transparently his own; the chameleon-like behavior he excoriates is the behavior he has already displayed when he blithely overswears the oaths of the previous moment. The fierce appropriativeness against which he warns her is even now directed at her as he twice implores her to "stay here," that is both in England and here on the page where he would fix her so that he himself could be fixed in relation to her. In the end the independence of which he so often boasts can only take form on the stages he sets. In short, it isn't independence at all, but one more fragile creation of a power that undoes him even as he exercises it.

He exercises it for the last time in a virtuoso performance. First, he imagines her asleep, that is, in the perfect passive posture. Then, he inscribes a scene on the blank tablet of her consciousness, a scene in which *he* dies a death that is triply screened, first by its occurrence in a dream and second by its status as something *reported* by her to a nurse when she awakens, and third by the fact that the dream is one he is warning her *not* to have: Do not, he says, fright thy nurse by crying out, "Oh, oh / Nurse, O my love is slain, I saw him go / O'er the white Alps alone; I saw him, I, / Assailed, fight, taken, stabbed, bleed, fall, and die" (51–54). It is a tribute to the poet's powers that this passage is often praised by commentators for its immediacy and sincerity of feeling, but in fact it is a triumph of illusionistic art. No small part of that art is the figure of the Nurse who, as the audience to the dreamer's cries, establishes a role, a textual place, that we as readers can occupy, indeed *must* occupy; as we occupy it we forget what we have just been told, not only that none of this is happening, but that the speaker is forbidding it to happen. The power of the Nurse to draw us in is a function in part of her late appearance; she seems to be independent of the issues and concerns that have possessed the poem to this point. In fact, however, she is, like everything else in the poem, a rewriting of a previously written form, for although we may not recognize her, we have met her before in line 16: "Thee only worthy to nurse in my mind." The line has two readings: (1) only the memory of you will nurse in me a desire to return, and (2) you are worthy, i.e. substantial, only when my mind nurses you and gives you form. In this second reading, the verb is a muted equivalent of everything that masculine persuasive force stands for, and when the verb turns up in the dream, now transformed into its noun, it/she is the representative *in* the scene of the force that is conjuring it up. That force, that impetuous rage, that indifferent interpretive lust, occupies every role, plays all the parts, sets the scene, lights it, frames it and then glosses it with a commentary. But, of course, that is just the trouble. By playing *all* the parts, the practitioner of masculine persuasive force denies himself a part of *his own;* by filling every space, he leaves himself with no place to stand, no place that is not already occupied by the theatrics that have become his essence. In a final irony, this moment of spectacular illusion does in fact enact his death, his disappearance as anything but a continually changing figure on a succession of illusionistic stages.

"ALL SIGNS OF LOATHING"

That irony is the subject of the *Satires,* despite the still influential account of them as spoken in the voice of one who "consistently defends the spiritual values of simplicity, peace, constancy, and truth."[15] Certainly there is much talk of these virtues in the poems, but they are invoked at the very moments at which the speaker is displaying their opposites; rather than naming his achievements, they name the states from which he is always and already distant, the state of being one thing (simplicity), of being that thing without conflict (in peace), and of being that thing forever and truly. The satires record the desperate and always failing effort of the first-person voice to distinguish himself from the variability and corruption – alteration from an original – he sees around him. The basic and (literally) self-defeating gesture of these poems is enacted in the very first lines of *Satire I*:

> Away thou fondling motley humourist,
> Leave me . . .

The phrase "fondling motley humourist" is made up of words that point to the same quality, instability; a humorist is a person of irregular behavior, "a fantastical or whimsical person" (*OED*); a fondling is a fool, someone dazed, incapable of focusing (in an earlier manuscript Donne wrote "changeling"); and motley is what a fool wears because a cloth "composed of elements of diverse or varied character" (*OED*) perfectly suits one who is without a center. It also suits the traditional figure of the satirist, the writer of a random discourse who moves from one topic to another in ways that display no abiding rationale; the linking definition of satire as "*satura* medley" – a full dish of mixed fruit indiscriminately heaped up – was a standard one in the period and linked the satirist both with the court fool (as he appears, for example, in *King Lear*) and with the "mirror" or recorder figure who reflects the disorder of a world without coherence and has no coherence of his own. (Here one might cite Skelton's Parrot.) In short, what the first-person voice pushes away or tries (in an impossible effort) to push away is himself; rather than saying, as he would like to, "Get thee behind me, Satan," he is saying (in perfect *self*-contradiction), "Get thee behind me, me." From the beginning, he is protecting and defending an identity – a separateness from flux and surface – that he never really has.

In what follows, each declaration of distance and isolation is undermined even as it is produced. In line 11 he vows *not* to leave the "constant company" of his library; but in the previous line that company is said to include "Giddy fantastic poets," an acknowledgment that at once belies the claim of constancy and points once again to the giddiness (absence of stability) of the speaker, who is after all practicing poetry at this very moment. In line 12 he is betrayed even by his own syntax:

> Shall I leave all this constant company,
> And follow headlong, wild uncertain thee?

Who is "headlong" – that is, madly impetuous – the motley humorist or the speaker who (at least rhetorically) disdains him? Since "headlong" can either be an adverb modifying "I" or an adjective modifying "thee," it is impossible to tell, and this impossibility faithfully reflects the absence of the difference the speaker repeatedly invokes.

The claim of difference is further (and fatally) undermined when the speaker without any explanation decides that he will follow along after all. As if to reaffirm his self-respect (and his self), he asks for assurances that he will not be left alone in the street ("First swear . . . / Thou wilt not leave me" [13–15]), but this weak (and, as he himself knows, futile) gesture only underlines the extent of his capitulation: the distance between "leave me" and "don't leave" has been traveled in only fifteen lines; the stutter rhythm of push away / embrace is now instantiated in the poem's narrative as the now indistinguishable pair prepares to exit together. Before they do, the speaker rehearses the dangers he hopes to avoid, but his recital of them is so detailed and knowledgeable that he seems already to have fallen to them, and when he once again reasserts his difference from the world he is about to enter – "With God, and with the Muses I confer" (48) – one cannot take him seriously. Immediately after uttering this line he says, "But" and performs the action he vowed never to perform in line 1:

> I shut my chamber door, and come, let's go.
> (52)

Yet even here he hesitates, pausing on the threshold (which he has long since crossed) to analyze an action that he himself finds inexplicable; after all, he knows his man too well to believe that he will be faithful, and he knows too that any fickleness will be accomplished by a justification for "why, when, or with whom thou wouldst go" (65). The real question, however, is why the *speaker* would go in the face of such knowledge, and he poses the question himself in the very act of going:

> But how shall I be pardoned my offence
> That thus have sinned against my conscience.
> (66–67)

There is no answer, merely the report that, finally, "we are in the street" (67), but the answer is all too obvious: if by conscience he means an inner integrity – an identity that holds itself aloof against all external temptations and assaults – then conscience is what he has not had ever since his first words revealed a mind divided against itself. Ironically, that mind is now unified (if that is the right word) when it accepts (certainly not the right word) its implication in the giddy and the variable, and ventures out into the world to encounter other versions of himself, others who, like him, are "many-colored" and forever on the move. The fiction that it is not he but his fickle companion who refuses to stand still (86) is rhetorically maintained by the distinction of pronouns, but even that distinction is collapsed in the final lines:

> He quarreled, fought, bled; and turned out of door
> Directly came to me hanging the head,
> And constantly a while must keep his bed.
> (110–112)

That is, he comes *home*, where he lives, to the speaker, and he comes "directly," as if by instinct, and as he comes he shares with the speaker the pronoun "me" – is it "comes to me while hanging his head" or "comes to me who am hanging my head"? The attribution of "constancy" is mocked not only by the immediate qualification of "a while," but by everything that has transpired in a poem where inconstancy rules and most spectacularly rules the voice who would thrust it from him ("Away . . .").

In *Satire 2* the spectacle of a self-divided being continuing to claim a spurious independence is even more pronounced. Here, the speaker begins by firmly distinguishing himself from the town which he does "hate / Perfectly" (1–2). The perfection of his hatred and the distance it implies are compromised, however, when he specifies it more precisely: he hates those who wield words, and he hates especially poets, and among poets he hates those who have transferred their verbal arts to the public sphere in order to manipulate the law. "Words, words, which would tear / The tender labyrinth of a soft maid's ear" (57–58), perform their seductions in a much wider field – in the court, the courts, the management of estates – until they threaten to "compass all our land" (77).

The question, of course, is that of the speaker's place in this dark vision. What is the status of *his* words? The answer is given with perfect ambiguity in the poem's last lines:

> . . . but my words none draws
> Within the vast reach of the huge statute laws.
> (111–112)

Does this mean, as A.J. Smith takes it to, that the satirist's words alone escape the reach of a corrupted law?[16] Or is Wesley Milgate right to see this as another declaration (and claim) of a difference between the speaker and those he indicts?[17] And if that is at least a possible reading, isn't it, as John Lauritsen insists, an instance of protesting too much: "the satirist . . . attempts to exculpate himself from a charge that no one has made . . . assuring no one so much as himself that he . . . is one person and Coscus quite another, that his dread of Coscus is not in fact a mirror image of his own guilt, that his fear of Coscus is not ultimately a fear of . . . his own perversion of the word."[18] Or could these lines (as Arthur Marotti suggests) be a complaint that no one is paying attention to him, that his words, unlike Coscus's, are ineffectual, and that his vaunted independence is something he would gladly lose if he could only gain a portion of the spoils won by others?[19] There is no answer to these questions – this is another of those poems which, as Herz says, "simply will not resolve" – and in the absence of an answer (or in the presence of too many) the speaker's claim not to have been compassed by what encompasses everyone and everything else in the land is without firm support.[20]

Moreover, insofar as the speaker's relationship to the world he scorns is precarious, so is Donne's, for nothing in the poem authorizes us to perform the saving and stabilizing move of formalist criticism in which a sharp distinction between the poet and his persona allows the former to stand outside the predicament of the latter. In Donne's poems, as Herz observes, "inside and outside are no longer clearly fixed points,"[21] and therefore we cannot with any confidence locate a place in which the poet is securely established as a controlling presence. This is particularly true of *Satire 4*, a poem in which the speaker plays with the dangers of displaying Catholic sympathies in a way that cannot be separated from the danger Donne – the Catholic-in-the-course-of-becoming-an-Anglican – risks in presenting such a speaker. Is it the satiric voice who begins by declaring "Well; I may now receive" and then labors to render the suggestion of a forbidden ceremony metaphorical and jesting, or is it Donne? One simply cannot tell in a poem in which, as Thomas Hester observes, the "consistent glances at the predicament of the Catholic in Elizabethan England" are always "equivocal."[22] That equivocality is not only a feature of the relationships *within* the poem, but characterizes the relationship between the poem and its maker; just as we don't know whether the speaker intends something serious by his references to Jesuitical practices or is merely producing them, in order to frighten away his importunate interlocutors, so we don't know whether Donne, in the same references, is alluding to "his own situation"[23] or merely fleshing out the situation of a fictive drama.

What we do know is that once again a Donne poem presents a speaker who refuses to recognize himself in the indictment he makes of others. In this case, the indictment is of those who go to court, which is the very first thing the speaker does in an action he finds as inexplicable as we do:

> My mind, neither with pride's itch, nor yet hath been
> Poisoned with love to see, or be seen.
> I had no suit there, nor new suit to show,
> Yet went to Court.
>
> (5–8)

The claim is, as in the earlier poems, a claim of interiority – he need not show himself in order to acquire value; he is content with what he is in himself – and in order to maintain the claim, he at once minimizes his sin and renders it something external by calling it "my sin of going" (12). Characterized that way, the sin seems accidental to an inner being it does not touch, something that "happens" to that being before it is even aware. Of course he knows what the commission of this little sin will suggest to some, that he is "As prone to all ill, and of good as forget- / ful, as proud, as lustful, and as much in debt, / As vain, as witless, and as false as they / Which dwell at Court, for once going that way" (13–16); but by insisting on the "once," on the anomalous nature of the event, he pushes the accusation away and reaffirms his status as something apart from the scene he unwillingly enters.

It is in the service of the same affirmation that he labels everything and everyone he meets "strange" and a "stranger," indeed "Stranger than strangers" (23). That is to say, nothing I saw is like *me*, an assertion belied by the very first person he encounters; that person wears coarse clothes which leave him bare (30); he "speaks all tongues" (35) and has none of his own; rather he is "Made of th' accents" (37), a confection of "pedant's motley" (40). He is, in short, a satirist, affectedly coarse, deliberately ill-attired, a mirror of everything around him, an indiscriminate mixture. The speaker has met himself, and he responds in language that at once admits the kinship and disclaims it:

> He names me, and comes to me; I whisper, "God!
> How have I sinned, that thy wrath's furious rod,
> This fellow, chooseth me?"
> (49–51)

"He names me" is literal in its identification of the two, but of course in so exclaiming the speaker intends only wonder at so unlikely an act of recognition; but then he performs (unknowingly) the same recognition when he "names" the stranger "thy wrath's furious rod," for this is still another standard description of the satirist and his purpose. Unable to free himself from this unwelcome companion, he has recourse to behavior that will he hopes drive the wretch away: "I belch, spew, spit, / Look pale, and sickly" (109–110); but this is precisely the aspect the "stranger" already bears, and it is no wonder that upon meeting it in the speaker "he thrusts on more" (111). The "more" he produces is a compendium of stock satiric themes – "He names a price for every office paid; / He saith, our laws thrive ill, because delayed; / That offices are entailed" (121–123) – and as he listens to this version of himself even the speaker is close to seeing the truth:

> ... hearing him, I found
> That as burnt venomed lechers do grow sound
> By giving others their sores, I might grow
> Guilty ...
> (133–136)

Guilty, that is, not simply of going, but of being, or rather of nonbeing.

The thought is too horrible and he thrusts it away with a gesture that is its own allegory:

> ... I did show
> All signs of loathing.
> (136–137)

"All signs of loathing" is a formulation that definitively begs the question both for the speaker and for Donne. "Signs" of loathing are precisely external indications of something that may be otherwise; whether the speaker *really* loathes is something we don't know and something *he* doesn't know either. The same holds for Donne: the entire poem constitutes *his* sign of loathing, *his* declaration of distance from the world he delineates and from the voice he projects: "This is not me but my creature; this is not my world, but the world in which my creature is implicated in ways that he does not know; I, like you, know; I am in control." But the only evidence he might cite in support of this declaration and its claim (the claim to be in possession of himself in contrast to his creature, who is not) are his signs of loathing, his production of words, his *show;* but whether or not anything lies behind the show, whether the *signs* of loathing stand in for an authentic loathing or whether they constitute a ruse by which the true nature of Donne's impure being is concealed from us and from himself in exactly the manner of his fictional (or is it true?) surrogate, is something we cannot determine. *And neither can he.* As in the elegies, the foregrounding of the power of signs and of their tendency to "compass all the land" catches the foregrounder in its backwash, depriving him of any independence of the forces he (supposedly) commands. The more persuasive is his account and exercise of verbal power the less able is he to situate himself in a space it does not fill, and he is left as we are, wondering if there is or could be anything real – anything other than artifice – in his performance (a word that perfectly captures the dilemma).

"TRUE GRIEFE"

The relationship between the exercise of power and the claims to independence and sincerity continues to be thematized in the *Holy Sonnets,* although in these poems Donne occupies (or tries to occupy) the position of the creature and yields the role of the shaper to God. That difference, however, is finally less significant than one might suppose since the God Donne imagines is remarkably like the protagonist he presents (and I would say *is*) in the elegies, a jealous and overbearing master who brooks no rivals and will go to any lengths (even to the extent of depriving Donne of his wife) in order to secure his rights. It is as if Donne could only imagine a God in his own image, and therefore a God who acts in relation to him as he acts in relation to others, as a self-aggrandizing bully. To be sure, in the sonnets the speaker rather than exerting masculine persuasive force begs to be its object ("Batter my heart, three person'd God"), but this rearrangement of roles only emphasizes the durability of the basic Donnean situation and gives it an odd and unpleasant twist: the woman is now asking for it ("enthrall me," "ravish me"). One might almost think that the purpose of the sonnets, in Donne's mind, is retroactively to justify (by baptizing) the impulses to cruelty and violence (not to say misogyny) he displays so lavishly in his earlier poetry. In an important sense "Thou hast made me and shall thy work decay" is simply a rewriting of "Nature's lay idiot," which might itself be titled: "I have made you, and shall *my* work decay?" The plot is the same, an original artificer now threatened by a rival artisan ("our old subtle foe so tempteth me"), and a complaint against change in the name of a control that would be absolute. Of course, in the "sacred" version the complaint is uttered not by the about-to-be-supplanted creator, but by the creature eager to remain subject to his power ("not one houre I can myself sustaine"); nevertheless, the relational structure of the scene is the same, a structure in which masochism (and now sado-masochism) is elevated to a principle and glorified, earlier in the name of a frankly secular power, here in the name of a power that is (supposedly) divine. The fact that Donne now assumes the posture of a woman and like the church of "Show me deare Christ thy spouse" spreads his legs (or cheeks) is worthy of note, but to note it is not to indicate a significant (and praiseworthy) change in his attitude toward women and power; it is rather to indicate how strongly that attitude informs a poetry whose center is supposedly elsewhere.

Moreover, even as Donne casts himself in the female role, he betrays an inability to maintain that role in the face of a fierce and familiar desire to be master of his self, even of a self whose creaturely nature he is in the process of acknowledging. In a poem like "As due by many titles I resigne / My selfe to thee," the gesture of resignation is at the same time a reaffirmation of the resigner's independence: considering well the situation, it seems

proper that I choose to be subservient to you. As Hester has observed, this
is not so much a resigning, but a re-signing, the production of a signature
and therefore of a claim of ownership, if not of the self that was, as he says,
"made" (1.2), then of the act by which that self is laid down (a distinction
without a difference).[24] Ostensibly the poem is an extended plea to be
possessed (in every sense) by God, but in fact it is a desperate attempt to
leave something that will say, like Kilroy, "Donne was here."

That desperation is the explicit subject of "If faithfull soules be alike
glorifi'd," a first line that enacts in miniature everything that follows it.[25]
As it is first read, the question seems to be whether or not all faithful souls
are glorified in the same way (are they alike?), but then the first two words
of the second line – "As Angels" – reveal that the likeness being put into
question is between all faithful souls (now assumed to be glorified alike,
but without any content specified for that likeness) and angels who are
themselves glorified alike but perhaps not in the same manner (alike) as
are faithful souls. If the pressure of interrogation falls on the notion of
likeness and therefore on the issue of identity (one must know what
something or someone uniquely is before one can say for certain whether
or not it or he or she is like or unlike something or someone else), then the
interrogation is from the very first in deep trouble when the word "alike,"
meaning "not different," turns out to be different from itself in the
passage from line 1 to line 2.

The trouble is compounded as line 2 further unfolds:.

> As Angels, then my fathers soule doth see

Whether or not his father's soul sees is still in doubt since the entire
construction remains ruled by "If"; and the fact of his father's being a
Catholic reinvigorates the question that had been left behind in the turn
of the second line: are faithful souls glorified alike even if they are faithful
to papism? As a result, the status of his father's vision is doubly obscure;
we don't know whether it is like the vision of other, more safely, faithful
souls, and we don't know, should it pass that test, whether it is as
perspicuous as the vision of angels.

It is in the context of that unsure vision that we meet the sight it may or
may not see: "That valiantly I hels wide mouth o'erstride" (4). The line
presents itself as an assertion of the way things really are – despite
appearances I stand firm against the temptations of the world, flesh, and
devil – but in the context of what precedes it, the assertion remains only a
claim until it is confirmed by one who sees *through* appearances to the
inner reality they obscure. Since, however, the question of whether his

father is one who sees in that penetrating way has been left conspicuously open, neither he nor we can be sure of that confirmation, and there remains the suspicion that behind the sign of purity, behind the verbal report of spiritual valor, there is nothing – the suspicion that the truth about him is no deeper or more stable than his surface representation of it. It is this dreadful possibility that Donne (one could say "the speaker," but it will come down to Donne in the end) raises explicitly in the next four lines:

> But if our mindes to these soules be descry'd
> By circumstances, and by signes that be
> Apparent in us, not immediately,
> How shall my mindes white truth to them be try'd?
> (5–8)

That is, if my father and other glorified souls (if he is, in fact, glorified and if all faithful souls are glorified alike) descry just as we on earth do, through a variety of glasses darkly, by means of signs, of representations, of what shows (is "Apparent"), then there is no way that anyone will ever know what's inside me or indeed if there *is* anything inside me. A "white truth" is a truth without color, without coverings, without commentary, but if colored, covered and textualized truths are all anyone can see, then the white truth of his mind will continue to be an untried claim, and one moreover that is suspect, given the innumerable examples of those who feign commitments they do not have:

> They see idolatrous lovers weepe and mourne,
> And vile blasphemous Conjurers to call
> On Jesus name, and Pharisaicall
> Dissemblers feigne devotion.
> (9–12)

Anyone *can say* they are faithful or sincere or "white," but such sayings, proffered as evidence of a truth beyond (or behind) signs, are themselves signs and never more suspicious than when they present the trappings of holiness. It is at this point (if not before) that the precarious situation of the poem becomes obvious; as a structure of signs it has done all the things it itself identifies as strategies of dissembling: it has wept, mourned, dramatized devotion, and then, as if it were following its own script, the poem closes by performing the most reprehensible of these strategies; it calls on Jesus' name:

> ... Then turne
> O pensive soule, to God, for he knowes best
> Thy true griefe, for he put it in my breast.
> (12–14)

There are at least two levels on which this is an unsatisfactory conclusion. First, there is no reason to believe that the turn to God is anything but one more instance of feigned devotion, one more *performance* of a piety for which the evidence remains circumstantial (that is, theatrical) and apparent, a matter of signs and show. To be sure, the structure of the sonnet lends these lines the aura of a final summing up, of a pronouncement ("Then") detached from the gestures that precede it; however, nothing prevents us from reading the pronouncement itself as one more gesture, and therefore as a claim no more supported than the claim (that he valiantly o'erstrides hell's mouth) it is brought in to support. And even if we were to credit the sincerity of these lines and regard them not as dramatic projections but as spontaneous ejaculations, they would not provide what the poem has been seeking, a perspective from which we could discern once and for all what, if anything, was inside him; for all the lines say is that whatever there is in his breast, God knows it, which means of course that we don't, and that we are left at the end with the same doubt that his "true griefe" (here just one more "untry'd" claim) may be false, a confection of signs and appearances. As in the elegies and the satires, the relentless assertion and demonstration of the power of signs to bring their own referents into being – to counterfeit love and grief and piety – undermines the implicit claim of *this* producer of signs to be real, to be anything more than an effect of the resources he purports to control.

Again, the large question is, does Donne *know* this? Does he stand apart from the corrosive forces his speakers fail to escape? An affirmative answer to this question has always been the strategy of choice in Donne criticism. One argues, as Roger Rollin recently has done, that while the sonnets are "sick poems," poems infected by spiritual malaise, confusions, and unacknowledged rationalizations, they are intended by Donne to be both diagnostic and salutary, "preventive medicine ... meant to be exemplary to disease-prone readers."[26] In other words, the poems are diseased, the speakers are diseased and the readers are diseased, but Donne is not. What, aside from the tradition in which authors are always accorded an extraordinary measure of control and awareness, authorizes this claimed exemption? What the poems show us is theatricality triumphant, and it is hard to see how one can move from the repeated dramatization of that triumph to the identification of a consciousness that is not itself dramaturgic (and thus suspect in all the ways it records) but real, purely present, valiantly o'erstriding the abyss of textuality. It is easy to see why readers might desire to identify such a consciousness, for there would then be a state (of awareness, control and self-possession) to which they could at least aspire, but the desire can only be realized in an act of construction that is no less fragile than the constructions it would transcend. The reader in short must engage in an act of self-persuasion, which will, if he performs it, replicate and extend the act Donne himself performs in writing the poem. Far from being the distant and calm physician to readers that Rollin projects, Donne is his poem's first reader, the desperate audience of its hoped-for effect. Not only is he trying to convince readers of his ultimate sincerity – of his mind's white truth – he is trying to convince himself.

This is spectacularly the case in "What if this present were the worlds last night?" This first line might well open one of the sermons Donne was later to write; it is obviously theatrical and invites us to imagine (or to be) an audience before whom this proposition will be elaborated in the service of some homiletic point. But in the second line everything changes abruptly. The theatricalism is continued, but the stage has shrunk from one on which Donne speaks to many of a (literally) cosmic question to a wholly interior setting populated only by versions of Donne:

> Marke in my heart, O Soule, where thou dost dwell,
> The picture of Christ crucified, and tell
> Whether that countenance can thee affright?
> (2–4)

Donne addresses his own soul and asks it to look in his heart, where will be found a picture he has put there, either for purposes of meditation or in the manner of a lover who hangs portraits of his lady in a mental gallery. But the meditation is curious in the way we have already noted: Donne does not direct it at his beloved, whether secular or spiritual, but to another part of himself. Although Christ's picture is foregrounded, especially in the lines (5–7) that rehearse its beauties in a sacred parody of the traditional blazon, in the context of the poem's communicative scene, the picture – not to mention the person it portrays – is off to the side as everything transpires between the speaker and his soul. The gesture is a familiar one in Donne's poetry; it is the contraction into one space of everything in the world ("All here in one bed lay"), which is simultaneously the exclusion of everything in the world ("I could eclipse and cloud them with a wink");[27] but here it seems prideful and perhaps worse, for it recharacterizes the Last Judgment as a moment staged and performed entirely by himself: produced by Donne, interior design by Donne, case pled by Donne, decision rendered by Donne. Again, as in the elegies, Donne occupies every role on his poem's stage, and since the stage is interior, it is insulated from any correcting reference other than the one it allows. Thus protected from any outside perspective and from the intrusion of any voice he has not ventriloquized, Donne can confidently ask the poem's urgent question:

> And can that tongue adjudge thee unto hell,
> Which pray'd forgivenesse for his foes fierce spight?
> (7–8)

The question's logic assumes a distinction between "that tongue" and "thee" (i.e., me), but since Donne is here all tongues, the distinction is merely verbal and cannot be the basis of any real suspense. The answer is inevitable and it immediately arrives: "No, no" (9). But as John Stachniewski acutely observes, "the argument of Donne's poems is often so strained that it alerts us to its opposite, the emotion or mental state in defiance of which the argumentative process was set to work."[28] Here, the mental state the poem tries to avoid is uncertainty, but its pressure is felt in the exaggerated intensity with which the "No, no" denies it. Uncertainty and instability return with a vengeance in the final lines:

> . . . but as in my idolatrie
> I said to all my profane mistresses,
> Beauty, of pitty, foulnesse onely is
> A signe of rigour: so I say to thee,
> To wicked spirits are horrid shapes assign'd,
> This beauteous forme assures a pitious minde.
> (9–14)

In the rhetoric of this complex statement, Donne's idolatry is in the past, but his words also point to the idolatry he has been committing in the poem, the idolatry of passing judgment on himself in a court whose furniture he has carefully arranged. The assertion that he is *not* now in his idolatry is undermined by the fact that he here says the very same things he used to say when he was. As he himself acknowledges, what he says is part of a seductive strategy, more or less on the level recommended in "The Anagram": if your beloved's countenance is forbidding and harsh, impute to her a benign interior; and if her aspect is "pitious," impute to her a consistency of form and content. In this poem, the suspect logic is even more suspect because it is directed at himself: the referent of "thee" is his own soul, the addressee since line 2. The soul is asked to read from the signifying surface of Christ's picture to his intention, but since that surface is one that Donne himself has as-signed, the confident assertion of the last line has no support other than itself.

Indeed, the line says as much in either of its two textual versions, "This beauteous forme *assures* a pitious minde" or "This beauteous forme *assumes* a pitious minde."[29] In either variant, "This beauteous forme" refers not only to the form Donne has assigned to Christ's picture, but to the form of the poem itself; it is the poem's verbal felicity and nothing else that is doing either the assuring (which thus is no more than whistling in the dark) or the assuming (which as a word at least has the grace to name the weakness of the action it performs). The poem ends in the bravado that marks some of the other sonnets (e.g., "Death be not proud"), but the triumph of the rhetorical flourish (so reminiscent of the ending of every one of the *Songs and Sonnets*) only calls attention to its insubstantiality. Once again, the strong demonstration of verbal power – of the ability to make any proposition seem plausible so long as one doesn't examine it too closely – undermines its own effects. In the end, the poet always pulls it off but that only means that he could have pulled it off in the opposite direction, and *that* only means that the conclusion he forces is good only for the theatrical moment of its production. This is true not only for his readers but for himself; as the poem concludes, he is no more assured of what he assumes than anyone else, neither of the "pitious minde" of his savior, nor of the spiritual stability he looks to infer from the savior's picture. The effort of self-persuasion – which is also at bottom the effort to confirm to himself that he is a self, someone who exceeds the theatrical production of signs and shows – fails in exactly the measure that his rhetorical effort succeeds. The better he is at what he does with words, the less able he is to claim (or believe) that behind the words – o'erstriding the abyss – stands a self-possessed being.

The realization of radical instability ("the horror, the horror") is given full expression in "Oh, to vex me, contraryes meete in one," a poem that desires to face the specter down, but in the end is overwhelmed by it. The problem is succinctly enacted in the first line: if contraries meet in one, then one is not one – an entity that survives the passing of time – but two or many. This would-be-one looks back on its history and sees only a succession of poses – contrition, devotion, fear – no one of which is sufficiently sustained to serve as the center he would like to be able to claim:

> ... to day
> In prayers, and flattering speaches I court God:
> To morrow I quake with true feare of his rod.
> (9–11)

These lines at once report on and reproduce the dilemma: "prayers" seems innocent enough until "flattering speaches" retroactively questions the sincerity of the gesture; and the same phrase spreads forward to infect the assertion of line 11; when he quakes with "true fear," is the adjective a tribute to his artistry, to his ability to simulate an emotion in a way that convinces spectators (including himself) of its truth, or is the fear true in a deeper sense, one that would allow us to posit a moment (however fleeting) of authenticity in the midst of so many performances? The question is of course unanswerable, although as the poem ends (both with a bang and a whimper) there is one last attempt to draw the kind of line that would make an answer possible:

> So my devout fitts come and go away
> Like a fantastique Ague: save that here
> Those are my best dayes, when I shake with feare.
> (12–14)

"Devout fitts" recapitulates the problem: can devotion be genuine – heartfelt – if it comes and goes like the ever-changing scene of a fever? In the continual alternation of contradictory spiritual states, no one moment seems any more securely "true" than any other. Nevertheless the poem proceeds to declare an exception with "save that . . . " On one level, the exception is to the comparison between spiritual and physical health: while in the illness of the body the best days are the days when convulsions subside, in spiritual matters the best days are marked by fearful agitation.[30] But the exception Donne here tries to smuggle in is one that would attribute authenticity to the fits he displays on some days as opposed to others: my life may be characterized by changeful humors, but among those humors one speaks the genuine me. In order for that claim to be strongly received, however, the last line must be disengaged from everything that has preceded it and be marked in some way with the difference it attempts so boldly to declare. But no such mark is available, and as we read it the line is drawn into the pattern from which it would distinguish itself. Either it refers backward to the "true fear" of line 11, already identified as a theatrical production, or, if we give the word "here" full force, it refers to itself – I am at this very moment of writing shaking with true fear – and asks us to accept as unperformed and spontaneous the obviously artful conclusion to a sonnet. In either case, one cannot rule out a reading in which the best days are the days when he best simulates the appropriate emotion ("look at how good I am at shaking with fear"), and we are as far from an emotion that is not simulated – from an emotion produced other than theatrically by someone other than a wholly theatrical being – as we were when he uttered the first self-pitying line, "Oh, to vex me ... "

Reading this same poem, Anne Ferry makes observations similar to mine but reaches a different conclusion. She takes the poem's lesson to be "that what is grounded inward in [the speaker's] heart is at a distance from language used to describe it, which cannot render it truly," and she generalizes this lesson into a Donnean theory of sincerity:

> ... what is in the heart cannot be interpreted or judged by outward signs, among which language is included, even when they are sincere. Inward states cannot therefore be truly shown, even by the speaker's own utterance in prayers or poems, cannot be defined by them, even to himself.[31]

Ferry assumes what it seems to me these poems put continually into question, that the "inward experience" or "*real self*" is in fact there and the deficiency lies with the medium that cannot faithfully transcribe it. I have argued that the problem with language in these poems is not that it is too weak to do something, but that it is so strong that it does everything, exercising its power to such an extent that nothing, including the agent of that exercise, is left outside its sphere. I am not offering *this* as the insight Donne wishes to convey as opposed to the insight Ferry urges, but, rather, saying that it is not an insight at all – in the sense of something Donne commands – but the problematic in which he remains caught even when he (or especially when he) is able to name it, as he does in this passage from a sermon delivered during his final illness:

> The way of Rhetorique in working upon weake men, ... is to empty [the understanding] of former apprehensions and opinions, and to shape that beliefe, with which it had possessed it self before, and then when it is thus melted, to powre it into new molds, ... to stamp and imprint new formes, new images, new opinions in it.[32]

Once again Donne identifies, this time by its proper name, the activity he has practiced all his life, an activity propelled by a force that knows no resistance and simply writes over (overswears) whatever meanings and forms some previous, equally unstoppable, force has inscribed. Once again, he attempts to assert his distance from that force even as he exercises it and reports on its exercise, attempts to possess it without being possessed by it. And once again the attempt takes the form of an act of displacement by means of which his fears are pushed onto others, not this time onto women or Frenchmen or Italians, but onto "weake men." Weak men are men whose convictions are so malleable, so weakly founded, that they can be shaped and reshaped by the skilled rhetorician who becomes, in an implied opposition, the very type of the strong man. But as we have seen, in the story that Donne's poems repeatedly enact, the skillful rhetorician always ends up becoming the victim/casualty of his own skill, and no more so than at those moments when his powers are at their height. The stronger he is, the more force-full, the more taken up by the desire for mastery, the less he is anything like "himself." The lesson of masculine persuasive force is that it can only be deployed at the cost of everything it purports to incarnate – domination, independence, assertion, masculinity itself.

In much of Donne criticism that lesson has been lost or at least obscured by a concerted effort to put Donne in possession of his poetry and therefore of himself. The result has been a series of critical romances of which Donne is the hero (valiantly o'erstriding the abyss). Ferry gives us one romance: the poet, ahead of his times, labors to realize a modern conception of the inner life. An older criticism gave us the romance of immediacy and the unified sensibility: the felt particulars of lived experience are conveyed by a verse that is at once tactilely sensuous and intellectually bracing. Often this romance was folded into another, the romance of voice in which a singular and distinctive Donne breaks through convention to achieve a hitherto unknown authenticity of expression. At mid-century the invention of the persona produced the romance of craft: Donne surveys the range of psychological experience and creates for our edification and delight a succession of flawed speakers. And the most recent scholarship, vigorously rejecting immediacy, voice, authenticity and craft as lures and alibis, tempts us instead with the romance of postmodernism, of a Donne who is "rigorously skeptical, endlessly self-critical, posing more questions than he answers."[33] (This last is particularly attractive insofar as it transforms obsessive behavior into existential heroism of the kind academics like to celebrate because they think, mistakenly, that they exemplify it.) As different as they are, these romances all make the mistake of placing Donne outside the (verbal) forces he sets in motion and thus making him a figure of control. In the reading offered here, Donne is always folded back into the dilemmas he articulates, and indeed it is the very articulation of those dilemmas – the supposed bringing of them to self-consciousness – that gives them renewed and devouring life.

NOTES

1 C.S. Lewis, "Donne and Love Poetry in the Seventeenth Century," in *Seventeenth Century English Poetry: Modern Essays in Criticism*, ed. William Keast (New York: Oxford University Press, 1962), 98, 96.

2 Judith Herz, "'An Excellent Exercise of Wit that Speaks So Well of Ill': Donne and the Poetics of Concealment," in *The Eagle and the Dove: Reassessing John Donne*, ed. Claude J. Summers and Ted-Larry Pebworth (Columbia, MO.: University of Missouri Press, 1986), 5.

3 *John Donne: The Complete English Poems*, ed. A.J. Smith (Baltimore: Penguin Books, 1971). All further citations of the elegies and the satires are taken from this text.

4 Thomas Docherty, *John Donne, Undone* (New York: Methuen, 1986), 68.

5 Arthur F. Marotti, *John Donne, Coterie Poet* (Madison: University of Wisconsin Press, 1986), 48.

6 Jacques Derrida, "Signature Event Context," trans. Samuel Weber and Jeffrey Mehlman, *Glyph* 1 (1977), 182, 185.

7 For a brilliant discussion of Chaos as it operates in Renaissance literature in general and in Milton's *Paradise Lost* in particular, see Regina Schwartz, "Milton's Hostile Chaos: '... And the Sea Was No More'," *ELH* 52 (1985), 337–374.

8 Wilbur Sanders, *Donne's Poetry* (Cambridge University Press, 1971), 41.

9 Marotti, *John Donne*, 308.

10 Helen Gardner, ed., *The Elegies and the Songs and Sonnets* (Oxford: Clarendon Press, 1965), 137.

11 Marotti, *John Donne*, 308.

12 Sanders, *Donne's Poetry*, 41.

13 Docherty, *John Donne*, 60.

14 See on this point ibid., 200–201. Docherty writes, "Male lovers look into the mirror of their lover's eye, or womb, and see the reflection of themselves (or of their sons, as representations of themselves), thus supposedly guaranteeing a stable, transhistorical male identity; and such eternal 'sameness,' identity, slips into 'truth'" (p. 200).

15 N.J.C. Andreason, "Theme and Structure in Donne's *Satyres*," in *Essential Articles: Donne's Poetry*, ed. John R. Roberts (Hamden, Conn.: Archon Books, 1975), 412.

16 A.J. Smith, *The English Poems*, 479.

17 Wesley Milgate, ed., *The Satires, Epigrams and Verse Letters* (Oxford: Clarendon Press, 1967), 139.

18 John Lauritsen, "Donne's *Satyres*: The Drama of Self-Discovery," *SEL* 16 (Winter 1976), 125.

19 Marotti, *John Donne*, 40.

20 Herz, "Poetics of Concealment," 5.

21 Ibid., 6.

22 Thomas Hester, *Kinde Pitty and Brave Scorn: John Donne's Satyres* (Durham: Duke University Press, 1982), 74.

23 Ibid., 74.
24 M. Thomas Hester, "Re-Signing the Text of the Self: Donne's 'As due by many titles'," in *"Bright Shootes of Everlastingnesse": The Seventeenth-Century Religious Lyric*, ed. Claude J. Summers and Ted-Larry Pebworth (Columbia, MO.: University of Missouri Press, 1987), 69. See also Docherty, *John Donne*, 139.
25 All citations from the *Holy Sonnets* are taken from *John Donne: The Divine Poems*, ed. Helen Gardner (Oxford: Clarendon Press, 1964).
26 Roger Rollin, "'Fantastic Ague': The *Holy Sonnets* and Religious Melancholy," in *The Eagle and the Dove: Reassessing John Donne*, ed. Claude Summers and Ted-Larry Pebworth (Columbia, MO.: University of Missouri Press, 1986), 131.
27 "The Sun Rising," ll.20, 13.
28 John Stachniewski, "John Donne: The Despair of the 'Holy Sonnets'," *ELH* 48 (1981), 691.
29 All manuscripts read *assures*, but the 1633 edition reads *assumes*.
30 Anne Ferry, *The "Inward" Language* (Chicago: University of Chicago Press, 1983), 242–243.
31 Ibid., 243, 249.
32 *Sermons*, ed. George R. Potter and Evelyn M. Simpson, 10 vols. (Berkeley: University of California Press, 1953–62), II, 282–283.
33 Docherty, *John Donne*, 29.

CHAPTER 12

How Hobbes works

In *Milton and the Culture of Violence* (1994) and in many other important writings, Michael Lieb has been concerned to show us what he sometimes calls the "darker, more unsettling side of Milton's personality" and Milton's God.[1] While poems like *Lycidas* and "At a Solemn Music" end in visions of a universal harmony of undifferentiated voices free of discord and jarring notes, Milton, Lieb tells us, was throughout his life haunted by the fear of the "barbarous dissonance" that attended the dismemberment of Orpheus.[2] The poet, in Lieb's account of him, was "desperate to avoid" the "return to the world of Chaos" – that "universal hubbub wild / Of stunning sounds and voices all confus'd" (*PL* II, 951–952) – that Orpheus's death at the hands of a "wild Rout" (*PL* VII, 34) symbolized for him. Milton's response to the specter of violent chaos is to assert against it a faith in a power even more dreadful. Lieb quotes the place in *De doctrina Christiana* where Milton urges the practice of *timor dei*, "reverencing God as the supreme Father and Judge of all men, and fearing above all to offend him."[3] Assaulted by forces that threaten to overwhelm him, the Miltonic "I," says Lieb, always "seeks refuge in a power beyond itself."[4] That power, however, resides elsewhere – Lieb cites *Samson Agonistes*: "our living Dread who dwells / In *Silo* his great sanctuary" (1673–1674) – and one must affirm it in the face of *visibilia* that do not unambiguously declare it.

The strength to do so, if one has it, comes not from the world – which, considered in itself rather than as the creation of a power it cannot contain, points in too many moral directions – but from an internal resource that must be actively and willfully summoned. The danger is that the outward surface of things – mere forms – will overwhelm or obscure an inner truth that surfaces do not display; this inner truth, if recalled and clung to, not only dispels surfaces but also reconfigures them. The clearest example is the Lady in *A Mask*, who, surrounded by darkness and beset by a "thousand fantasies" of "beck'ning shadows dire" (205, 207), nevertheless relies on the anchor of her "virtuous mind" (211) and is rewarded both by a vision – "thou unblemish't form of Chastity / I see ye visibly" (215–216) – and by an alteration in the physical landscape – "there does a sable cloud / Turn forth her silver lining on the night" (223–224).

Milton is always imagining his heroines and heroes this way (including himself, as in the concluding sentences of *The Ready and Easy Way*), as solitary figures "In darkness, and with dangers compassed round" (*PL* VII, 27) who reject the evidence of things seen and stake everything on a loyalty (to the God of dread) for which there is often no empirical support. The model is Abdiel, who alone dissents from the infernal council – Satan calls him a "seditious angel" (*PL* VI, 152) – and receives this praise from his Lord: "for this was all thy care / To stand approved in sight of God, though worlds / Judged thee perverse" (*PL* VI, 35–37). Abdiel, the Lady, the young Jesus in *Paradise Regain'd*, the poet in *Lycidas*, the Samson who finally frees himself from positive law, Milton in the *Apology* – they all exemplify Milton's conviction that "obedience to the Spirit of God, rather then to the faire seeming pretences of men, is the best and most dutifull order that a Christian can observe."[5] The word "order" is tendentious, for behind it is the recognition that in the eyes of those who abide by the order of worldly appearances ("the faire seeming pretences of men"), the lone dissenter will be seen as a figure of *dis*order.[6] The hero of faith in Milton's prose and poetry is always the one who marches not only to a different but also to an inaudible drummer and refuses to measure himself or herself "by other mens measures" (YP 1, 904–905).

Other men's measures, by contrast, are the cornerstones of the philosophy of Thomas Hobbes (1588–1679), which receives its fullest expression in *Leviathan* (1651). For Hobbes, the private man who follows the inner promptings of his faith and prefers them always to public procedures and decorum is a figure not of heroism but of danger. It is he and others like him who precipitate and justify rebellion against established authority and thus bring about a condition of "continuall feare" and a way of life that is "solitary," but not nobly so as Milton would have it, for it is "poor, nasty, brutish, and short."[7] Where Milton distrusts surfaces because they distract the virtuous man and lead him away from the proper devotion to an internalized spirit, Hobbes valorizes and honors surfaces because they alone can protect us from the political fantasies of those who consult their own hearts and conclude from what they find there that it is necessary and good to kill a king.

Like Milton, Hobbes fears a return to chaos, but he identifies the coming of chaos with just what Milton celebrates – an antinomian virtue that knows no law except for the law written on the fleshy tables of the individual heart. Milton believes that discipline and order must come from within and cannot be imposed by external forms; a nation of transformed and regenerate people will naturally produce good and pious actions, just as from a "sincere heart" the appropriate praise of God will "unbidden come into the outward gesture" (YP 1, 941). Hobbes believes that external forms are all that stand between us and the war of all against all and that the claim of sincerity, because it is available to everyone and defies public verification, licenses everyone's crimes against life and property. Milton yearns for a transformation of vision in which everyone will be like the Lady of whom *A Mask* says, "Sure something holy lodges in that breast" (246). Hobbes devises a technology of administration, not in order to encourage vision, but to hold it at bay. Milton worships a God who is removed from human ways and must be arduously sought and found only by a few chosen persons. Hobbes presents for our worship and fear a "Mortall God" (227) who is the artificial construction of those who choose, for entirely prudential reasons, to obey him. In short, if Milton, as I have argued elsewhere, works from the inside out, Hobbes works exclusively on the outside and regards the inside as a realm to be avoided at (literally) all costs.[8]

The judgment of history has been kinder to the regicide than to the arch-formalist, but in what follows I shall suggest that there may be more to say for Hobbes than is sometimes assumed.

I.

Hobbes works by dismissing as absurd what many of his readers will think of as obvious. This strategy is typically deployed with a flourish and always points in the same direction. Here is an example from chapter 7 of part 1 of *Leviathan*. It centers on the idea of conscience, although that word does not appear until the middle of the passage where it is redefined in a way that makes Hobbes's usual point. The sequence begins with an account of how public knowledge of a fact – knowledge based on what Hobbes has earlier called "settl[ed] significations" (105), definitions generally agreed upon and placed at the beginning of any train of reasoning – binds men to certain verbal, and finally moral, actions: "When two, or more, men, know of one and the same fact, they are said to be Conscious of it one to another; which is as much to know it together" (132). That is to say, their knowledge of the fact is not an internal private matter – neither man looks inward for a verification of it – but a matter of public record, and as a matter of public record available to anyone, independently of his personal inclinations, biases or desires. It follows then, says Hobbes, that one who would deny this fact or replace it with some fanciful substitute has willfully departed from what he consciously knows to be true and deserves to be condemned. It is at this point that the word "conscience" is first used: "It was, and ever will be reputed a very Evill act, for any man to speak against his *Conscience*, or to corrupt or force another to do so" (132). What is surprising is that the phrase "speak against his conscience" would usually be taken to refer to someone who surrenders his or her private judgment of what morality requires to some merely public formula. It is in this spirit, for example, that Milton's Samson responds to the demand that he come and entertain the Philistine nobility with feats of strength. He refuses, and when the Messenger warns that the Lords will be offended, and that he should take care to "Regard thyself," he retorts, "My self? My conscience and internal peace" (133–134). Or, in other words: "My first obligation is to the law written on the fleshy tables of my heart and not to the law of any state, be it either Hebrew or Philistine. I will not act against my conscience in deference to the accident of political authority."

For Hobbes, however, conscience is violated precisely when one does what Samson does – prefer the guidance within to the guidance provided by publicly formulated definitions and obligations. Hobbes knows that the Miltonic sense of conscience is now the standard one, but he regards it as a corruption. Once, he tells us, conscience was understood as he understands it – a conscientious observance of the laws as they have been set down and published – but at some point "men made use of the same word metaphorically for the knowledge of their own secret facts and secret thoughts" (132). That is, men departed from what they were conscious of *together* – departed from meanings that in no way depend on private perceptions – and opted instead for the meanings concocted in the laboratory of their own individual ideas and imaginings. Earlier, Hobbes has defined "metaphorically" as using words "in other sense than they were ordained for" (102). The ordination in question is not by God, but by agreed upon conventions. "Conscience" is made metaphorical when it is taken to refer to something unavailable to public inspection, and, once made metaphorical, the word then gives rise to and legitimates a metaphorical world where nothing is fixed, and everyone is free – by this perverted law of conscience – to assign meaning and value in any way that pleases: "Men, vehemently in love with their own new opinions, (although never so absurd), and obstinately bent to maintain them, gave

those their opinions also that reverenced name of Conscience" (132).[9]
Misuse a word, and the next thing you know, private desires have invaded
the sphere of public stability. Depart from a settled signification, and you
are on the way to legitimizing the worst actions. As Hobbes observes in a
later chapter (he has his eye on 1649), any man who wants to kill his king
need only first "call him [a] Tyrant"; for then he does not have to admit to
"*Regicide,* that is killing of a King," but only to "*Tyrannicide* that is,
killing of a Tyrant" (369). A little change in vocabulary, and what is
unlawful is made lawful and an entire government is brought down.

   Hobbes's entire philosophy and method can be extrapolated from these
small examples. The method is simultaneously to introduce and scoff
at standard meanings and concepts to which his readers are likely to be
attached. You think that the word "conscience" refers to an inner voice
that must be obeyed if you are to be moral? No, that is the very definition
of "*im*morality," as anyone with a grain of sense should know. You think
that "tyrannicide" is the name of a rational and defensible action? No,
"tyrannicide" is a rhetorical device employed by men who would hide
from you, and perhaps from themselves, the perversity and absurdity of
what they propose. The philosophy is a philosophy of surfaces – of the
superiority of procedural and conventional notions to substantive and
internal ones. If any quarter whatsoever is given to private desires, idio-
syncratic (nonpublic) definitions, religious revelations, or grand moral
imperatives, the structure that holds things together and keeps men's
instincts for plunder and self-aggrandizement in check will crack and
tumble. The reason is simple: private desires, subject-centered definitions,
religiously inspired agendas, comprehensive moral schemes are by definition plural – manifestations of the "difference in mens passions" that lead
"some mens thoughts [to] run one way, some another" (135) – and in the
absence of any natural or hard-wired measure of precedence and superiority, such a measure must be artificially devised ("artificial" is Hobbes's
favorite honorific), and if it is to do its job, that measure must be as empty
of substantive aspiration as possible. The trouble, however, is that in its
present state our moral vocabulary is too full of substance, and therefore it
must be purged of the pretensions that make it not only useless (because it
has no single referent) but subversive (because it licenses precisely what
must be curbed, the sway of private judgments). Hence the strategy,
enacted over and over, of first invoking a word or phrase in its now impure
form and then rescuing it from the corruption of positive morality.

   Sometimes the strategy is performed almost as an aside, as when
Hobbes begins a list of "absurd significations" with familiar examples like

a "round Quadrangle" or "accidents of Bread in cheese" but ends it with "A *free Subject;* a *free-Will;* or any *Free,* but free from being hindered by opposition" (113). I know, he is saying, that many of you will believe that being free is the most desirable of states, the hallmark of your dignity; but think about the phrase "free subject": how can you be a subject, that is, a person living under magistrates and laws, and be free? It makes no sense; it is, as Hobbes says (it is his favorite word of opprobrium), "absurd." And on the other hand, if you take "free" literally – that is, in the only way it should be taken, in the corporeal (not spiritual) sense of "free from being hindered," free to do anything you like without any restraint whatsoever – then you are by this definition free to be a menace to your neighbors as they, in turn, are free to be menaces to you. Far from being desirable, the life of freedom is the worst imaginable, as hordes of what Hobbes terms "masterlesse men" (266) go their marauding way without hindrance; the life of freedom is the life of total vulnerability and nonstop anxiety.

Later, this small moment – it is, after all, a point made in the service of another – is expanded into a full chapter entitled "Of the Liberty of Subjects" (the title itself is a Hobbesian joke) (261–274). Here the argument is spelled out. Just as people corrupt the notion of conscience when they make it a private virtue rather than a resolution conscientiously to adhere to public understandings, so do they misconceive ("abuse") liberty and give it a "specious name" when they take it as a "Private Inheritance, and Birth right," and fail to understand that liberty "is the right of the Publique only" (267). The liberty of which we should make "frequent and honorable mention," says Hobbes, "is not the Libertie of Particular men; but the Libertie of the Commonwealth," which is at liberty to defend its borders and interests and thereby to protect the citizens who live not in liberty but in obedience to the sovereign's laws. It is "not that any particular men had the Libertie to resist their own Representative" – which would be the case were liberty a personal birthright and not a condition (the condition of being free to move around) secured by the *general* institution of public restraints – "but that their representative had the libertie to resist or invade other people" (267). If resistance were the right of every man according to what he was pleased to call his "conscience," that is, if there was a "full and absolute Libertie in every Particular man," if men always had the liberty of "doing what their own reasons shall suggest," the result would be "no inheritance, to transmit to the Son, nor to expect from the Father; no propriety of Goods or Lands; no security" (266). How can anyone desire *that* liberty "by which all other men may be masters of their lives" (264) and not be "absurd"?

The absurdity follows from the mistake of defining liberty as "an exemption from Lawes" in favor of some inner law invoked as a higher authority (264); the true meaning of liberty can be nothing but the "corporall Liberty" of not being "imprisoned, or restrained, with walls or chayns" (264, 262). *That* liberty, Hobbes points out, is enjoyed by every citizen who has not been incarcerated for failing to respect the corporal (not essential) liberty of fellow citizens (by stealing, assaulting, embezzling and so on), and therefore it is once again absurd "for men" – that is, those who live within the constraints of the law – "to clamor as they doe, for the Liberty they so manifestly [already] enjoy" (264). In order to keep things straight, Hobbes observes, all you have to do is refrain from applying "the words *Free* and *Liberty*" to "anything but *Bodies*" (262). Any other application will be metaphorical and open the way to internalizing a concept whose true meaning and utility must remain public and external. Either liberty – properly understood as the liberty to walk in the streets and "buy, and sell, and otherwise contract with one another" (264) – is already the possession of those who abide by established authority, or liberty is the name of an anarchic right to go one's own way with no regard for the ways of others, and as such must be repudiated either as a political condition or a legitimate aspiration.[10] One must give up liberty in this second sense in order to secure it in the first. Unless every man lays down his "*Right,* of doing anything he liketh," he will have no defense against another who would assert "his own Right to the same" (190).

2.

It is clear from these passages that getting the definition of liberty (or freedom or conscience or tyrannicide) wrong is not simply to have made a conceptual or philosophical error, but to have endangered the good order and security of the society. Let the wrong ideas get into people's heads and there is no telling what they will do, although you can be pretty sure that what they do will be bad. That is why Hobbes follows the paragraphs parsing the correct and incorrect understandings of liberty with a call for indoctrination and censorship. For, he says, "when the same errour [of taking liberty in a private rather than a public sense] is confirmed by the authority of men in reputation for their writings in this subject, it is no wonder if it produce sedition, and change of Government" (267). Especially dangerous are those "Greek, and Latine Authors" who teach that "*no man is* Free *in any other Government*" than a democracy, and that therefore it is lawful and virtuous to depose one's monarch. Those who read in these authors,

From their childhood have gotten a habit (under a false shew of Liberty) of favoring tumults, and of licentious controlling the actions of their Sovereigns; and again of controlling those controllers, with the effusion of so much blood; as I think I may truly say, there was never any thing so deerly bought, as these Western parts have bought the learning of the Greek and Latine tongues. (267–268)

And the remedy? Care by the sovereign that the right and not the wrong doctrines are taught and read:

[The sovereign must] be Judge of what Opinions and Doctrines are averse, and what conducing to Peace; and consequently, on what occasions, how farre, and what men are to be trusted with-all, in speaking to Multitudes of people; and who shall examine the Doctrines of all bookes before they be published. For the Actions of men proceed from their Opinions; and in the wel governing of Opinions, consisteth the well governing of mens Actions. (233)

This conclusion follows from everything that has preceded it – from the discussions of conscience, freedom, liberty and countless other matters; given the relentless unfolding of Hobbes's argument, it makes perfect sense. But once again it is a sense deliberately counter to the sense that usually accompanies the rejection of censorship in the liberal tradition of which Hobbes is one founder. In that tradition, the question: "Why allow the free publication of opinions and doctrines?" has always been answered with the reasons Milton gives in his *Areopagitica* – to encourage dissent, to prevent the state from criminalizing criticism of itself, to provide self-governing citizens with the information necessary to make informed decisions, to foster civic virtue and judgment by allowing opposing views to contend with one another in a free and open encounter. But these are all *bad* reasons if you distrust and fear the very abilities a regime of unfettered publication promises to produce (because you fear and distrust the unfettered energies of humanity), if you fear that dissent will lead to dissatisfaction with the present order of things, if you fear that a state that allows itself to be challenged will lose its authority and its ability to keep the peace, if you regard the notion of citizens governing themselves with horror because each of them will want to go in a different direction with no one to stop them, if you identify civic virtue with obedience to established authority and regard private judgments, especially those that have been well developed and exercised, as the source of all troubles.

But what, one might ask, about truth? In Milton's *Areopagitica*, and in every free expression defense that has followed his, the importance of facilitating and encouraging the search for truth is always a main reason for rejecting censorship. Since we are all fallible, the argument goes, and since we are all prone to mistake our necessarily partial views for the true ones, it is necessary that there be a mechanism for ensuring that no view that has the potential of advancing the search for truth will be suppressed: "If it come to prohibiting, there is not ought more likely to be prohibited than truth itself; whose first appearance to our eyes bleared and dimm'd with prejudice and custom, is more unsightly and unplausible than many errors" (YP II, 565). Hobbes is ready for this objection and indeed raises it himself in the same paragraph: "And though in matter of Doctrine, nothing ought to be regarded but the Truth; yet this is not repugnant to the regulating of the same by Peace. For doctrine repugnant to Peace, can no more be True, than Peace and Concord can be against the Law of Nature" (233). Hobbes agrees that if it repressed the truth, regulation would be censorship, and therefore bad; but, he reasons, since the highest truth of all is the truth that peace and stability must always be preserved, any regulation of opinions tending to tumult and sedition is not a violation of truth's primacy, but a protection of it. What he has done here is substitute for the idea of *searching* for the truth – a truth by definition not fully available to us now – the idea of *hewing* to a truth that has been stipulated in advance. Rather than being a mysterious and elusive entity whose location is always shifting – Milton's definition – truth in Hobbes's argument is quite simply and formally defined as that which conduces to peace. The questions "What is Truth?" and "Is this or that assertion true?" are no longer deep questions – remember, Hobbes is the philosopher of surfaces – provoking sophisticated metaphysical contortions, but easy and automatic questions. Is the assertion, whatever it is, in harmony with the imperative of peace? If the answer is yes, it is true; if the answer is no, it isn't.

Once again Hobbes has taken a supposedly substantive concept – in this case *the* substantive concept – and made it into a matter of a settled convention which, once established, gives operational force to the judgment that something is or is not true. In another chapter, exactly the same formalization or "thinning" of a substantive value is performed with respect to the question: "Is it or is it not just?" In some philosophies, the quest for justice – undertaken within the conviction that justice cannot be identified with existing positive law – takes a long and tortured and uncertain path. In Hobbes's philosophy, justice is found quickly and unproblematically in the idea of contract. It is easy to see why contract would be the branch of law Hobbes finds congenial. A contract is an agreement between persons who bind themselves to reciprocal actions as they are stipulated by the terms of a writing. A breach occurs when one of the parties ceases to abide by the terms; that party is then subject to a penalty. The sequence is entirely formal in that no independent assessment of the terms – no question like: "Are they fair?" or: "Do they square with religious or moral or social norms?" – is to the point; for the point is simply whether or not someone has or has not kept his or her word irrespective of the wisdom or prudence of having given it in the first place. You cannot receive either the credit for having kept your word or blame for having failed to keep it unless there is a public record of your word that can serve as the measure for assessing your actions. That is to say, the possibility of doing something good or bad exists not in the abstract – in some overarching moral system – but only in relation to a published contract. Morality, or at least this part of it, follows from certain speech acts and has no substantive form.

Hobbes says all this and more in a brilliant paragraph (202). First, he explains what the moral life is like before there are covenants: "Where no Covenant hath preceded, there hath no Right been transferred, and every man hath right to every thing." In the state of nature, where there is no natural bar to the fulfilling of one's desires, nothing prevents a man from believing that everything should belong to him; everyone can justify his desires to himself, and no independent public norm sets limits to those desires and labels them legitimate or illegitimate. "Consequently," says Hobbes, "no action can be Unjust." But once contractual terms have been formulated and agreed to by two or more, those terms immediately define the proper limits of desire and determine what will subsequently be deemed lawful and unlawful behavior. "But when a Covenant is made, then to break it is *Unjust*." All you need is a compact in relation to which you can default, and "unjust" becomes a possible description of your action where before the only descriptions available were successful and unsuccessful (you got away with it or you didn't). It follows then, says Hobbes, that "the definition of INJUSTICE, is no other than *the not Performance of Covenant*." By "no other than," he means no *more* than; there is no deep moral content to injustice, just the fact of not having abided by your word, whatever it is and in whatever circumstances you gave it. It is an entirely procedural account of injustice, and along with it comes an entirely procedural, nonsubstantive account of justice: "And whatever is not Unjust, is JUST." No agonizing debates about conflicting duties or about the tension between natural law and positive law; no grand battles between utilitarian and normative justifications for action.

Just a simple question: Is the action in accordance with the covenant? (Not the wise covenant or the fair covenant or the mutually beneficial covenant, but the agreed-upon covenant.) If the answer is yes, the action – however you might like or dislike its consequences – is just; if not, unjust. That's all there is to it, just as all there is to the truth of a doctrine is its conformity to the imperative of seeking peace.[11]

For Hobbes, this point is the whole of morality and is introduced as his third law of nature: *"That men performe their Covenants made"* (201). Just do what you said you would do, and you earn the description "moral." What drops out in this view is any inquiry into whether what you have pledged to do and done is good by some independent measure.[12] And that is why Johann Sommerville declares, "it is doubtful whether it makes sense to describe Hobbes as having any genuine moral system at all."[13] By "genuine" Sommerville means a system the content of which would be a set of general normative obligations which is prior to, and can be invoked as a check on, any particular act – including the act of entering into a covenant – we might perform. To this, Hobbes would reply that the problem with any such "genuine moral system" is that there is more than one, indeed as many as there are people with different passions, and that therefore one would purchase moral depth at the cost of surface stability – at the cost, that is, of conflict, and, eventually, of civil war.[14] The way to stabilize surfaces – to provide for the orderly conduct of domestic, civic and commercial business – is to remain resolutely on the level of surfaces, on the level of conventional forms (of stipulated meanings, of negotiated terms of contract, of political allegiance) whose chief recommendation is not that they correspond to reality or are in touch with goodness and virtue, but that they have been publicly proclaimed and so can serve as the artificial constraint made necessary by the unavailability of a natural constraint everyone would recognize and obey.

The only requirements are publicity and perspicuousness: if the definitions of words are settled and generally known, if the terms of contract are unambiguous and published, if the hierarchy of political authority is clear and not subject to dispute, life will work irrespective of whether the definitions, the terms and the political arrangements have the content God and nature would approve (who's to know?). When people flourish in a state, says Hobbes, it is not because the man who rules them has the "right" – because of his superior wisdom and virtue – to rule them, but because he is the man "they obey" (380). The moral status of the one who is obeyed is irrelevant to the function he performs, the function of assuring "concord of the Subjects" (380).[15] In Milton's view, if the one chosen ceases to be wise and a person of integrity, he should be removed. In Hobbes's account, removal of a sovereign is justified only if he is not keeping up his end of the bargain; that is, if he is no longer able to protect those who swear fealty to him: "Take away in any kind of State the Obedience (and consequently the concord of the People), and they shall not onley not flourish, but in short time be dissolved" (380). And, by the same reasoning, when a legal system flourishes, it is not because it embodies or reflects the ideal of justice, but because it has set up procedures by which citizens can order their lives and avoid penalties.

Earlier in the *Leviathan*, Hobbes provides a parallel account of the growth and establishment of knowledge. When science flourishes, he explains, it is because words have been precisely defined and then combined by rules of "Connexion" into "general Affirmations" (the generality being entirely conventional, a matter of adhering to what has been set down), leading finally to a "Conclusion" that follows not from the shape of the world or from a Platonic idea of nature, but from the order of discourse. But, warns Hobbes, "if the first ground of such Discourse be not Definitions; or if the Definitions be not rightly joined ... then the End or Conclusion is ... OPINION" (131), no more than what some private person said; and if opinion is unchecked and allowed to proliferate, you will soon find yourself "wandering amongst innumerable absurdities; and their end, contention and sedition" (117). Always the same lesson: absurdities are ready at any moment to enter and disrupt discourse and life. The only way to keep them at bay is to resist the temptation of the private and the substantive and put your faith – a word deliberately chosen – in the public enforcement of artificial, stipulated conventions.[16]

Everything, then, depends on the order of words, but at the same time the order of words is the source of danger. Salvation is linguistic, but so is disaster. Both parts of this lesson are spelled out in the fourth chapter of *Leviathan*, where Hobbes tells us first that there is "nothing in the world Universall but Names" (102), and second that the rightness of the names is synthetic not natural; the world does not suggest them; rather, their imposition (his word) and subsequent combining of them into general affirmations delivers to us a world – entirely discursive – about which we can then reason: "By this imposition of names ... we turn the reckoning of the consequences of things imagined in the mind, into a reckoning of the consequences of Appellations" (103). The mind registers some images – the residue of "*decaying sense*" Hobbes has explained earlier (88) – and the same mind brings order to that random profusion by first coming up with, and then adhering to, the names it has set down. Once the order of names has been established (the reasoning is exactly the same as the reasoning that derives justice from contract), it is then possible to say of an assertion that it is true or false – not because some thing in the world pronounces either verdict, but because some name artificially instituted now stands as a measure of accuracy or its opposite. "For," says Hobbes in a pronouncement as postmodern as anything said by Richard Rorty, who indeed says exactly the same thing, "*True* and *False* are attributes of Speech, not of Things. And where Speech is not [that is, where there is no conventional system of signification], there is neither *Truth* nor *Falsehood*" (105).[17] Without an in-place system of signification, an artificial system devised by people with no privileged relationship to the world, true and false statements about the world (forever removed from direct inspection) cannot be made.

The methodological conclusion follows immediately: "Seeing then that *truth* consisteth in the right ordering of names ... a man that seeketh precise *truth*, had need to remember what every name he uses stands for," not because he will thereby be in touch with the thing the name refers to, but because in a world where everything is in motion, where experience is made up of sense impressions decaying even as they register, where people are driven by the diverse desires of their diverse passions, there has to be something stable in relation to which mental life and civic life can be organized, and that something can only be artificially devised names and the strict logic by which they are combined and connected. The person who loses a grip on that conventional stability loses meaning, truth and everything else: "He will find himselfe entangled in words, as a bird in lime-twiggs; the more he struggles, the more belimed" (105). This is not a warning against the danger of being seduced by words into forgetting about things on the model of Cato's *rem tene, verba sequentur* ("hold to the thing, the words will follow"). Hobbes's advice is exactly the reverse: hold to the words, and things will follow and will sit still long enough for you to begin and conclude your reckonings. The precise truth Hobbes promises is not the truth of things, of an independent reality, but the truth that follows upon precision (and consistency) in definitions. The truth of things, Hobbes says, is absolute and unconditioned, but it cannot be ours. The truth that can be ours is entirely discursive and entirely "Conditionall": "No man can know by Discourse, that this, or that, is, has been or will be, which is to know absolutely [without mediation]; but onely if this [some settled verbal signification] be, That is ... which is to know conditionally; and that not the consequence of one thing to another; but of one name of a thing, to another name of the same thing" (131).

As Victoria Silver puts it, "In Hobbes's view science does not manipulate facts, but words; its formulae do not describe the operations of external bodies, but rather the mind's concepts; its predictions remain conditional upon a precise, concrete use of language ... and not upon a close and repeated observation of some world beyond ideas."[18]

3.

It is this ability to manipulate words and build out of them descriptive and predictive structures that distinguishes human beings from animals. Both humans and beasts, says Hobbes, react to an experienced effect in the same way: "wee seek the causes, or means that produce it" (96). So when a loud noise is made in the vicinity of a human and a dog, both will look around and try to identify its source, and if the noise is unpleasant both will move away from the source once it has been identified. But the human will then proceed to mental actions beyond the dog's capacity. The human might ask, Who is responsible for this noise? Do I have a legal remedy? If I build a wall around my house could I keep it out? Should I move to another neighborhood? In short, the human projects into the long-term future and makes plans. Rather than simply registering an effect, "Wee seek all the [other] possible effects, that by it can be produced; that is to say, we imagine what we could do with it," and this imagination, which Hobbes identifies with curiosity, is unique "to man onely" and withheld from an animal "that has no other Passion but sensuall, such as are hunger, thirst, lust and anger" (96). Only humans have the capacity of "designe," otherwise known as "the faculty of Invention" (96). This faculty, in excess of the "five Senses" we share with animals, is not natural but "acquired, and encreased by study and industry" (98). What enables us to acquire it and go far beyond what animals can do in the way of planning is speech: "For besides Sense, and Thoughts, and the Trayne of thoughts, the mind of man has no other motion" and is in this no different from the beast. But "by the help of Speech and Method, the same Facultyes may be improved to such a height, as to distinguish men from all other living creatures" (99).

It is a happy story and an old one, told first by Cicero in the *De inventione* and *De oratore* and repeated by every humanist who follows him: the arts of speech and eloquence civilize.[19] But it is a story of humanity's perfectibility and the possibility of substantive moral progress, and Hobbes will not let it stand.[20] He drops the other shoe in the fifth chapter, where he revisits what he had said in chapter 3, "That a Man did excell all other Animals in this faculty, that when he conceived any thing whatsoever, he was apt to enquire the consequences of it, and what effects he could do with it" (113). "Apt to enquire" means apt to speculate, imagine, and devise. But, Hobbes quickly adds, "This priviledge" – of being able to think creatively – "is allayed by another, by the priviledge of Absurdity to which no living creature is subject, but man onely; and of men those are of all most subject to it, that professe Philosophy."

Why? Because philosophers are least content with the "Definitions, or Explications of . . . names" currently in use (113). Philosophers, rather than hewing to what has been conventionally settled, wish above all else to go beyond what is conventionally settled, and their ability to do so causes endless troubles in the form of metaphorical flights of fancy, definitions made up out of whole cloth, and projects which because they float free of any "orderly Method" (115) threaten the stability both of reckonings and political administration. If only humans were like animals, and had "no other direction, than their particular judgments" – judgments of the moment and therefore not built up into a narrative or a vision of life – and "appetites" (225). If only humans were, like animals, without the gift and burden of speech, "that art of words, by which some men can represent to others, that which is Good, in the likenesse of Evill; and Evill, in the likenesse of Good; and augment, or diminish the apparent greatnesse of Good and Evill [thereby] discontenting men, and troubling their peace at their pleasure" (226). Animals, because they lack reason and cannot generalize from the present moment of satisfaction or distress to a theory of the just distribution of goods and honors, have no sense of private injury and no capacity for being unhappy with the present arrangement of things.

[Animals] do not see, or think they see, any fault, in the administration of their common businesse; wheras amongst men, there are very many, that think themselves wiser, and abler to govern the Publique, better than the rest; and these strive to reform and innovate [hear the scorn], one this way, another that way; and thereby to bring it into Distraction and Civill warre. (226)

In short, and with apologies to *My Fair Lady*, why can't a man be more like an animal?

Two answers to this question have already been given – reason and speech, faculties that mark a superiority that is dearly bought. To these Hobbes adds a third – equality, that most cherished of Enlightenment doctrines. What happens to equality in his hands is what happens in other chapters to freedom and liberty. It is stripped of its substantive aura and redescribed as a physical fact with no moral implications. The physical fact (and the new definition of equality) is that "though there bee found one man sometimes manifestly stronger in body, or of quicker mind then another; yet when all is reckoned together, the difference between man, and man, is not so considerable" (183). That is to say, people are roughly equal in bodily and mental endowments. That's all there is to equality; it is not an abstract condition that confers an abstract right, but an inconvenient empirical fact that presents us with problems of political management. For if every person is more or less equally endowed, there is no measure *in nature* for adjudicating the claims of one as opposed to another: "The difference between man, and man, is not so considerable, as that one man can thereupon claim to himselfe any benefit, to which another may not pretend, as well as he" (183). Whereas in the animal kingdom precedence follows natural abilities – the strong take things from the weak, the swift outrun the slow – in the world of human beings precedence is continuously disputed and there are no natural marks by which it might be determined: "The question who is the better man has no place in the condition of meer Nature" (211). If people were born with the signs of superiority and inferiority emblazoned on their persons (here is the entire history of heredity and racism), the distinctions better and worse, deserving and undeserving, master and servant, would declare themselves. In the absence of any such signs, everyone is justified in believing that he or she is the one who should lead, possess and rule: "From this equality of ability, ariseth equality of hope in the attaining of our ends. And therefore if any two men desire the same thing, which nevertheless they cannot both enjoy, they become enemies; and in the way to their End ... endeavour to destroy, or subdue one an other" (184).

Equality in this account is not, as it is in the Enlightenment tradition following Milton and Locke, a reason for denying one person the right to rule over another. Rather, it is the reverse. Instead of subscribing to the proposition that everyone is created equal and therefore absolute authority is against nature, Hobbes says that everyone is created equal and therefore absolute authority is absolutely necessary. If nature will not tell us who is superior and deserving of rule, we must supply nature's defect by stipulating to the superiority of some person who will occupy the role of sovereign – not because the person deserves it, but because we need it. We must, that is, establish a precedence rooted in nothing more substantive than our declaration of it; we must establish a "common Power to feare" (187). Without such a power firmly ensconced, the passions and desires of those who are to all appearances equal will go unchecked, for they will not "know a Law that forbids them" (187). Without that law, without the imposition of conventional and artificial constraints, "nothing can be Unjust" and the "notions of Right and Wrong, Justice and Injustice have ... no place" (188).

'CONCLUSION'

Here, in the concluding paragraphs of this chapter, I finally reach the thesis for which Hobbes is most often remembered and most often excoriated:

> The only way to erect such a Common Power, as may be able to defend [men] from the injuries of one another, and thereby to secure them in such sort, that by their owne industrie ... they may nourish themselves and live contentedly; is to conferre all their power and strength upon one Man ... and therin to submit their Wills every one to his Will, and their Judgments to his Judgment ... This is the Generation of that great LEVIATHAN ... of that *Mortall God*, to which wee owe under the *Immortal God*, our peace and defense. (227)

I did not introduce the thesis earlier because, in isolation, at the beginning of an explication, it would have struck the reader, as it strikes so many who first hear of it, as at once preposterous and evil. I would have then ignored the lesson Hobbes learned from Euclid, as Aubrey tells it: that a proposition nakedly offered may seem impossible, but if it comes at the end of a succession of proofs, it will seem inevitable.[21] As I trust it is now evident, the proposition of a sovereign will is no more or less startling than the proposition that conscience is a public matter, not a private one, and therefore requires a public, that is, conventional, baseline. Indeed, it is the same proposition, issuing from the same repudiation of substance in favor of artificially stipulated form. Once one gets the hang of the basic move – exchange a substantive vocabulary for a vocabulary of bodies and motions, take away the putative depth and interiority of concepts like conscience, justice, injustice, better, worse, true, false, liberty, freedom, merit and equality – and once one grounds that basic move in an account of human nature – variable, competitive, voracious and radically insecure – absolutely everything follows and seems, if I can use the word, natural.

Michael Oakshott, responding to those who seek and fail to find an architecture in Hobbes's thought, observes, "the coherence of his philosophy, the system of it, lies not in an architectonic structure but in a single 'passionate thought' that pervades its parts."[22] "Passionate thought" is Hobbes's phrase; it appears near the beginning of *Leviathan*, where it serves both as a general direction for composition and as a description of how *this* composition works. What is required, says Hobbes, if discourse, thought and life are not to "wander . . . as in a Dream" (95), is a "Passionate Thought to govern and direct those that follow," an end and point kept always in mind and acting "as the thing that directs all your thoughts" (96). *Leviathan* answers perfectly to this description, and this perfection is the object both of Victoria Silver's praise and complaint. The praise is for the tightness of the performance, for the degree to which the prose generates, from sentence to sentence, an intelligibility that leaves no seams or cracks that might disrupt it.[23] So powerful is the effect that the "source of all true statement and the criterion of self-evidence in *Leviathan* is its own terminology" (366). The complaint is for the very same thing. Hobbes's argument, says Silver, "is consumed by the obsessive definition and reiteration of terms, often to the detriment of its ostensible science, which degenerates into verbal engineering."[24] Degenerates? Verbal engineering, as Silver well knows, is the entire point, not because Hobbes is trying to put something over on the reader, but because, as he passionately believes, no other engineering, grounded in something more substantial than words and the conclusions they compel, is available. There is, according to Hobbes, nothing to degenerate from, and it can hardly be a criticism of *Leviathan* that its own performance is, as Silver also sees, an instance of what it urges. The fact that on its own terms Hobbes's masterwork is irrefutable should be the occasion not of complaint, but of wonder and awe.

Of course we may challenge those terms and ask, after explaining how Hobbes's argument works, whether or not it works in the world beyond its own rhetorical unfolding. Many, from the very day of its publication, have judged that it does not, and have said that the argument fails at its core because, as Jean Hampton insists, the right of subjects to determine whether or not the sovereign's rule does in fact contribute to their self-preservation and so fulfills the contract, is a fatal undermining of the sovereign power on which the entire scheme rests: "Indeed as long as the subjects retain the right to preserve themselves in a commonwealth" – and self-preservation is the reason for setting up the authority in the first place – "they cannot be said to have surrendered *anything* to the sovereign," and, consequently, Hobbes is unable "to make the sovereign's rule permanent and secure."[25] But Hobbes knows this at least as well as Hampton and her predecessors, and – surprise, surprise – he builds it into his exposition:

But as men, for the atteyning of peace, and conservation of themselves thereby, have made an Artificiall Man . . . so also have they made Artificiall Chains, called

Civill Lawes, which they themselves, by mutuall covenants, have fastened at one end, to the lips of that Man ... to whom they have given the Soveraigne Power; and at the other end to their own Ears. These Bonds, in their own nature but weak, may nevertheless be made to hold, by the danger, though not by the difficulty, of breaking them. (263–264)

That is to say, I know how fragile are both the argument I am making and the strategy that argument recommends. It all depends on the willingness of the unbridled will to bridle itself, to submit for no substantive reason, but for a prudential reason, to an authority it alone upholds. Nothing is easier than the breaking of these bonds, and nothing is more disastrously consequential. Put this way, the Hobbesian creed bears an uncanny resemblance to the faith-based creed proclaimed by his great opposite, John Milton. In a key passage, Milton's Raphael observes that the only guarantee of the happiness of free agents is an act of obedience rooted in nothing firmer than itself: "On other surety none" (*PL* v, 538).[26] On this point the arch-antinomian apostle of the inside and the arch-formalist champion of the outside agree. The security of the world is in peril at every moment, and the slightest wrong movement – eating an apple, or deciding to call a king a tyrant – can bring everything crashing down, as it, in fact, did. Of course, the difference between the two remains: one stakes everything on an internal law that has no necessary external form; the other clings desperately to external forms and fears any invocation of the internal as a prelude to chaos. But even in this opposition, they stand allied against the facile rationalists, the believers in perspicuous and easy political solutions, of their day and ours.

NOTES

1 Michael Lieb, *Milton and the Culture of Violence* (Ithaca: Cornell University Press, 1994), 10.
2 John Milton, *Paradise Lost*, vii, 32, in *John Milton: Complete Poems and Major Prose*, ed. Merritt Y. Hughes (New York: Odyssey Press, 1957). All quotations of Milton's poetry come from this edition; quotations of *Paradise Lost* are noted parenthetically as *PL* by book and line(s).
3 Michael Lieb, *Theological Milton: Deity, Discourse, and Heresy in the Miltonic Canon* (Pittsburgh: Duquesne University Press, 2006), 193.
4 Lieb, *Milton and the Culture of Violence*, 69.
5 John Milton, *An Apology against a Pamphlet*, in *The Complete Prose Works of John Milton*, 8 vols. in 10, ed. Don M. Wolfe et al. (New Haven: Yale University Press, 1953–1982), I, 937. All quotations of Milton's prose come from this edition and are noted parenthetically as YP by volume and page.

6 Compare Bunyan: "Things to come, and carnal sense, are . . . strangers to one another." See John Bunyan, *The Pilgrim's Progress*, ed. James Wharey; rev. ed. Roger Shattuck (Oxford: Oxford University Press, 1960), 32.

7 Thomas Hobbes, *Leviathan*, ed. C.B. Macpherson (Harmondsworth, England: Penguin Books, 1968), 186. All quotations of *Leviathan* come from this edition and are noted parenthetically.

8 Stanley Fish, *How Milton Works* (Cambridge, MA: Belknap Press of Harvard University Press, 2001), 24.

9 On this point, see David Panagia, *The Poetics of Political Thinking* (Durham, NC: Duke University Press, 2006), 41.

10 Mary Dietz, "Hobbes's Subject as Citizen," in *Thomas Hobbes and Political Theory*, ed. Mary G. Dietz (Lawrence: University Press of Kansas, 1990), observes correctly that "insofar as the virtues of Hobbes's citizen cultivate a disposition toward obedience to Leviathan, they conspire to deprive the citizen of precisely the sort of liberty that distinguished classical republicanism – a liberty Hobbes deemed specious" (112).

11 For a brilliant discussion of Hobbes's view of contract and its relationship to other views held by his contemporaries and predecessors, see Victoria Kahn, *Wayward Contracts: The Crisis of Political Obligation in England, 1640–1674* (Princeton: Princeton University Press, 2004). Kahn observes that in Hobbes's account of contract, "The contemporary discourses of natural law[,] covenant theology, and the common law appear, but each is systematically undermined" (155). She further notes, "To define breach of contract in formal terms as a logical and linguistic absurdity would have been shocking to Hobbes's contemporaries," who would have learned from Aristotle and Aquinas that "the idea that promises should be kept was a maxim of the moral law" (156). Kahn links Hobbes's position with the famous Slade's Case (1604): "If in the older view of obligation, promises were to be kept because of a transcendent moral law . . . in Slade promises were to be kept because they had been articulated in the shared medium of language and ratified by the exchange of other material signs" (47).

12 M.M. Goldsmith, *Hobbes's Science of Politics* (New York: Columbia University Press, 1966), points out that Hobbes is a legal positivist, which means that he "denies that laws must be just, right, moral, and good in order to be laws. Instead law is distinguished by procedural . . . test" (274).

13 Johann Sommerville, "Hobbes on Political Obligation," in *Leviathan*, ed. R. Flathman and D. Johnston (New York: Norton, 1997), 334.

14 Richard Tuck, *Hobbes: A Very Short Introduction* (Oxford: Oxford University Press, 1989), explains that Hobbes "treated *moral* terms in exactly the same way he had treated color terms: though common language and common sense might lead us to think that something is really and objectively good, in the same way as we might think something is really and objectively red, in fact such ideas are illusions and fantasies, features of the insides of our heads only" (63). This relativism, Tuck notes, need not lead to toleration on the reasoning that everyone's judgments are equally unauthorized. It might lead

instead to absolutism, on the reasoning that in the absence of a perspicuous authority in nature, we must invent one: "Moral relativism, thought through properly, might lead ... to the Leviathan" (130).

15 Milton's position is exactly the opposite. In *The Tenure of Kings and Magistrates*, he tells a more virtue-centered story of the origin of political authority. When humans first perceived the need for some form of governance, "they communicated and deriv'd [the authority] either to one, whom for the eminence of his wisdom and integrity they chose above the rest, or to more then one, whom they thought of equal deserving" (YP III, 199).

16 See, on this point, Bernard Gert, "Hobbes's Psychology," in *The Cambridge Companion to Hobbes*, ed. Tom Sorell (Cambridge: Cambridge University Press, 1966): "What was really important for Hobbes was to use words in such a way that everyone would agree that the terms referred to the same thing. He did not want to use words that were primarily expressions of the attitudes of the person using them" (163).

17 See Richard Rorty, *Contingency, Irony, and Solidarity* (Cambridge: Cambridge University Press, 1989): "To say that truth is not out there is simply to say that where there are no sentences there is no truth ... The world is out there, but descriptions of the world are not" (5).

18 Victoria Silver, "The Fiction of Self-Evidence in Hobbes's *Leviathan*," *ELH, A Journal of English Literary History* 55 (1988), 360.

19 Marcus Tullius Cicero, *On Invention*, in *On Invention. The Best Kind of Orator. Topics*, trans. H.M. Hubbell (London: Loeb Classical Library, 1949), 1.1.1–3. Marcus Tullius Cicero, *On the Orator, Books I–II*, trans. E.W. Sutton and H. Rackham (London: Loeb Classical Library, 1949), 1.8.33.

20 Rousseau tells still another story, one in which civilization corrupts the noble savage by socializing him to the point where the authenticity of his own inner existence disappears and is replaced by the artificial conventions insisted on by society. His fear is Hobbes's desire.

21 John Aubrey, *Brief Lives*, ed. O.L. Dick (London: Secker and Warburg, 1949), lxv.

22 Michael Oakshott, *Hobbes on Civil Association* (Oxford: Basil Blackwell, 1975), 17.

23 Sheldon Wolin, "Hobbes and the Culture of Despotism," in Dietz, *Thomas Hobbes and Political Theory*, observes that "Hobbes was not trying to persuade his readers but to compel them. The logical structure of his argument is a sequence of stark compulsions forcing on his reader–citizen the choice between controlled violence and violent oblivion" (26). In the same volume James Farr explains that Hobbes's "ideal reader ... is the person persuadable in the ways of truth and peace, as Hobbes understood them." He adds, "Should Hobbes actually persuade readers he would not have only authored some new doctrines but created new vessels for them" ("Hobbes and the Politics of Biblical Interpretation," 188).

24 Silver, "The Fiction of Self-Evidence," 371.

25 Jean Hampton, "The Failure of Hobbes's Social Contract," in Flathman and Johnston, *Leviathan*, 354, 357.

26 See Fish, *How Milton Works*, 511–573.

Index